Praise for *Wolfe Trap*, Book One of the Clay Wolfe / Port Essex Mysteries:

"Set on the midcoast of Maine, *Wolfe Trap* introduces us to an eccentric and interesting cast of Maine characters in this first installment in the Port Essex Mystery series. This gripping plot moves with lightning speed until it's explosive and thrilling conclusion. Here we have murder, drug-smuggling lobstermen, heavy drinking, art theft and budding romance. Despite our hero's hard-drinking and prolific womanizing, Clay Wolfe is a sympathetic and likable character. Cost's jam-packed plot should appeal to all lovers of private detective fiction. I eagerly look forward to next book in this series."

—JOSEPH SOUZA, acclaimed author
of *The Perfect Daughter*

Novels by Matt Cost
aka **Matthew Langdon Cost**

Historical Fiction

I Am Cuba: Fidel Castro and the Cuban Revolution

The Goff Langdon Mainely Mysteries

Mainely Power

Mainely Fear

Mainely Money

The Clay Wolfe / Port Essex Mysteries

Wolfe Trap

Mind Trap

Mouse Trap

WOLFE TRAP

— A Clay Wolfe / Port Essex Mystery —

MATT COST

Encircle Publications

Farmington, Maine, U.S.A.

Wolfe Trap © 2021 Matt Cost

Paperback ISBN-13: 978-1-64599-169-4
Hardcover ISBN-13: 978-1-64599-170-0
E-book ISBN-13: 978-1-64599-171-7
Kindle ISBN-13: 978-1-64599-172-4

Encircle editor: Cynthia Brackett-Vincent
Cover design: Deirdre Wait
Cover images © Getty Images

Published by:

Encircle Publications
PO Box 187
Farmington, ME 04938

info@encirclepub.com
http://encirclepub.com

Acknowledgments

If you are reading this, I thank you, for without readers, writers would be obsolete.

I am grateful to my mother, Penelope McAlevey, and father, Charles Cost, who have always been my first readers and critics.

Much appreciation to the various friends and relatives who have also read my work and given helpful advice.

I'd like to offer a big hand to my wife, Deborah Harper Cost, and children, Brittany, Pearson, Miranda, and Ryan, who have always had my back.

I'd like to tip my hat to my editor, Michael Sanders, who has worked with me on several novels now, and always makes my writing the best that it can be.

Thank you to Encircle Publishing, and the amazing duo of Cynthia Bracket-Vincent and Eddie Vincent for giving me this opportunity to be published. Also, kudos to Deirdre Wait for the fantastic cover art.

Dedication

To Encircle Publications for making my writing dreams come true.

Chapter 1

"I want you to find the person who supplied the drugs that killed my grandbaby."

Clay Wolfe eyed the woman across the desk from him. She was either about sixty years old—or a rather rough forty-five, rode hard and put away wet. He guessed the latter. She was thin, petite, with a shocking pink tube top encasing her Lilliputian bosom, and a jean skirt wrapped around a diminutive waist from which sprouted birdlike legs. As she spoke, she carelessly waved an unlit cigarette.

His receptionist had texted him minutes earlier asking when he was getting into the office, as there was a client waiting. Clay had just finished reading the paper at the diner, so he'd flipped a twenty onto the table to cover his breakfast and then walked the few steps down the street to his private detective agency.

Clay was just six feet tall and 180 pounds. His hair was dirty blond, his eyes that rare combination of blue and green that seemed to change back and forth, like an opal in the sunlight. He sported a goatee and mustache that appeared the result of a few days of neglect, but in reality, was a look he cultivated with his trimmer. His shirt was carefully pressed under a waistcoat, with slim-fit jeans completing the ensemble.

"Let's start at the beginning," he said. "I'm Clay Wolfe."

"Crystal Landry." She ignored his proffered hand.

He would have offered her coffee, but he guessed by her agitated movements and flickering eyes that she didn't need any caffeine. He hoped he didn't have to dissuade her from lighting the cigarette. They sat in his office, back behind the reception area, a bathroom off to one side completing the premises of Clay Wolfe, Private Detective.

"Do you live in Port Essex, Crystal?"

"Yeah, out in Botany Village." This was a trailer park up the hill on the outskirts of downtown.

"How long you been there?"

"You writing a fuckin' book?"

Clay didn't deign to reply. If nothing else, he was a patient man. That might go hand in hand with jaded and cynical.

The majority of his cases were insurance fraud, one of his biggest employees being the shipyard in Bath. He was called in to investigate disability and workman's compensation claims, just to make sure the employees were telling the truth about their injuries. More often than not, John Doe was lying about being incapacitated, unable to walk, bend over, lift heavy objects, or what not. But, when there was doubt or when an "injury" had dragged on too long, it was up to Clay to get the proof that instead of being laid up at home, these employees were actually gallivanting on the beaches of Florida or some such thing.

"Okay, okay," she said. "Don't know why you need to know how long, but whatever. About five years now."

"How old is…was your granddaughter, Crystal?" Clay wondered if he looked as weary as this woman. He knew he sometimes felt it, having left the Boston Police Department about a year earlier after shooting a man, with all the stress and emotional upheaval that had entailed.

"She was six months on the dot the day she died." A hard tear tumbled down her cheek.

"And how did she die?"

"She overdosed on fuckin' drugs, I already told you." Crystal stood as if to lunge at him, but then began pacing in an office that would've made Sam Spade jealous—if Spade didn't dismiss it out of hand as pretentious, that is.

The office was not only spacious and well-appointed, but its main feature was a stunning picture window overlooking Essex Harbor. There was a torn and ragged leather couch on which Clay had grabbed many a nap, and where he'd even slept the night through a few times. His desk was made of cherrywood and gleamed a deep red, more from the efforts of his receptionist than his own. On the left was another desk with his computer and printer, while the right-side had two tall gray filing cabinets. There were two L.L.Bean Lodge armchairs of rich brown leather similar to the couch, but much less worn, facing him.

"What drug?" Of all the addictions Clay had struggled with throughout his life, drugs had never been one of them. Unless you included alcohol.

"Heroin."

"How did a six-month-old baby get heroin?"

"How the fuck d'you think?"

Clay sat stone-faced and waited. The second source of clients for Clay was from clients who were the victims of cheating spouses. Maine was a no-fault divorce state, but he was still hired to find proof of infidelities. More often than not these flings resulted in a few black eyes and reconciliation, or were used to void prenuptial agreements, or otherwise mitigate damaging divorce settlements. Port Essex was an intriguing mix of hard-working poor, prosperous fishermen, and incredibly wealthy families who spent their time enjoying the oceanfront views when they weren't in Florida or some other warmer clime in winter.

"I wasn't the best mother. God knows that." Crystal returned to her seat, sitting forward across the desk, her hands tapping lightly on the wood, the cigarette tucked precariously behind her ear. "Her dad ditched us. I had more than my share of boyfriends. Did some drugs. But I've been clean now for three years."

"Congratulations." He looked her over again, nodding at his earlier guess about her age. Heroin would do that to a person, destroy their looks and age them beyond their years.

After his parents and grandmother had died, Clay's grandpops had hired a woman to be his nanny. She had not been unlike this woman in her toughness, if perhaps a bit more refined in language. He hadn't thought about his nanny in over twenty years and made a mental note to ask Gene about her.

Crystal stared intently at him. "I got people that count on me, you know?"

"Tell me about what happened to your granddaughter."

"Her name was Ariel."

"And she was your daughter's daughter?"

"Yes. Kelly Anne was my third child. Of five."

Clay looked at the waif-like woman in her mid-forties and wondered how she'd possibly given birth five times. "Kelly Anne," Clay repeated, writing it down.

"Yep. Kelly Anne. I named her for that lady who almost won season one of *Survivor*. That broad kicked ass."

"The reality show?"

"You own a television, Mr. Wolfe?"

Clay did own a television, but he had never watched *Survivor*, or made it more than five minutes into any other so-called reality show. He preferred movies and Netflix series. Anything without commercials, as a matter of fact.

"And Kelly Anne was using heroin?" he asked.

"I suppose so." Crystal began rocking back and forth in her chair. "She'd leave little Ariel with me a few nights a week, you know, and I didn't know what she was getting up to."

Clay doubted that the woman was ignorant of her daughter's habits. Maybe Crystal Landry was no longer a user, but she was still an enabler, still an inhabitant of that world where heroin or Oxy was just a part of daily life, your own or someone you knew.

"Are you married?" he asked.

"No," she said. "I got a boyfriend. He's a lobsterman."

"How did Ariel overdose on heroin, Crystal?"

"She didn't mean to kill her."

"What happened, Crystal?"

"The baby was teething, you know? Crying and screaming all night? She thought it would help to wipe her gums with the residue from the baggies, you know? Just a little bit of it to soothe the pain. And it worked. Right up until it didn't."

Clay remembered reading something about this in the newspaper, now feeling the same sort of disgust he'd felt the first time. He grunted. Leaned back. Crossed his arms over his chest and sighed. He knew that opioids had become a serious problem over the past years. Thousands had died, just in Maine alone, not to mention the rest of the country.

In many cases, babies were born to addicted parents, and if they weren't messed up at birth—well then, they were soon growing up in a druggie household, or slightly better, the state's overburdened and underfunded foster care system. Once in a great while kids would get into their parents' stash and overdose, but that was rare. It seemed that druggies were good at not leaving their heroin, or Oxy, or whatever, lying around. It was too important to them.

But, in this case, it had been a baby who had died, not by some mistake, but by ignorance. Clay remembered seeing the picture of the mother in the newspaper. Kelly Anne had the twisted and scarred look of a habitual user. It was not in Clay to try to find evidence for the woman's proof of innocence. He knew she was guilty just from the picture.

"Your daughter was medicating your granddaughter's gums with heroin over several weeks? And she overdosed?" He said baldly, wanting to be clear that he had the correct story.

"I know she did wrong, but she was all messed up, you know?" Tears were now running freely down Crystal's face. "Addiction ain't an easy thing to overcome, Mr. Wolfe, and they keep pushing it on you. I know. I been there."

"And you want me to find evidence to exonerate your daughter from the death?" he asked.

"Exonerate?"

"To prove it was not her fault."

"It was her fuckin' fault, goddammit." Crystal slammed her tiny fist on the desk in fury. "Ain't you listening?"

"What is it you want from me?" His words had a slight edge to them.

Crystal hiccupped a huge sob, and then gritted her teeth. Clay watched as she visibly regained her composure.

"The world ain't always black and white, Mr. Wolfe," she said after a minute.

He shrugged. "It would be helpful if you would be black and white about what, exactly, it is that you want me to do," he said.

"I know my daughter is guilty of killing her little girl. Little Ariel. She was my precious angel. Looked just like me, she did." Crystal wiped her eyes. "But so is the person who was selling the heroin to my daughter and her good-for-nothing boyfriend. They are just as guilty."

"Just to be clear," Clay said. "You want me to find who was supplying the heroin to your daughter?"

"My daughter is going to jail, Mr. Wolfe. That I know. But ain't the dealer just as guilty as her? I want him to pay for the crime as well."

"Any idea who might've been dealing to her?"

"No. I told you. I been done with all that nonsense, done some time now, don't hang with that crowd."

"Your daughter down at Two Bridges?" Clay asked. It was the county jail and courthouse in Wiscasset.

"She got out on bail yesterday."

"She got out?" He was incredulous.

"Yeah, it was just a misdemeanor. She got to go back to court at some time."

"When did the baby, little Ariel, die?"

"About two weeks ago."

"And they let Kelly Anne out?"

"On bail. Sure enough. The lawyer said something about how there was no exact crime for what she did except child endangerment or something."

"Do you know where she's staying?"

"Nope. Her boyfriend done kicked her out. DHS took her two older kids and put them into the foster program."

Clay sighed. "Fifty bucks an hour, plus expenses," he said. This was half his going rate, but what the hell. He doubted he'd even see that out of this lady.

"I got $120 on me right now, Mr. Wolfe. My check comes in Friday, and I can get you another fifty."

He quickly tallied how much of his time this would account for and made a decision. Perhaps running down a small-time drug dealer in Port Essex, Maine, was just what the doctor had ordered to cure Clay's doldrums. He was already tired of looking for proof of lying employees and cheating spouses. That and acting as a bodyguard for people who didn't actually need one, which was his third major source of income. These were often men who thought they were more important than they were. Then there were the husbands who hired him to keep an eye on wives supposedly for safety, but in reality, his presence that of a glorified babysitter to make sure they stayed in line. Perhaps chasing down local drug dealers would have some rejuvenating effect on his soul. Plus, Crystal Landry reminded him of his nanny, who he had called Nan-Ju. Clay idly wondered if her name had actually been Julie. Again, he needed to ask Gene about her.

"Okay, Crystal." Clay took fifty from her, pushing seventy back at her. "I'll see what I can do."

Chapter 2

STILL TUESDAY, JUNE 30TH

Clay walked Crystal out and down the stairs. His office was on the second floor of a building that had been a boating supply store, but now housed a gift shop/gallery. They had no use for the second floor, and thus it had remained empty for about a year, until Clay had returned to town looking for just such a location. Actually, he had been looking for a dingy, windowless shithole like Sam Spade's digs. But when he saw the view? Kudos to Spade, but modern times meant better views, or something like that.

As he came back up the stairs, he took a second to admire the inscription on the door. CLAY WOLFE, PRIVATE DETECTIVE. Pushing open the door, Clay was met with the bouncing tune of "Along Came Betty" played by Art Blakey and the Jazz Messengers. Benny Golson, who composed the piece, was gamboling along on the tenor sax like a five o'clock shadow.

Baylee Baker, his receptionist, was at her desk pretending to be busy while in reality just waiting to hear the dirt on the new client. He liked that she was a jazz fan. Clay pretended to head straight back into his office but was met with a not-so-fast-mister look. She was seven inches over five feet and had dark brown eyes that matched her hair.

"Got something for me?" Clay asked.

"You going to tell me about the new client?" Baylee's smile never quite filled itself out and disappeared quicker than it arrived. "She doesn't look like your normal customer."

"You remember that lady who killed her baby by rubbing heroin on the little girl's gums?"

"Sure," she said. "Kelly Anne Landry."

"That was the grandmother of the baby. Kelly Anne's mother."

"Young for a grandmother."

"From thirty feet away, she looks like a lot of class. From 10 feet away she looks like something made up to be seen from thirty feet away," Clay growled in his best Phillip Marlowe impression. He couldn't remember which of Hammett's books the line was from, but it was so good he'd remembered it.

"I would've guessed she was all of forty."

"Kelly Anne Landry is her third child. Don't let her diminutive figure fool you. You get closer, her face tells another tale."

"Let me guess. Her precious daughter didn't do it at all. She's taking the fall for the baby-daddy."

"Not at all," Clay said. He was well aware of Baylee's sensitivity to domestic abuse. After all, she had been one such victim, having shot and killed her abuser and husband just a year earlier. "She seems to accept that her daughter did what she did. What she wants to know is who was supplying Kelly Anne with the heroin."

"Yeah, drug abuse certainly seems to be all over the news these days. But who would have thought Port Essex?" Baylee looked away. "Pretty scary stuff."

"I sure saw some things in Boston I don't care to ever see again," Clay said.

"Worse than a mother rubbing heroin laced with fentanyl on the gums of her baby girl?"

"No," he admitted. "That's rock bottom."

"Why do you think it's become such a problem?"

"I guess it has to do with all the doctors pushing opioids over the past years."

"What was the big one in the news a few months back? Purdue Pharma?" Baylee's hair was pulled back in a bun. She wore a white sweater over her blouse, as Clay liked to keep the office cool in the winter and downright cold in the summer.

"The Sackler family. Made billions off OxyContin."

"That is, until they went bankrupt in the face of thousands of lawsuits."

"Bankrupt?" Clay raised an eyebrow. "You mean another way for the one percent to protect their money. They got so much hidden in offshore accounts that those islands are sinking with the weight of it."

"*Those* are the ones that you should go after, Clay Wolfe." She gave that fluttering half-smile.

He muttered something that might have been a curse under his breath. "The Sackler family will be living like kings in some paradise long after hell freezes over."

"Which isn't looking real good, now is it? Not with global warming and all that."

Clay contemplated the concept that hell would not be freezing over any time soon, at least not with the current administration's backtracking of environmental concerns. Hell was bound to stay hot for the immediate future.

"Look, I'm going to jump right on this case," he said after a moment. "Do we have anything pressing on the agenda?"

"You're supposed to be in Woolwich today watching Gary Stout. He took a medical leave from BIW for his back and is pressing for workman's comp. They're not so sure it's on the up and up." Baylee scrolled down the screen. "Also, you're supposed to get started checking up on Allison Daigle's husband to see if he is working late nights or boffing his secretary. That's about it until next week."

"Can you see if Don wants to pick up a few extra bucks? If he's available, have him go down and keep an eye on Stout's back. Remind him to bring his camera." Clay used Don occasionally to do surveillance and stake outs when he had other cases vying for his attention.

"He does tend to forget that the telescopic lens provides better visuals for the customer than his cell phone," Baylee said.

"I should be able to swing by Allen Daigle's office later and check up on him."

"Where do you plan on starting your investigation, Mr. Wolfe?"

"Where else? At the bar, of course."

Clay was still grinning as he pushed his way through the swinging doors of the Seal Bar and Tavern a few minutes later. Of course, he had to remember to not throw his 1950's gumshoe slang around outside of the office, especially in this day and age of political correctness. He understood this and agreed with it, but it was still fun to rile Baylee with objectionable and outdated zingers. Usually, she gave as good as she got, and he wondered vaguely what had put her off her game lately.

The Seal Bar was, for ten months of the year anyway, a local hangout on the harbor. The months of July and August saw the regulars pushed across the street, away from the water up the hill to a more local bar, Lucky Linda's, making way for the summer crowd, which was comprised of both the wealthy residents and the tourists. The distinction was that the wealthy owned a home here while the tourists just rented.

Port Essex was possibly the most beautiful place in the world for those two glorious months, and those of means recognized this, choosing to own a house here as one in their stable of homes around the world. Most of these mansions were across the harbor from the Seal Bar, which was located in the downtown area of small businesses—mostly restaurants, motels, bars, and gift shops. A walking bridge traversed the inlet connecting this downtown with the far side for those who didn't want to search for parking.

And then, of course, there were the tourists who rolled into town for a few days to a week and ran amok trying desperately to fill every second of their vacation with memorable images they could post to social media to show how exceptional their lives really were. Families that clogged the sidewalks window shopping while complaining about being bored. Men who came to play golf, get drunk, and wreak havoc. Pretentious couples who thought that everything was so quaint and would stop a crowd to get a selfie at the drop of a hat. Of course, all of these people were catered to and welcomed. They may not have been the beating heart of Port Essex, but their wallets were certainly the veins that brought the money streaming in. In September, the locals would all sigh a big gasp of relief, count their money, and budget to survive until the following July.

So, for two months, the Seal Bar and Tavern catered to the wealthy and the tourists, putting up with these people from away for the greenbacks they brought to the local economy. The bar, located to the left once inside the door, was a square with stools all the way around occupied mostly by locals, at least at this time of day. With the upcoming Fourth of July weekend, generally recognized as the start of the summer season, the regulars would soon migrate to Lucky Linda's. But as yet, there were still seven or eight of them sitting around making small talk with each other and the bartender, who was being kept busy filling drink orders from the restaurant, which swooped out towards the harbor and the views. These tables were filled with the early tourist lunch crowd, trading mediocre food for the exceptional view.

Clay slid into a seat next to a man who was as wise as he was wizened. If lines on a face could be read as adventures lived, then Joe Murphy had seen the world. In reality, he'd not been out of the state since arriving on a boat fleeing the violence of his native Ireland some fifty years earlier. Clay didn't know anything about those years of the man's life, only guessing that he'd been a member of the IRA, and that he'd decided to emigrate rather than die. He'd gotten his clamming license, at some point became a citizen, and lived a simple life.

Now, at seventy-four, he spent all day, every day, on a barstool. Clay had never seen the man drunk, but then he wasn't sure if he knew what Joe Murphy looked like sober, either. At first, he'd assumed he was just another poor, broken-down drunk cadging rotgut liquor, but then discovered the man drank Jameson's exclusively, which was too expensive for the normal government-check drinker. Perhaps he'd socked away a few shekels over the years.

"Clay Wolfe! Aye, me fella, what's the story?" Murphy asked. He occasionally slipped into an Irish brogue, though whether purposefully or subconsciously it was difficult to tell. The last fifty years had, for the most part, obscured his Irish birth.

"Murph. Just thought I'd get myself a drink. Can I buy you one?"

"So, this has nothing to do with your new client?"

"And who would that be?"

"Crystal Landry. Mother of the Wicked Witch of the West."

"How…?" Clay began and then stopped himself. This was why he was here. This man knew everything in town, often before it even happened. "Two Jameson's," he said to the bartender instead.

"Now, lawyers will do anything for money." Murphy cast his sparkling blue eyes at Clay, in his glance a question. "Is that true for private detectives?"

"What do you mean?" Clay took a nip of the Jameson. It was good. Too good.

"I'm asking if you're going to dig around and try to prove that baby killer is innocent?" Murphy had not yet touched the drink the bartender had set in front of him.

"I guess I'd do just about anything for the right money," Clay lied. "But in this case, Crystal wants me to bring the people dealing the drugs to the police. You know, then the cops can hookem-and-bookem, throw them in the hoosegow to share a cell with her daughter, the Wicked Witch of the West, as you call her."

"Ah, a noble cause, then."

"Yep. Although, I'd have preferred one that actually paid."

"Aye, lad, it is always nice to be paid well for doing good." Murphy grabbed his whiskey tumbler and clicked Clay's glass. "Let me know if that ever happens, for that would be news around this place. Can't imagine Crystal Landry has enough money for booze *and* your fees, not with her part-time laundromat job."

"I think I just spent the entire advance on these two fine Irish whiskies," Clay said.

"You ever wonder why people call money 'clams'?"

"Hadn't ever thought about it."

Murphy tipped his head back and let the remainder of the brown liquor slide down his throat. "It's because there *is* money in clams."

Yeah, right, Clay thought to himself. If you wanted to work the odd hours of the tides bent over for hours at a time doing excruciatingly brutal work. But he had heard that if you were willing and able to do this, you could make a hundred grand a year, and that wasn't peanuts.

"You pretty much know everybody and everything in town," Clay said. "Maybe you can help me out with a few things."

"You know the wharf just past your office? At the old boatyard?" Murphy asked. He waited for Clay to nod before he continued. "I was thinking of doing a bit of fishing tomorrow morning. Maybe you'd like to join me?" He pinned Clay's eyes with his own and then let his gaze traverse the bar and the patrons sitting around, most of them as attentive to the two men's conversation as to the level of the booze in the glass in front of them.

"Yeah, sure," Clay said. "What time?"

"Sunrise is at 5:00 and high tide just past 7:00. What say we meet at 6:00?"

Clay nodded. 6:00 in the morning? It'd been awhile since he'd seen that time of the day. And here was this old codger who drank whiskey all day who was probably up then every morning, rain or shine, winter or summer. Clay began to get an inkling that the man might have been making more than a hundred grand a year from more than clamming.

"6:00 is good."

Murphy cast a knowing glance at him. "I'll bring a rod for you."

Clay forced himself from the stool and out the door. The Irish whiskey had been damn good. He crossed over Commercial Way and followed Cabot Street around and up the hill to the *Port Essex Register*. It was a daily paper that came out in the afternoon five days a week. Many of the stories were newswire from other publications, but a handful of reporters and editors scoped out the local news. He was betting that he knew exactly who it was who had covered the infant overdose.

There was a receptionist providing nominal protection from the public. It was mostly for show, as all the locals knew, for Sally would always launch into a good morning, and the regulars might ask after her kids, and whether her new puppy was past the chewing stage. Clay was a regular, so he spent a minute chatting before entering the newsroom, with advertising on one side and news on the other, about a dozen desks, altogether.

Marie Cloutier was the managing editor, whatever that meant, but on top of those duties she wrote more stories for the rag of a newspaper than anybody else. She had a pretty face, her hair curling around it in a bob, with glasses perched on her nose as she clattered away on a keyboard.

"Hello, Marie," Clay said.

She finished what she was doing, pressed her glasses firmly back on, and looked up. "Clay. How's your grandfather?"

He smiled. Of course, she'd known that Gene had been taken to Mid Coast Hospital. "He's fine. Shook himself up a bit, sprained his knee, but he's back home."

"How'd he fall?"

The story must not have been big enough to investigate that far. "Maybe you should ask him. He won't tell me, but I think there may have been a bottle, or a widow, involved, or perhaps both."

Cloutier laughed. "You must need something."

"I was just hoping you might be available for lunch. Even newshounds have to eat, am I right?"

"You know the way to my heart, Clay Wolfe. The deli next door sells beer now."

They did indeed, and one of them was the 120-minute IPA from Dogfish Head. That coupled with a chicken salad wrap and some Utz potato chips were soon on the way to their table, both of them having ordered the same thing.

"What do you need?" Cloutier asked.

"Can't a bloke just ask a pretty lass to lunch?"

"One would think, but in reality, no."

"What do you know about Kelly Anne Landry?"

"The heroin addict who killed her own baby?"

"That's the one."

"What do you want to know?"

"For starters, did she do the crime?" Clay asked.

The beers came out and they clinked bottles, disdaining the glasses offered, and tipped back a slug. Clay didn't know a lot of women who enjoyed beer, but Marie Cloutier was one, and she could keep up her end with most men.

"Sure looks that way. Boyfriend copped her to the whole thing," Cloutier said.

"Maybe he's lying to protect himself?"

"Could be, but I don't think Dylan Thompson is smart enough. He was pretty detailed, including how she assured him it wasn't a problem, as she'd done it with both her older children, and they were just fine."

"Do you know where I can find him?"

"He's got a trailer in Botany Village," Cloutier said.

"The same park as Crystal Landry?" Clay asked in surprise.

"Yep. She watched the kids quite a bit, usually at her place."

"But he kicked Kelly Anne out?"

The wraps arrived and Cloutier took an enormous bite. "More like he didn't let her back in the door when she got out of jail." She liked food and beer and cigarettes and was unapologetic about it.

"That brings me to the question of how the hell is she out on bail? She killed a baby and is out less than two weeks later?"

"All they could charge her with was child endangerment, and Maine doesn't have any felony charges for that particular heinous crime." She shook her head ruefully, "Go figure. Most serious charge they can levy against her is a Class D misdemeanor that carries a maximum penalty of one year in jail and up to $2,000 in fines."

"For killing a baby?"

"The DA doesn't think they can make anything more serious stick."

"That's messed up," Clay said.

"Damn straight it is," Cloutier replied.

Clay took a bite and washed it down with some beer. He idly wondered if the deli now served beer, whether or not they had to change their business designation. Did this make them a pub? A tavern?

"How about you tell me why you want to know all this?" Cloutier asked. "Don't tell me you're working for Kelly Anne to prove her innocence?"

"I've been hired to find the person or people who supplied Kelly Anne Landry with the heroin that killed her baby girl." Clay chewed another bite.

"Hired? By who?"

"The grandmother hired me."

"Crystal Landry? Does she think her precious daughter will be freed when the real bad guys are found?" Cloutier finished her wrap and began eyeing Clay's.

"I don't know. If pressed, I'd guess that it's half vengeance and half easing her conscience, that her daughter was manipulated, you know, the victim of the drug dealers."

"I guess I can see that. But most people would say it's not guns that kill people, but people that kill people." Cloutier was one of the few people in Port Essex who openly supported gun control legislation. "So, following that along, it's not the drugs but the person who killed little Ariel Landry. And that person is no other than Kelly Anne."

"You better be careful what you write," Clay said. "You start putting words on paper that say guns and drugs are bad, well then, you're going to make a lot of enemies around here."

"How do you feel about guns, Clay Wolfe?"

"I own one," he said. "But it only has thirteen shots, and I didn't mind waiting a few weeks to get it."

"I guess you *were* a homicide detective, not that the bobbies over in the UK seem to need guns to keep the peace."

"If it makes you feel better, it is safely tucked away separate from the ammo that goes with it."

"And how do you feel about drugs?" Cloutier moved the subject on, knowing that Clay's abrupt departure from the Boston PD after having killed a man in the line of duty was still a raw wound. A fact that he'd shared with her after a few too many drinks one night.

Clay pushed over the second half of his wrap. "Guess I don't have a problem with weed, not that I enjoy it, but the opioids running rampant? Heroin? OxyContin? Bath salts? Guess I could do without them in my town."

"You getting paid to run these drug dealers to ground?"

"Fifty big ones." He rolled his eyes. "As in dollars."

"What else you need to know?"

"Tell me about the case."

Cloutier chawed off half of his wrap in one bite, chewing loudly. "The baby had been left with the grandmother, Crystal Landry. She called 911, and the paramedics showed up because the little girl stopped breathing. They were unable to resuscitate her. Cause of death was initially unknown, but then the Maine Medical Examiner's Office informed the police that test results showed the little girl died from fentanyl intoxication. You know what fentanyl is?"

"Something they mix with heroin?"

"It's a potent synthetic painkiller that is often mixed with heroin to give it more kick. It's the largest cause of fatal overdoses out there. The ME also said it had been ingested directly. At first, the mom, Kelly Anne, denied any knowledge of how it could've happened, but then the boyfriend copped a plea and told the investigating officer he saw her rubbing the residue from their baggies on the baby's gums several times, and that she'd told him not to worry about it, as she'd done it before with her older kids."

"Where are the siblings at now?" Clay asked.

"Don't know. Most likely wards of the state."

"And the boyfriend?"

"He hasn't been charged with anything. Not yet."

"Is he telling the truth?"

"I know it sounds judgy, but he really is too dumb to lie."

"You know where Kelly Anne is?"

"You should be able to check the courthouse records. Think she has to give an address to get out on bail."

"Yeah, just trying to save myself a drive." Clay looked at the bill, stuck his card in, and handed it to the waitress.

"You know anything about the drug scene in Port Essex?" Cloutier asked.

"Not really my thing."

"Can't say I know much more than you. All I know is it's getting bad. Seems like we've been flooded with the shit lately."

"Yeah, I guess it's time for me to crawl into the seedy underbelly of Port Essex and see what I can find."

They walked to the door and out into the sunlight of the last day of June. "Whatever I can do to help, Clay," Cloutier said. "But one thing remains the same. Kelly Anne Landry is a fucking baby killer, and that is unforgivable."

Chapter 3

STILL TUESDAY, JUNE 30TH

Jake Lobbins climbed into his pickup truck with trepidation. He had come to hate Tuesdays when he had to make the delivery. He felt safe out on the water, but something about dry land made his legs quake, and of course, he had to deal with the bosses. He looked over his shoulder at his forty-five-foot boat, the *Lob-Star*, and just the sight of her gave him a burst of confidence that allowed him to face his fears. Most people named their fishing boats after their mothers, wives, or daughters. Women's names. Not Jake. The most important thing in his life had been his glory days of high school football. Now it was this boat. Five more years and it would be paid off. Just five more years.

The garbage bag on the floor of the passenger seat was filled with eighty packages of heroin. Each of these consisted of ten grams. When broken up into single use baggies and sold at $10 a pop, that was $160,000.

A year earlier, Jake had thrown a disc in his back, hauling traps. He had no insurance, so he ignored it as long as he could. Not once did he admit to himself that Obamacare might have been a good thing, had he maintained his coverage once the mandatory participation had been abolished. As the monthly premiums irked him, he'd let his policy lapse and again returned to the ranks of the uninsured. After all, he'd rationalized, no use throwing money away.

And then the injury. He'd ignored it for a month, but soon he was unable to work, and was forced to go to the Urgent Care, where some quack told him he needed surgery. By the time it was all over, it had cost him $80,000—eighty grand he didn't have. He'd been able to get an equity loan, putting *Lob-Star* up as collateral. None of this was the real problem.

The real problem was the sixty pills of OxyContin the doctor had sent him home with. Three pills a day for twenty days. After five days he was back to work. He had to earn a living, after all. The pain was still lingering when the bottle was empty, and the desire for the numbing effect was raging. Unable to get a prescription, he started paying $15 a pill on the street. Every day these little white miracles diminished in effect, until he was popping ten a day just to remain always on the edge of misery.

He'd been on the verge of defaulting on the boat payments. There was some drinking to go along with the meds, not a good combination. Somewhere in there his wife had left, taking his two young boys with her. Jake Lobbins was contemplating suicide when the strange dude with the acrid breath and eyes the color of a dead mackerel approached him with an offer. And suddenly there was a way out. All he had to do was become a drug mule. His plan was to cut his daily pill consumption by one every week until he was free and clear of his addiction.

Today's drop was set at the Knox Cove Grill, just this side of the bridge over to Spruce Island. It was only a few minutes' walk from where he moored his boat at the Knox Wharf, but Jake had product to deliver, and he didn't think walking down the street with it was advisable. He pulled his truck into the parking lot of the restaurant and got out, making sure to lock the doors. He usually never bothered, but it seemed a good idea with a garbage bag full of heroin.

The man with the acrid breath and the Lieutenant were at a table, already eating. That was fine with Jake. He had no appetite anyway. He looked out the window past them at Knox Cove sparkling in the sunshine of this March day. He'd grown up just across the way and had been fishing there almost since before he could stand. When new owners had bought this grill a few years back, they'd adopted the moniker of the cove and put it on a sign over the door. Before that, it had been Dale's Grub for years.

"Jake, sit down." The Lieutenant's eyes were chillingly blue.

He sat down. He'd learned to listen to their orders, something he'd never been very good at in other circumstances. Not with his parents, or the football coach in high school, and not with his wife. It was probably why he had followed in his father's footsteps and become a lobsterman. Out on the water, he was his own boss. His two cousins worked for him, followed his orders. They had been plenty happy enough to earn more money by pulling heroin from the traps to go with the lobsters. As far as they knew, the only difference was they didn't have to measure the length of the heroin bags to determine whether or not to keep them. Jake could imagine the two dolts throwing the bags back in the water for being too short. Of course, being a mule was more lucrative than being a lobsterman, especially if you weren't pissing it all away on Oxy.

Early on, Jake had missed a drop, being too tired to deal with it, and had woken in the middle of the night with a gun pressed to his forehead. On the other end of it had been the man with the acrid breath. Jake got the message.

"Something to eat? Drink?" The Lieutenant asked.

"I'll have a Bud."

The Lieutenant waved the waiter over and placed the order. "Everything smooth on the water?"

"The traps were full. I have the…lobsters…in the front of the truck for you."

"Excellent." Acrid Breath trapped him with intense blue eyes. "Any problems?"

"Everything is fine."

"Your cousins happy with the arrangements?" Acrid Breath asked harshly.

"They're all good," Jake said. "You good with my end?"

"You are doing a great job, Jake, keep it up."

"Anything I should know?"

"There is one little hiccup," The Lieutenant said.

"Hiccup?"

"Did you hear about the little girl who died?" Acrid Breath asked.

"What little girl?"

"Just a baby, really. I think she was six months old."

"In Port Essex?" Jake was flummoxed as to where this was going.

"Yeah, out to Botany Village." Acrid Breath was busy popping fried clams into his mouth.

"What's that got to do with anything?"

"Supposedly her mother was wiping heroin from the empty baggies on the baby's gums to shut her up." Acrid Breath smiled, as if the image gave him pleasure.

"What?" Jake wasn't much for watching the fake news or reading the newspaper. "Was it...?"

"Relax, Jake. I'm heading up the investigation, for now at least. The State Police are involved, but I can control that end. There's nothing to worry about." The Lieutenant spoke in clipped words, each syllable delivered as if stamped from a machine. "It was an accidental death and not a murder. The Staties will soon go away and leave it in my hands."

This did not appease Jake. He was indirectly responsible for the death of a little girl. "How old did you say she was?"

"Under a year." Lieutenant Smith said. "The grandmother hired a private detective to investigate where the drugs came from. A man by the name of Clay Wolfe."

"Clay?"

"That's the one. Just thought you should know in case he comes poking around."

"Why would he come out here? Does he know something?"

"Relax, Jake. He knows nothing. I just wanted to give you a heads up."

Jake thought about his two young boys. He only got to see them on Sundays. He wondered again about killing himself but knew that he was too much of a coward to do that. It would be so simple. Take the *Lob-Star* out to the deep water where he pulled the traps full of lobsters and drugs. Attach a cinder block to his leg and simply step over the side and let the icy water embrace him.

"Perhaps we could take a break until things cool down?" Jake asked.

Acrid Breath lived up to the name Jake had given him, barking out a cackle that was a cross between a seal and a wounded seagull. While the sound was an offense to Jake's ears, it was more the man's breath, washing over him like a toxic cloud of smoke from burning tires, that repulsed him.

"We can't take a break, Jake," The Lieutenant said patiently. "What about our regular clients? They would be forced to go elsewhere. What about our dealers? We provide a service, and any interruptions would have rippling and devastating repercussions."

"Don't the state police handle all the murders in Maine?" Jake asked.

"This wasn't a homicide, Jake. It was an accidental death. Besides, they won't want to touch it, not with a ten-foot pole. I'm in charge of the investigation, and they're happy to distance themselves." The Lieutenant slammed down a shot of tequila. It was the second, while a third, still full, remained on the table.

"And this private detective? Clay Wolfe?"

"You know him?" Acrid Breath asked.

"Went to school with him. Played ball with him. He was the quarterback last time Port Essex won the state championship." Jake hadn't spoken to Clay since he'd come back to town about a year ago. He'd seen him around a few times, mostly at the bars, but had slunk back into the shadows.

"Well, I'll be," Acrid Breath said. "What position you play?"

"Linebacker," Jake said. "Some offensive line."

"You two keep up?" The question had an underlying hint of violence twisting through it.

"Nah, not for years."

"He's a fucking Walmart cop who likes to tip the bottle. He won't be any bother at all." Acrid Breath was twirling a steak knife in his hand as he spoke.

Jake wondered why the man had a steak knife if he'd ordered clams. "Okay, then," he said. "When's the next drop?" He wondered about reaching across the table, grabbing the knife, and driving it into the man's throat.

"Next Tuesday. You should begin hauling the traps by 6:00 a.m."

It was always Tuesday, but Jake liked to make sure. "You got something for me?"

Acrid Breath pulled a plastic bag from the floor and set it on the table in front of Jake. "You going to drink your beer?"

Jake guzzled the Budweiser down and picked up the bag and headed for the door. Acrid Breath followed him while the Lieutenant finished the tequila and paid the bill. After he slid the garbage bag into the backseat of 2019 GMC Yukon Denali with tinted windows, Acrid Breath grabbed Jake by the elbow, and leaned in, his putrid breath thick and suffocating, and told him he best just keep following instructions if he knew what was good for him.

Once back in the truck, Jake dug underneath the cash in the bag with shaking fingers and pulled out the vial of sixty 20-mg. OxyContin pills. Try as he might, he couldn't make them last a full week, and by next Monday he'd be trembling and in need of his weekly hook-up. He popped two into his mouth and washed them down with the cold coffee in his travel mug. He could, of course, purchase more on his own, but he was trying very hard to not do that. The cash in the bag would pay his cousins for their part and bite into his boat loan and health care costs, leaving just enough for weekly expenses.

He did have income from lobsters as well, but this past year had not been a banner one. Between the late molting that caused a shortage during the lucrative summer months when tourists bought lobster rolls like hot dogs, the ridiculous price of bait after the poor pogy catches, and the new quota on herring, he'd barely broken even. It wasn't cheap to power the boat for the forty-five-mile ride out into the Atlantic Ocean. And, then of course, there was child support and alimony.

Jake stopped at the store and bought a twelve-pack of Bud and a pack of smokes. He planned on going home and drinking himself to sleep. This was not a result of the day running drugs, the meeting with Acrid Breath and the Lieutenant, or the news of the baby who died. It was just what he did every night now.

Chapter 4

STILL TUESDAY, JUNE 30TH

Clay had always liked the view of Port Essex from the top of the hill here by the *Daily Register*. He took a moment to take a gander at the town laid out before him like a postcard. The population of 16,000 year-round residents swelled to 24,000 in the two upcoming months. On this midafternoon weekday leading up to the holiday weekend, people filled the sidewalks, and cars jammed the small winding streets. With the Fourth of July on a Saturday this year, he dreaded the crowds that would stream into his town over the coming days, crowds who would linger until after Labor Day weekend, generally seen as the end of the tourist season.

And it *was* his town. He'd been born here. Had grown up here. Sure, he had gone away. Had needed to leave. Clay had wanted to be a cop ever since his parents died. So, he'd gone to Boston University, got his BS in Criminal Justice, joined Boston PD as a beat cop, attended the police academy, passed his Civil Service Exam, and was a homicide detective by age twenty-nine. He hadn't understood what he was missing until he returned. It was sort of like when he'd wrenched his knee his junior year in football. He didn't know how bad it was until it was better.

On days like this it was almost hard to believe that Port Essex was real. The harbor was glittering before him like a diamond necklace wrapped carefully around the swanlike neck of a beautiful woman.

Businesses, from fancy galleries to gritty storefronts selling T-shirts, beach toys, and drug paraphernalia, adorned this side of the harbor. And most important of all, inside of each of these places real people worked. Men and women you could talk to without them looking over your shoulder with eyes glazed over, or pulling out their cell phone to check messages, social media alerts, or the weather.

Across the curving inlet were magnificent homes with a few restaurants scattered throughout, and just to keep it humble, a rough and tumble lobster wharf littered with traps, ropes, and bins, the breeze carrying the tang of the sea and the faint reek of rotting bait. And, while these wealthy occupants were only summer residents, they were people who understood quality of life. They didn't feel the need to work fourteen hours a day to be accomplished. They didn't want the glitz and lights of Las Vegas or Miami.

These were the things that Clay had come to understand in the year he'd been home. At the same time, he couldn't quite shake the feeling that he'd come back with his tail between his legs like a beaten dog, unable to make it in the real world. Not that he was treated this way by the residents of Port Essex. He seldom had a drink at a bar where somebody didn't want to relive some moment of that state football championship season, or when someone would introduce him as the Boston homicide detective who'd decided to come home to ply his wares as a private investigator. No, it was only he, Clay Wolfe, who knew the disdain he felt in running away from life in the city to return to the safety of small-town Maine. But, dammit, he liked it here.

He said hello to a few people as he wended his way back to his office on the waterfront. The sun was out, and summer was nigh, but an anchor was attached to his soul. He was, after all, investigating the death of a baby whose life was taken by heroin, or to be more exact, heroin laced with fentanyl. Beneath the fairy-tale charms of this village he called home was a darker, desperate place that he had already begun to wade into, and he was not yet certain how close it would come to drowning him.

"Hey Baylee, what's happening on the home front?" he asked upon entering his second-floor office.

"Business as usual. Busy keeping this place afloat while you gallivant around playing detective," she replied with a wicked grin.

"Playing?" Clay asked. "You have no idea what a day I've had." He hoped the breath mints covered the smell of liquor and beer on his breath. "You uncover who's trafficking heroin here in Port Essex?"

"Not much luck tracking down any drug dealers. But I got you an address for the boyfriend."

"Great." Clay's phone buzzed in his pocket, but he refrained from checking it, as he personally was annoyed by people always checking their phones while talking with another. It was probably Marie with the same information that Baylee had just offered up. "But if we could skip that step and solve the case, I could put it to rest and turn to paying clients."

"If I solved everything then I'd probably deserve the big office with a view, and you'd be out here greeting customers and answering the phone."

"I'm sure you'd be better than me at my job, but I'd certainly be worse than you at yours," Clay said.

"You okay with me leaving a few minutes before 4:00? I have an appointment."

"Sure. If I'm not here, just lock up."

"Are you ever here?"

"Crimes aren't solved at a desk." Clay knew this wasn't true and that many crooks were undone by men and women at computers or in forensics labs. "What's your appointment?"

"Therapy," Baylee said after a short pause.

Clay nodded. None of his business. But he wasn't very good about keeping his big yap shut. "What for?" He thought he already knew, but how did one casually ask, 'for killing your husband'?

"Just somebody to talk to."

"You can talk to me," Clay said. "I've got big ears, and I've been known to shut up for at least a whole minute at a time."

"Thanks."

"You know why I came back to Port Essex?"

"You missed the place?" Baylee asked.

Clay gave her a half-smile that lit up his face. "That too, but I came back because I was dealing with killing a man."

"Yeah, I read about it online," she said.

"He was a bad man."

"Nobody deserves to die, though, do they?" she asked.

"Nobody deserves to die, but some need to," he replied.

"Did it help, killing the man?"

"What do you mean?"

"Did it make the world a better place?"

"Maybe a smidgen." How had they gotten to talking about him? Clay wondered. And, were they talking about him? Or were they talking about both of them? "But it didn't solve the bigger issue, which was sex trafficking. I had the ringleader dead to rights, but the bastard had a team of lawyers that got the charges dismissed."

"The bastards always get away, don't they?" she asked grimly.

"Not always," he said. He didn't add, 'not if you kill the fuckers.'

The phone rang, and Baylee picked it up. Clay took the chance to pull his cell phone out. There was a text from Donna.

You free to get together at 4?

He pecked out a quick reply.

Sure. Your place?

Of course, he knew that it would be, but he didn't want to be an assumer.

Yep.

Came the reply.

"You want Don to stay watching Stout until lights out tonight?" Baylee was holding her hand over the receiver of the retro rotary dial phone. Don was keeping an eye on the BIW employee out on a workman's comp claim.

"Yeah, sure. See if he can get a peek inside. See if he's doing cartwheels in the kitchen."

Baylee passed on the request and then hung up. "How'd it make you feel?" she asked.

"What?"

"Killing somebody."

"I felt like I'd done a service to the world," he said.

"Really?"

Clay looked at her wide eyes and knew he couldn't lie. "Nah, not really. I felt…I feel like shit. If I didn't keep reenacting it in my dreams at night, I might be over it."

"Yeah, I know what you mean," she whispered.

"If I hadn't plugged him, he would've killed me," Clay said.

"Yes, he would have. If not that night, then soon. It was only a matter of time."

Again, Clay was not sure which of them they were talking about. "Nothing we can do about it now. That cat isn't going back in that bag."

"I'm going to head out a bit early and grab some coffee on the way, if that's okay?" Baylee asked.

Clay checked the time on his phone. It was quarter to 4:00. "Yeah, I've got an appointment at 4:00 as well. I'll walk you out."

"Who you appointing with?" she asked as they walked down the wooden stairs.

"Undercover work," he replied.

"Whatever that means," she said. "Don't forget to check in on Daigle tonight."

"Got it. I'm going home to get my Jeep. Which way you going?"

"Downtown." Baylee turned and took several steps, and then stopped and turned back. "Clay? Thanks for talking."

"Sure thing. Maybe we can have a drink sometime and talk more."

"Isn't there a company policy about no fraternizing outside of work between owner and employee?"

"I'll check the manual and get back to you. Of course, that may be a while as I have to go write the manual first."

Clay was fifteen minutes late to Donna's house. She lived around the harbor on the edge of the wealthy estates, a house that was just far enough from the water or any kind of view to make it not quite one of them. There was a bottle of Hornito's Black Barrel tequila and two shot glasses on the table next to her chair on the covered porch. One had a trace of the dark amber liquid in the bottom. She poured two more.

"You're late," she said.

"Summer at 4:00 in Port Essex? I'm lucky to have made it at all. I could've walked faster."

She stood and handed him a shot glass. "Consider this buying you a drink. I have to be somewhere in an hour." She slammed back her glass with a toss of the hand and a tip of the head.

Clay shrugged and followed suit. Whiskey in the morning. Beer at lunch. Tequila before sex. All in a good day's work. He followed Donna into the house and down the hall to her bedroom. She already had her shirt and bra off and was looking at herself in the mirror. She had strong shoulders and muscular arms with a stomach you could bounce a quarter off of, as she'd urged him to do on several occasions as proof.

He'd met her six months ago at the Pelican Perch, but he sometimes felt that it was less than chance, and that he was the prey and she the huntress. He'd never seen her back there since. She'd bought him a drink, invited him back to her place, and made the first move. Clay was not used to such an aggressive woman. He found he didn't mind, and as a matter of fact, kind of liked it. It was such a relief to have a woman in his life who didn't go through a checklist as if to prove to herself that she wasn't a slut. Donna liked sex and made no bones about it.

In the past half-year, he'd barely cracked the outer shell that protected whatever it was that made her tick. This, Clay knew, because he'd created his own, purposefully insulating his frangible inner self. This veneer kept him from developing deeper relationships, he knew, but he had as yet to find the desire to peel back his own shell. And now, with Donna? So far, it seemed, there was no need, because she seemed to desire little more than physical contact.

"Do you think I'm gaining weight?" she asked.

"Not an ounce." Clay sat on the edge of the bed and removed his Hubbard dress shoes, polished brown leather he buffed every other day.

"My boobs aren't sagging?"

"Going the other way if anything." They were ample and firm, he thought, but gravity might have its way with them in another ten years.

She removed her gun and lay it on the bureau, and then slid out of her pants. She was wearing blue lace panties that matched the cool color of her eyes. She undid her hair tie and shook out her blonde frosted locks. "You're just trying to get into my pants," she said.

"Seems to be working."

Clay removed his checkered waistcoat and draped it on the seat of the chair at the vanity. He unbuttoned his shirt and hung it carefully over the back. Donna came over and undid his belt and jerked open his jeans, sliding them down to his ankles.

"You're too slow," she said. "I told you I'm on the clock." She turned him and shoved him onto the bed, pulling his pants off with a wrench. She reached inside his boxers and grabbed him with her hand. "That's what I'm talking about."

Sex was fast and furious as always. Afterwards she lit up a cigarette. "I heard you got a new case today."

"Yeah? Where'd you hear that?"

"I got my sources." She smiled coyly.

"What'd you hear?" he asked.

"That doper's mother hired you to find who sold her daughter the drugs."

"No secrets in this town."

"You got any leads?"

"I just got the case," he said. "You got anything I should know about it?"

"Couldn't tell you if I did." She looked at him quizzically, and he wasn't sure if she was serious. "Besides," she continued, and this time he had no doubt, "I think you should let the police handle it." Donna stood up, sliding into her panties with one fluid motion. "Get dressed. I got to be somewhere in ten."

"Hell, you want to leave me some cash?" he asked.

"What do you need?" she asked.

Clay stood and began to dress. What single guy would be upset about sex with no strings attached, he asked himself? Wham, bam, thank you ma'am. Except he felt like he might be the ma'am in this situation.

"Hey," she said as he was about to get into his Jeep. "You keep me informed of any progress you make on that doper case."

He climbed into the Jeep. The top and doors were off and would stay that way for the summer. If it rained, he could put up the soft top, but more often than not, that was reason enough to not drive anywhere. He pecked out a quick text to Westy.

Beer at the Pelican Perch in 20?

Clay was sitting in traffic on Commercial Way when his phone buzzed.

Already here.

the message said.

Weston Beck had been Clay's best friend since the third grade. They had gone through all the rites of passage together. Sports. Homework. Drinking. Marijuana. Dating. Fights. Clay had been the quarterback and Westy the running back carrying Port Essex to the state championship in 2001. That same fall brought the New York City terrorist attacks, and it was that event that sent the two boys maturing into men in different directions.

Upon high school graduation, Clay prepared to attend Boston University choosing a Criminal Justice major, and Westy found a mentor for the Physical Screening Test to get into the Navy's SEAL program. While Clay navigated the classroom, parties, and affairs with numerous women in his first semester, Westy was attending boot camp in Great Lakes, Illinois.

In the Spring semester, Clay was rushing a fraternity, and becoming a brother through a haze of alcohol during Hell Week. Westy was in the midst of the SEALs' version of Hell Week, a 120-hour odyssey that involved little sleep while traversing over 200 miles in running, swimming, and paddling exercises, as well as things such as underwater knot tying.

When Clay graduated college, Westy was overseas, and the two fell out of touch. Even after they had reconnected years later, Westy never shared his experiences as a SEAL, and Clay knew better than to ask. The man did not talk about it.

The Pelican Perch was on the point just past Clay's office, a finger of land that separated Essex Harbor from Knox Cove and offered a stunning view of the shimmering Atlantic all the way to Ireland. Spruce Island was off to the right, while downtown Port Essex was back to the left. Clay climbed the three flights of rickety stairs to the outdoor bar on the restaurant's roof.

Westy was at the bar with a Budweiser in front of him. He was only six inches over five feet, but his shoulders were wider than most doorways, his chest resembling a barrel. His left arm was fully tatted up—a Viking warrior, various knots, then two SEAL emblems, first the bone frog signaling homage to a fallen comrade, and finally the menacing, elemental symbol of these special naval members, the trident. The images took on a life of their own in the rippling muscles of his arms. His hair was short and tight on top, but an impressive beard sprouted from his face, wild and groomed at the same time.

Clay slid into the seat next to him. "Stowaway," he said to the bartender.

"Wolfe-dog," Westy said.

Clay fist-bumped him. "Where you been hiding at, man?"

"Working for a living."

"What are you catching?"

"Getting the last of the mackerel for the season. Saturday, I got a bluefin tuna. Four hundred pounds."

"Dang, Westy, that's some good money."

"Put up one helluva fight. Can't imagine catching a real big one."

"How's the wife and son?" Clay took a third of the beer down with a single swig.

"Fair to middlin'. Probably wondering where I'm at, about now." Westy was not much of a chatterbox.

"Doing any diving?"

"Nah, too busy as of late, but I'm going to go out this Sunday, if you want to come along?"

"I'll see what I got going on."

Clay knew that the question was more polite than sincere. He would just hamper Westy in the water. Of course, the man had done a twenty-four-week basic underwater demolition program as part of his SEAL training, while Clay's only qualification had taken the form of a week-long certification in Bermuda.

"Cheating hearts of America keeping you busy?" Westy asked.

"Actually, I got hired to run a drug dealer to ground."

"Yeah?" Westy turned and faced Clay. "Fucking Miami Vice, huh?"

"Pretty much the same thing."

"Come to think of it, you dress like Don Johnson, 'cept you favor those prissy vest things and not his sports jacket."

"I'll take that as a compliment."

"Not intended as one."

"Who was his partner?"

"Don Johnson's? No idea."

"My point, exactly. Dress for success, my friend. Not that that isn't a fine-looking black tank-top and Target jeans."

Westy suddenly narrowed his eyes. "You're feeling pretty cocky," he said. "Where you coming from?"

"I was working."

"You know, for a private detective, you're a pretty shitty liar. You been batter-dipping the corn dog." Westy slapped Clay on the back with a hand like a shovel. "Hooking up with that mystery lady of yours, I take it. Good for you."

"What do you know about drugs in town?" Clay asked, steering their talk to safer ground. He didn't really want to talk about the regular hook-ups with Donna. Besides, how had Westy caught on so quickly, he wondered?

"You looking for Viagra?"

"Can we stay focused, please? And no, I don't need any help in that department, thank you very much. I'm looking for who's dealing heroin."

"Isn't arresting drug dealers a job for the police?"

"I guess they aren't getting it done."

"Who's your client?" Westy held up two fingers, signifying another round to the bartender.

"Crystal Landry. Her daughter thought it was a good idea to rub the residue from her heroin baggies onto her baby girl's gums to stop her from crying. The baby overdosed."

"Fuck. That'd be Kelly Anne. She's a real piece of work." Westy took a slug of his Bud. "I still don't get why you been hired."

Clay looked down the bar. There were a few regulars there, but nobody paying their conversation any mind. A man who appeared as if he'd come here mistakenly instead of the yacht club looked up and caught his glance. He tipped his tumbler of brown liquor and smiled.

"I think Grandma Landry wants somebody to share the blame with her daughter," Clay said in a lowered voice. "You got any knowledge on who might be dealing in town?"

"Maybe weed, but heroin? Shit no. You might try up to Lucky Linda's. That's a pretty sketchy crowd at night."

"You mean where Murphy and the old-timers hang out?"

"Yeah, that's the place. But you got to go there long after those old salts are gone. Whole new crowd after 10:00."

"You want to order some food, have a few drinks, and mosey over there later with me?" Clay asked.

Westy laughed like a tank firing. He stood up and tossed a twenty on the table. "Not me, partner. Faith is holding dinner for me, and I got to be out on the boat before the sun is up. Good luck to you."

Clay waved his friend away and looked at his phone to check the time. It was 6:30. He had over three hours to kill. Have some dinner. A few more drinks. He should hold back on those if he wanted to be less than a mess at Lucky Linda's, as he didn't make it much past 10:00 before turning in these days. He had to swing by Allen Daigle's office and see if he could catch the man with his hand in the cookie jar, or up his secretary's dress. As both parties were married, chances were that they were shacking up in a motel room somewhere, but Clay didn't think so. Daigle's wife said she had access to the credit card statement, and there weren't any surprise charges. Plus, he knew Daigle, and the man was too cheap to be paying for a room he was only going to use for a couple of hours. No, if he was cheating, it was at the office.

"Mind if I join you?" The misplaced yacht club man stood over the seat vacated by Westy. He had a blue blazer with gold buttons and a striped tie with anchors on it, both looking so goddamn luxurious, yet so simple, that Clay knew they cost thousands of dollars.

"Help yourself," Clay said.

"Niles Harrington." The man held out a hand.

"Clay Wolfe." He wanted to ask him if he was Niles Harrington the third but refrained.

"You're a private detective?"

"Yeah, sure. Who told you that?"

"The bartender." Niles sat down. "Can I buy you a drink?"

"Got one. Just ordered a burger."

Clay took a longer appraisal of the man. He was tall with a tanned face and blond hair combed back to reveal a long forehead. His teeth seemed unnaturally white, his eyes quite open and friendly.

"I don't mean to snoop into your business, Mr. Wolfe, but I heard you talking to your friend. I had made inquiries of the bartender earlier because it struck me that I might be in need of your skills." Niles tilted his glass and twirled the cubes and liquor as if struggling with how to proceed.

Clay assumed the man wanted to hire him as a bodyguard, which was often a plush assignment with a variety of perks, but he just didn't have time. "My docket is pretty full right now, Mr. Harrington."

"Please, call me Niles."

"If you call me Clay."

"My need does not require immediate attention, Clay."

"And what is your need, exactly, Niles?" Clay asked, feeling a little bit as if he was playing Jeeves to Niles' Bertie.

Niles took a nip of his drink and set the glass down as if having made up his mind. He reached into an inner pocket and pulled out a photograph. He set it down on the bar. "Do you know the work of Auguste Rodin?"

"The sculptor dude?"

"Yes. One of the most famous sculptors of all time. He lived in France during the late 19th and early 20th centuries."

Clay looked at the picture. It was the sculpted figure of a man. "Okay," he said.

"His most famous work, in my opinion, is the *Gates of Hell*. This was an amazingly intricate creation of the gates of hell as described by Dante in his famous work *Inferno*."

"Is there a point to this art lesson?" Clay asked.

"Bear with me, just for a moment," Niles said. "The *Gates of Hell* has over 200 individual figures adorning it. He later enlarged many of these figures as stand-alone creations. One such is the *Three Shades*, souls of the damned who stand above the *Gates of Hell* pointing at the inscription 'Abandon hope, all ye who enter here.'"

Clay was about to abandon all hope, but then his burger arrived. He was able to dig in while Niles continued on.

"Rodin ended up using the same figure in different poses for the *Three Shades*. An early model had one of the Shades in a pose that he eventually decided against. That relatively unknown early Shade was recently stolen from my house."

Clay set his burger down. "And this...Shade...is valuable?"

"It is worth many millions of dollars, Mr. Wolfe. But to me? It is priceless."

"And the police aren't having any luck?"

Niles raised his empty glass, and the bartender put two cubes in a fresh tumbler and grabbed the bottle of twenty-five year-old Bowmore. "Sure I can't interest you in a scotch?" he asked Clay.

"Sure. It will make a fine digestif to my meal," Clay said, taking another bite. He figured if he had to listen to the man's rambling, he might as well be enjoying a $50 single malt.

Niles raised two fingers at the bartender. "My grandfather was in the British 2nd Army during World War II. He was part of Operation Plunder that crossed the Rhine and shattered the last remnants of the German Army. At one point, his platoon was involved in a fierce fight at a farmhouse in the middle of the countryside. When it was all over, they had wiped out the Nazis taking refuge there. There were just a dozen men left alive in my grandfather's platoon."

"Kudos to your grandfather."

"The farmhouse contained a trove of art stolen from France. My grandfather walked away from there with The Shade."

"To stolen art." Clay raised his glass.

"Liberated art." Niles tapped his glass with Clay's.

"So, you can't go to the police," Clay said. "And you couldn't even have it insured?"

"No, and no."

"When was The Shade stolen, Niles?"

"I just discovered it missing this past Saturday."

"You're a sunbird, Niles?" The scotch lingered on Clay's lips, not a single harsh note, as if it were more a gentle caress of a woman's lips rather than liquor.

"A sunbird?"

"You know? The opposite of a snowbird. Somebody escaping the heat of the south for the cooler summers of Maine."

"Ah, I hadn't heard that before, very good. Yes, I suppose you could say I am a sunbird. My primary residence is in Houston, Texas. I spend most of July and August here in Port Essex. I had my man prepare the house for my arrival. He checks on the house weekly to make sure everything is in order while I am not here, but he of course didn't notice the missing Rodin sculpture. It could have occurred at any time over the winter."

"And you'd like me to find it? Maybe who stole it as well?" Niles nodded. Clay held out his hand as if to shake. "I charge $150 an hour plus expenses." He figured he ought to try and recoup the loss he was taking on the drug overdose case, and Niles certainly looked like he could afford it.

Niles shook Clay's hand and raised his glass. "To your success."

Chapter 5

STILL TUESDAY, JUNE 30TH

Baylee Baker walked away from her therapy session a bit disillusioned. A year ago, she'd shot and killed her husband, and even if it had been necessary, it was still a difficult burden to bear. At first, it had been good to talk to somebody about it. She had shared some with her friend, Tammy, but not the deeper and darker pieces. It was easier to open up to a complete stranger, sworn to silence, and one she paid for listening to her sob story. After a bit, Baylee came to realize that her 200 bucks an hour got her little else than a chance to talk.

"Dr. Rogers," Baylee said under her breath, "is nothing more than a quack."

At first, the venting, breathing into a paper bag, visualization, and other techniques had been helpful in coping with the overwhelming anxiety that would sweep through Baylee's body at any time of the day or night. When this no longer worked, Rogers had recommended Xanax for Baylee, connecting her with a local psychiatrist to write the script. After six months, the pair of them had begun to whittle the dosage down week by week. Something about it being addictive and not healthy for her in the long run.

Unbeknownst to her shrink, Baylee had found another means of obtaining Xanax. Where Dr. Rogers thought she'd been cutting back and using natural remedies, Baylee had actually been increasing her dosage to slow her fluttering heart and racing pulse. Now the final insult had been delivered. Doctor Rogers had totally cut her off and suggested two sessions a week, instead of just the one. Not that it mattered, for Baylee had made her own "appointment" to replace the lapsed prescription, one that she was on her way to right now. Of course, this man was neither doctor nor pharmacist, and most certainly did not accept health insurance.

There was a new coffee shop down an alley not too far from where her therapy session had been. As Baylee entered the small space, she thought of the irony of coming here to find a sedative instead of caffeine. She got a tea, more out of guilt than desire, and found a small table with two stools. The man was not here, so she buried her head in her phone, hoping nobody would recognize her. That would start the rumor mill turning, this being a small town. She could just imagine the talk that Baylee was dating again, just a year after killing her husband. The thought of dating Curtis made her shudder, not so much because of the lifeless eyes, but more for the terrible breath that smelled like the time all the pogies washed up on shore and rotted in the sun.

After a few minutes the chair across from her slid back and she looked up to see the man, who if she were honest, she would have to call her dealer. His irises were tiny, almost as black as his pupils, and were currently fixed intently upon her. His smooth-shaven head flowed like molten lava down his forehead to a ski-jump of a nose that flared dramatically up and out. But it was the sourness of his breath, a bitter, pungent odor, that repelled her the most. It was worse when the man laughed, a harsh barking noise that shot the stench like some chemical weapon across at her unprotected face.

"Baylee. You are looking beautiful this afternoon."

"Curtis," she replied. She did not know his last name.

"How have you been doing since last week?"

"I, uh, need more this week."

"No, I mean how has life been? How is your work?"

"My work?"

"Yes. You work for a private detective agency, don't you?"

She was quite certain that she'd never told him this. "Yes."

"You work for a man by the name of Clay Wolfe?" The man's birdlike eyes glared at her, utterly devoid of empathy.

"What does it matter to you who I work for?"

"It matters, Miss Baker, because we are engaged in an illegal activity. If you work for a private detective, that is something that I need to know."

"He doesn't know anything about this. He doesn't even know I'm on Xanax. Nobody does, except for my therapist and you, and now my therapist thinks I'm off, so just you, okay?"

At first Baylee had been angry, but she could feel the anxiety massing in her body, making her heart beat faster, her armpits suddenly wet in fear, and her breath catching in her throat. What if this man with the putrid breath cut her off on the same day her therapist had pulled the rug out, Baylee wondered? She wouldn't survive the night. Just this thought increased the trembling in her hands and made her dizzy. She tried breathing deeply while staring at a painting of a cow on the wall. *There is nothing to fear, there is nothing to fear, there is nothing to fear,* she repeated internally over and over.

"I just need to make certain that you will not share anything with your boss in regard to our…relationship," Curtis said.

"I won't," Baylee said. What relationship, she wondered? She took a sip of tea, using both hands to steady the mug against the shaking. "I don't want him to know any more than you do."

"What sort of cases does he work on, Baylee?" It seemed they were now back to a first-name basis.

"Usually insurance fraud or adultery," she said. "Sometimes he acts as a bodyguard."

Baylee failed to mention that just that day he'd been hired to find who was dealing heroin, particularly to that mother who'd killed her little girl with it. Could there be a connection here? But no, this man sold anxiety medicine, not heroin. He was, he had told her, a pharmaceutical salesman with excess samples looking to make a bit more money. That was a far cry from a heroin dealer. While he did wear a dapper suit, she had tried to imagine him in a doctor's office—and failed.

The man slid an envelope across the table.

"I need to double my order," Baylee said.

"This is all I have right now. I can have more for you this weekend."

"Okay." She slid an envelope with $60 in it back across the table.

He waved her off. "Keep it. This is on the house." He stood up and walked out the door.

Baylee melted back into her chair. Her skin was clammy. She thought she might vomit. With an effort, she went into the bathroom, washed her face, took a small cupped hand of water, and swallowed a two-milligram bar of Xanax.

•　　•　　•　　•

Lucky Linda's was filling up fast when Clay slid onto one of the last barstools available. It was hard to go backwards from expensive scotch to beer, but he gamely ordered a Bissell Brothers Substance, which was a brightly funky IPA. There were a lot of leather jackets in the room, and an equal number of overalls. Clay would guess that it was a cross between bikers and fishermen, with a third contingent of people—those who'd been thrown out of every other bar in town. AC/DC was cranking through the speakers, making talking all but impossible.

It had been some time since Clay had shoved himself into a seething mass of humanity, all of them amped up by alcohol and other stimulants and looking for sex, with maybe a bar fight or two thrown in for good measure. As a matter of fact, Lucky Linda's made him think of fraternity parties back in his college days. He'd had no idea that this raucous scene even existed in Port Essex.

Clay had been no stranger to bars in his life, but increasingly his idea of a good time was being with a couple of friends tipping back a few, all the while chatting or arguing about everything and nothing. Lately, he'd come to prefer the golf course, the porch overlooking the ocean at his grandfather's house, and the occasional happy hour with buddies.

Tattoos were a theme at Lucky Linda's, more so on the women than the men. The men outnumbered the women by about two to one, but the women made up for this numerical inferiority by being vocally superior. Across the bar, three women were screeching the lyrics to a Scorpions' song at the top of their lungs.

Clay scanned the room wondering what a drug dealer looked like in Port Essex. He had an inkling that they did not look like the street pharmacists in Boston. As far as he was concerned, half the people in here fit the image he'd conjured in his mind. He wasn't even sure if he was supposed to call it heroin, junk, white horse, dope, or any one of about fifty slang terms he'd found on the internet. He had been in homicide, after all, and not narcotics, even if the two often overlapped.

"You watch the game?" the guy next to him asked, nodding his head at the television where they were doing a recap of the Red Sox/ Yankees game from London.

"Saw some of it," Clay said. "Guess the Sox choked again?"

"London. Go figure. Seems a long way to go to play a baseball game."

They talked baseball, or rather, shouted back and forth over the din of the room. Clay realized he had brown liquor in front of him. He didn't remember ordering it, and his senses were dulled enough that he had no idea if it was the good stuff or the cheap stuff. He was hoping that he'd been wise enough to order Dewar's, or Jimmy Beam, for that matter. No sense spending good money when he couldn't appreciate it properly.

"Hey, you know where I can score some junk?" he asked his baseball pal as the bartender delivered another drink.

"Score some junk? What the fuck?" The guy glared at him, stood up, and walked off.

Perhaps this had been a bad idea, Clay thought, as a cute woman in her early thirties scooted into the empty seat. Either her T-shirt was too small or her breasts too large, but there were some major containment issues happening.

"Put whatever she's having on my tab," Clay said to the bartender.

"Thanks, honey," she said.

"I'm Clay," he said, holding out his hand.

"Tiffany," she said with a giggle. Several rose tattoos twirled up her arm disappearing under her sleeve, while an old-fashioned timepiece set to five o'clock was inked onto her wrist.

"You come here often, Tiffany?" Clay leaned in close to speak into her ear, her scent heavy in his nostrils.

"Just every night." Tiffany tossed her hair back with a shake of her head.

"Do you party?"

"Sure, I party. I'm here, aren't I?"

Clay convinced himself that he was just working up to asking if she knew any drug dealers that could hook him up, and that he wasn't actually flirting with her. She was ten years younger than he, and he would guess not a very interesting conversationalist. Of course, Clay was currently involved in a relationship that consisted solely of sex, so perhaps that was really his thing. But he knew it wasn't. An image of him telling Westy he was breaking off the no-strings-attached sex with the smoking hot blonde came to mind, and Clay chuckled aloud. Westy would have punched him immediately in the face.

"What's so funny?" Tiffany asked.

"Nothing," he said. "Hey, do you know where I can score some dope?"

"You mean weed?"

"No, I'm looking for heroin."

"I'm no fucking junkie." Tiffany grabbed her drink and walked off.

That was one sure way to prove he wasn't looking to get lucky at Linda's, Clay thought, as he watched the delicious Tiffany walk away.

"Lemonade," the bartender said.

Clay looked back around, thinking he was being cut off. "What?"

"You must not be from around here," the bartender said. "But here, it's called lemonade." He was drying a glass with a towel.

It took Clay's fuddled mind a bit to work through what was being said. "Do you know where I can score some…lemonade?"

"Check with those two over at the pool table." The bartender walked off.

Clay stood up, staggering slightly. He took a moment to gather his equilibrium and plot a path through the crowd before lurching off in the direction of the lone pool table. He passed by Tiffany who was talking with some guy, and she cast him a fuck off look.

"Anybody got winner?" Clay asked. He was not very good at pool. Darts was more his game.

The man about to shoot was short but extremely muscular, his upper torso showcased by his white wife-beater. He paused and looked up. "Chalkboard behind you."

Clay turned and viewed the list of names. "You mind if I ask you a question?"

Wife Beater straightened up. "What?"

"You know where I might score some lemonade?"

The second player, a tall stringy dude with a snake tattoo wrapping around his neck stepped forward and tapped Clay with his pool cue. "Ain't you that private detective? The one from the papers last fall?"

"I don't know what you're talking about," Clay said. "I need to score soon. I'm fucking jonesing here."

"And I *don't* know what you're talking about," Snake Tattoo said. "Get lost."

"Come on, man, help me out."

"I said get lost."

"I got money," Clay said.

Wife-Beater looked at the sheaf of twenties Clay had splayed out. "Round back," he said. "Next to the oak tree. Five minutes."

Clay started for the door, remembered the bartender had his credit card, and returned to settle up before exiting. It was dark out behind Lucky Linda's, a faint glow emanating from a dim light on the back of the building. There were seven vehicles crowded into space for five. It was too dark to discern which tree was an oak. He went and stood by the trees with a dumpster on his right and waited. It was less than a minute before he saw two figures come around the corner of the building.

"Watcha want?" Wife-Beater was now wearing a leather jacket.

"You guys selling heroin?" Clay wavered slightly.

"Let me see that money again," Wife-Beater said.

Clay pulled out a hundred dollars. "I need some information," he said.

Snake Tattoo ripped the money from his hands, and Wife-Beater punched him in the mouth. Clay lurched backwards, but then swung a roundhouse blow that caught the shorter man in the ear. The effort caused him to stagger, and Snake Tattoo clubbed him in the back of neck, knocking him to his knees. Wife-Beater stepped in and kicked him in the head, toppling him to the ground, and then both men started kicking him. Clay curled up into a ball and concentrated on not vomiting.

"We don't touch that fucking stuff," Wife-Beater said.

"You gonna get us killed saying we're dealing that shit." Snake Tattoo kicked him again. "The people selling the white horse are people you don't want to mess with."

"Who?" Clay asked.

A foot came down on his head, and the dim light wavered like an old bulb about to go out. Clay was dimly aware of them walking off. He closed his eyes for a moment.

"You want to find who's dealing, you gotta check the pots," a voice whispered in his ear.

Clay picked his head up, but there was nobody there.

Chapter 6

Murphy was already on the wharf when Clay arrived in the morning. It was 6:00 on the dot. The man was a solitary figure at the end of the old boat dock, his rod loose in his hand, the line dropping straight down. His only action was steadily raising and lowering the line about a foot at a time. The sun was a fully formed, fiery ball of yellow on the horizon.

"Hey, Murph," he said by way of warning as he walked up behind him.

"Morning, Clay."

"What are you fishing for?"

"I got me a Swedish Pimple Jig carrying a rather fine-looking shrimp hoping to tempt some dumb mackerel into jumping on board." The man's eyes sparkled with the same mischievousness as when drinking at the bar.

"Any luck?"

"Couple throw-backs." Murphy looked around at Clay. "Brought you a rod if you want to give it a shot."

"Yeah, I don't have a fishing license."

"Looks like you nicked your face shaving a few times," Murphy said. "And you didn't get any of the scruff off either."

"A couple of fellers took offense at me trying to buy heroin from them. They also took my money."

Murphy laughed, and Clay had a sudden vision of Lucky from Lucky Charms. He half-expected Murphy to say, 'they're magically delicious.'

"That's why they call it buying junk, I guess," Murphy said. "You learn anything?"

"Don't try to buy heroin from strangers at Lucky Linda's?"

"More of an OxyContin crowd there. You want to find heroin, you got to get out to the Side Door."

"Is that the place out by Botany Village?"

"Yeah, that's it. Around the corner from the homeless shelter."

"Got any names?"

Murphy looked at him. "Not for sure."

"I was taking a bit of a rest in the parking lot behind Lucky Linda's last night, and somebody whispered to me that if I wanted to find the drugs, then I should check the pots."

"The lobster pots?"

"That'd be my guess."

"Maybe the rumors are true," Murphy said.

"What's that?"

"I've heard a few whispers that Jake Lobbins is into something... illegal. He's been going out as far as forty-five miles, which isn't unusual in the winter, but he's still out a good twenty miles now. His two cousins work for him, and they've both been flashing money around. Jared bought himself a new F-150. He's been bragging he paid cash for it." There was not much that went on in town that Murphy didn't hear about, especially in the fishing community. The bonus of spending your day in the bar with your ears open.

"Maybe they just had a good year."

"Nobody had a good year in the lobster business. The molt was late, and the bait was expensive. Plus, I know the wholesaler, Jerry, who they sell to. Not a banner year for them."

"Where's Lobbins go out of?"

Murphy nodded his head to the right. "Just over there in Knox Cove. Jerry's Lobster Wharf."

"It's definitely worth checking into," Clay said. "Lobbins a big guy? Couple years younger than me?"

"Yeah. He was a stud linebacker a few years after you went off to college. Must've been a freshman or sophomore your senior year."

"Yeah, I remember him."

Murphy's rod suddenly bent over, and he reeled in a mackerel. The iridescent bluish green-backed fish with a silvery white underbelly was marked by twenty to thirty black bars running across the top half of its body.

"What else you need?" Murphy removed the mackerel from the lure and put it in his cooler of ice.

"You know where I can find Kelly Anne Landry?"

"She not staying with that loser boyfriend of hers?"

"Seems they had a falling out. Something about him turning her in for killing her baby."

Murphy dropped the line back down off the end of the wharf. "Don't know who she runs with, if anybody. I bet you ask around the Side Door, you might get something. Her mother got her a job at the Wash and Fold, but I'm betting she lost it while spending time in the slammer. Hell, she'll probably be at the Side Door this afternoon looking to trade a blow job for a drink or a fix. You might even get lucky if you play your cards right."

"Okay, thanks Murph, I owe you."

"For the blow job advice?"

"That, too."

"Been here a long time, Clay. Can't rightly say I'm happy with the drug problem coming in, killing so many people we know. Good luck to you."

Baylee came into the office at ten minutes before 9:00. Clay had been there for about two hours already, finishing up some paperwork. He heard the outer door open, and then her rustling around at her desk. He stepped to the door but paused a foot short of the opening, appreciating the vision of Baylee from afar.

Her hair was the color of caramel, currently twisted carefully in a bun. He'd only seen her twice with her locks unsheathed, such a lovely sight that he'd encouraged her to wear it down at the office, the milieu not exactly being corporate. He'd refrained, with difficulty, from repeating this, so as to not sound like some weirdo. But it was difficult, as he loved her hair cascading loosely down, a sight which often led to what Murphy would have called impure thoughts.

Baylee's hair was a compliment to her rich skin, tinted golden from her Native American heritage, her father's side tracing back to the Abenaki tribe who had inhabited these very shores. Her eyes, also brown, flashed between bewitching, provocative, mischievous, caring, and intelligent depending on the situation. Clay was still undecided if he had a preference.

The best part of Baylee Baker was that he could always count on her to give him her opinion and to tell him the truth. There was no waffling or sugar-coating. On several occasions she'd called him an ass and been perfectly correct. Clay shook his head.

"Good morning," he said, coming out of his inner lair.

"Morning, boss," Baylee said.

"I got us a new case last night."

"Is that the undercover work you were doing?"

Clay noticed her eyes were sleepy and her cheeks puffy. "No. I was down at the Pelican Perch, and some well-heeled dude approached me. He wants me to find a family heirloom that his grandpappy stole from the Nazis, who stole it from the French, and has now been stolen from him."

"Maybe the French came and took it back," Baylee said. "What's the heirloom?"

"A Shade."

"Like a lamp shade?"

"Apparently in The *Inferno*, which is the first part of the *Divine*

Comedy, or so the internet tells me, Dante refers to Three Shades who are souls damned to hell, and they hang out at the gates of hell and tell new arrivals to abandon all hope. This French guy, Auguste Rodin, made several versions of them for a sculpture called *The Gates of Hell*. One that he decided not to use, the *Fourth Shade* if you will, has been hanging out right here in Port Essex for the last seventy-some years."

"A fine place for souls damned to hell," Baylee said.

"Don't abandon all hope yet."

"So, it's a sculpture?"

"Yeah." Clay shrugged. "He's paying top dollar."

"Sounds better than hanging out with cheaters, druggies, and people committing insurance fraud." Baylee's walnut cheeks flushed slightly, and she shifted her eyes away from Clay.

"Something different," he said. "Anyway, I got to go out to his house in a bit and interview his property caretaker."

"Is our new client a sunbird?"

"Yeah, by way of Houston, Texas. Niles Harrington."

"The Third?" she asked.

Clay smiled. "Probably."

"You check up on Daigle last night?"

"Yep. Stopped over there at 8:00. Place locked up tight as a drum. Check in with his wife today and see what time he came home, could you?"

"Sure thing. How about Don?"

"He hasn't sent his report in. If you can get on him about that, that would be great. I'm taking it he didn't catch the man out back playing volleyball. We should stay on him the rest of the week, and then I'll check in with Bonny over at BIW and see what she wants to do."

"Okay, boss. How'd your undercover work go yesterday?"

An hour later, Clay found himself on the porch of a mansion on the shores of Penobscot Bay with a Bloody Mary in hand. He sat across from the property caretaker, Scott McKenny, and next to Niles Harrington. It was only 10:00 in the morning, but after the night he'd had, the drink seemed like a remarkably good idea. The porch ran the length of the back of the house overlooking the Atlantic Ocean. Several sailboats dotted the horizon, as well as a few fishing and pleasure boats. Clay thought he could see the silhouette of a liner moving across the very edge of his sight. Or maybe it was a cruise ship. A perfectly manicured lawn ran down to a rocky shoreline, and an American flag fluttered in the wind on the point of land.

"How long you been watching over the place, Mr. McKenny?" Clay asked.

"About ten years now, I reckon."

"What do you do here?"

"I guess just about everything. Landscape in the spring and summer. Rake in the fall. Plow in the winter. I come by once a week when Mr. Harrington isn't here."

"You have any employees?"

"I got a couple of guys do landscaping with me."

"Do they have access to the house?"

"No. I am the only one with a key."

Clay took a sip of the Bloody Mary. He realized there was a hot tub nestled into the rocks to the left. "When do you check in on the house?"

"Once a week, like I said." McKenny was a bulky man with a beard and small eyes.

"What day, Mr. McKenny?"

"Wednesdays, usually."

"What do you mean, usually?"

"Well, if I plow on a Sunday, I'll pop in and check and make sure things are all working smoothly."

"You knew Mr. Harrington was arriving this past weekend?" Clay asked. When the other man nodded, he continued, "So, you probably been working to get the place in tip-top shape the last few weeks."

"We were here almost every day for the past few weeks," Scott said.

"Did your landscape crew use the house for the bathroom? For breaks? Did you have them check and make sure everything was in order?"

"No, sir. That is my job and my job only."

Clay noticed the tell-tale to the lie. The man's eyes flickered away from his own then back again. He chose to ignore it, knowing the man would never admit to allowing his employees into the house on their own, not in front of Niles Harrington, anyway.

"And you never noticed The Shade missing?" Clay asked.

"The what?"

"My Rodin statue, Scott," Niles said.

"Oh, yeah, of course. No, I can't say I ever noticed it even when it was there."

"So, you don't know what it even looks like?"

"No, sir, I can't say I do."

"It is two feet high and sat right on the mantel in the study," Niles said.

"Can't say I been in there except to peek through the door and make sure some wild animal hadn't taken up habitat over the winter," McKenny said.

"You realize of course that you have to be the prime suspect?" Clay asked. "The alarm system is the best that money can buy. You are the only one who has access to the house while Mr. Harrington is gone. Is there anything you want to tell me?"

"I ain't no thief," McKenny said.

"Does anybody else have access to the house, Niles?" Clay asked.

"I have a few family members who use the cottage in my absence, but they have to check in with Scott to get the key and the alarm code," Niles said.

Clay knew that Niles had been divorced five years earlier, had two grown children, and three young grandchildren. There was no current Mrs. Harrington.

"So, is it possible that a visitor came, borrowed the key, made a copy, and also had the code for the alarm system?" Clay asked. It occurred to him that the theft just might be the work of a spoiled and wealthy adult child thinking they were entitled, and what better way to collect what they were due then to sell an extremely valuable art piece just sitting on the mantel. A piece their father couldn't even legally admit to owning, at that. The whole thing reeked of the spite of a jaded and resentful scion.

"We change the code every fall, and nobody has been here since the last update." Niles ran his fingers through his blond hair, smoothing it back over his head.

"Is that right, Mr. McKenny?" Clay looked at the caretaker. "None of Mr. Harrington's family has visited since last fall?"

"I guess that must be right." The caretaker's eyes flickered again.

"Perhaps you can put together a list of everybody who has used the place in the last few years other than yourself?" Clay finished off the Bloody Mary. "And I will need the names of your two employees and their contact information, Mr. McKenny." He made a mental note to ask the man whether or not either of Niles' children had asked for the access code since last fall.

Clay thought he'd have an early lunch at the Side Bar, but he caught a glimpse of a greasy cheeseburger with soggy fries passing by on a paper plate and thought better of it. Best to just have a drink. He chose a beer in a bottle just to be safe, not trusting the cleanliness of the glasses. There were seven people in the place. One pool table. Not much for light. The floors were sticky, suggesting that perhaps they always were, as it was only noontime. The bar was a rectangular slab of plywood. Clay sat gingerly upon one of the stools, hoping that his John Varvatos Star Bowery jeans wouldn't be ruined. Luckily, they were a shark grey, which should help in hiding whatever might be lingering on the stool from previous occupants.

"Kelly Anne Landry come in here?" Clay slid an Andrew Jackson across the bar.

"Yep." The bartender was a slender man of moderate height with very little definition to his body.

"When does she come in, usually?"

"Any time."

"Do you think she'll be in soon?"

"Maybe."

"Does she come in by herself?"

"Sometimes."

Clay slid another Andrew Jackson across the bar. He imagined this was more than the man would make in tips the entire day. "Can you give me the names of anybody she talks to?"

"Besides people she's hitting up to buy her a drink?"

"Anybody."

The bartender nodded, just a slight twitch of his chin. "She sometimes talks with the fellow over by the window."

Clay carefully shifted around to look. At a small table by the window sat a man and a woman. He did not recognize the woman. The man was Allen Daigle. The person he was supposed to be investigating who might be cheating on his wife. The woman was not his wife.

At that point, the door opened, letting the bright July sunshine sweep into the dark space that was the Side Bar. It was like one of those alien movies where a shadowy figure emerges from a brightly lit passageway, and the audience sits on the edge of their seats waiting to see what will materialize. And Kelly Anne Landry was indeed looking like an alien. Her appearance suggested that she'd had a rough go of it. Quitting heroin cold turkey in a jail cell was just short of waterboarding on the torture scale. Seven days of hell. It came fast and hard like a locomotive, but then it was over.

She came across the room to the bar and sat down, openly appraising Clay as a new victim to tempt into her spider web. Her hair may have been blonde at one point but was now a ragged brown and clumped into greasy coils. Kelly Anne stared at him from eyes that were sunken into her head like the sockets of a skull, except for the jagged-red streaks springing out in all directions from her gray irises. Of course, it was possible she'd looked like this before detoxing.

"Hey fellow, you want to buy a girl a drink?" she asked. "I'm a little tight on funds."

"Sure." Clay nodded at the bartender. He poured her a tequila. She motioned for him to continue, and Clay nodded again, and the slender man filled the tumbler to the brim with no ice. "I'm Clay Wolfe." He made no effort to hold out a hand.

"Kelly Anne." She leered at him.

"I was wondering if I might ask you a few questions?"

"Whatcha want?" Her voice could've been fingernails on a chalkboard. "I done told Curtis I got no money and no product." She twisted a greasy coil of hair as she said this.

"What product are we talking?" Clay asked.

Kelly Anne looked sideways at him. "Ya' didn't tell me what you're doing in here."

"Who is Curtis?"

"I don't know what you're talking about."

"Are you hungry?"

"Can I borrow fifteen bucks?"

Clay thought of lending her the money and then following her, for he was sure she would lead him straight to her drug dealer, but he couldn't quite see being a part of her descent into the grave. From the looks of it, she didn't have far to go.

"How about you answer some questions first, and then we'll see," he said.

"Ya tell me who you are, or I'm leaving."

Clay looked over at the bartender who was making no attempt to disguise his eavesdropping. He sure would like to know who this Curtis was, and what product Kelly Anne was speaking of, but he didn't think the conversation would last another minute if he didn't come clean.

"I am a private detective, Kelly Anne. Your mother hired me."

"Crystal hired you to prove my innocence?" Kelly Anne asked with genuine interest.

"Not exactly," Clay said.

"What the fuck's that mean?"

"Calm down, Kelly Anne, I'm trying to help," Clay said, thinking that the apple certainly hadn't fallen far from the tree in the case of the Landry mother and daughter.

"What did Crystal hire you to do?"

"She hired me to find out who sold you the drugs that killed Ariel."

"The bitch still thinks I did it, don't she?" Kelly Anne coughed, a dry hacking sound. "How about I hire you to prove my innocence? And prove that fucking weasel, Dylan, is the one who wiped heroin on my baby's gums?"

"Do you know if Dylan is home? I need to speak with him as well."

Kelly Anne leaned over so that her hot breath scalded his face. "How the fuck I know that? The bastard lies and puts me in jail and then goes free to do what he pleases. It ain't right. He's probably there banging his new squeeze."

"Who is his new squeeze?"

She put her hand on his leg. "How about I hire you?" she asked again.

"You already told me you have no money." Clay tried to steer the conversation back to the mysterious Curtis, the lack of money, and of product. At the same time, he carefully removed her hand from his knee.

"I can do other things for you." Kelly Anne pursed her blistered lips. "If you know what I mean?"

"Hire me for what?"

"To prove that Dylan Thompson, that little puke, is the one that killed my baby."

"I'll see what I can do. First, who did you buy the drugs from?"

"I didn't buy no heroin."

"You saying you weren't doing heroin?" Clay asked.

"I didn't say I wasn't chasing the dragon a bit here and there," Kelly Anne said. "But I never used a needle on my arm. Don't want to get AIDS now, do I?"

"So, who'd you buy it from?"

"Dylan bought it."

"Who was Dylan getting the heroin from?" Clay asked.

"I don't know."

"Was it a man by the name of Jake Lobbins?"

"Told you I don't know nothing about buying heroin." Kelly Anne's eyes fluttered over to the door that had again opened. Allen Daigle and the woman he was with were disappearing out through it.

Clay was in a quandary. Should he follow the man? Or stay and try to pry a shred of information out of this walking corpse of a woman? "If you want to prove your innocence, you're going to have to give me something."

"Dylan knows who the dealer is," she said. "You go and ask him."

"Okay, then," Clay said.

She looked coy, if that was possible. "He won't tell you shit," she said. "You best follow him. Once you catch him scoring, I bet the prick comes clean and tells the truth. Go do your private dick thing, and the truth will come out. Looks like your loss. I might not have to hire you after all." She cackled. "But I might reward you just the same."

Chapter 7

STILL WEDNESDAY, JULY 1ST

Clay walked out into the bright sunshine of the seventy-eight-degree day. This was just about as warm as he liked it, and he could only stomach this because of the gentle sea breeze cooling things down. He felt dirty from just being in the Side Bar, never mind his somewhat surreal conversation with Kelly Anne. He could use some sanity to cleanse the filth from his pores. Perhaps he'd see if Maria Cloutier wanted to do lunch again today, as he still hadn't eaten. Then he wondered about maybe going back to the office and taking Baylee out for lunch instead.

Just over a year earlier, Clay had been sitting in his newly-leased office with his feet up on the desk when Baylee Baker had walked in. She had come about the job he'd listed in the newspaper. Clay was old-school like that, having placed an advertisement in the Port Essex *Daily Register* for a full-time receptionist/secretary. He had hired the woman with the sad eyes on the spot, and she had started the next day.

This was just a few months after she had killed her husband. As he later learned piecemeal, they'd been married for five years and, like clockwork, once a month for those five years, he had beaten and raped her when he was drunk. She'd left him. He followed her. She filed for divorce. He fought it. She filed for a Protect from Abuse order, and, after several visits with the judge, was granted it. He showed up and beat and raped her two nights later. There were no witnesses. He had an alibi. He went free. She bought a gun legally.

The next time that George showed up at her house, she allowed him to beat her and rape her one final time. Then she shot him in the mouth and called the police. The prosecutor tried to get her to accept a manslaughter charge. She refused, finding a good lawyer through Clay's grandfather. The judge threw the case out and let her walk free. This, of course, was a quick recollection of the facts of her life, but these were the things Clay had found through online research, his connections in the police department and the courts, and conversations with his grandfather. She had never shared any information with him.

His ruminations on Baylee Baker were interrupted by a trunk slamming shut. He looked up and realized that Allen Daigle and the woman he'd been with were still in the parking lot. She had black hair cut short, was well-dressed, and wore practical shoes. He noticed this last bit as she walked with small mincing steps over to a Volvo. Daigle got in the driver's seat of his Corolla. When they drove off in two separate directions, Clay decided to follow the woman.

Had they come to the Side Bar after getting together for a tryst, Clay wondered as he followed the woman back towards Route 1? Port Essex was about twelve miles out a peninsula from this coastal corridor of Maine. In the middle of the day, a few days prior to July 4th, the traffic was still not bad, but come this weekend that twelve miles was at least an hour's drive. After about four miles she turned right onto a road that led back into a development of capes and colonials. They all had two-car garages and at least a half-acre of land. The woman pulled up the driveway of one such home and disappeared into the garage. Clay parked across the road and took down her address from the mailbox.

He wondered if perhaps Allen Daigle had not come home the previous night and this had just been the end of their rendezvous? He pecked out a text to Baylee.

Did you find out what time Allen Daigle got home last night?

What did he know about Allen Daigle other than that the man was a lawyer? Clay made a mental note to do some research.

His phone buzzed. A text from Baylee.

About 10. Why?

Just saw him at Side Bar with pretty woman who drives a Volvo and lives in suburbia.

Classy guy. I wish some guy would take me to the Side Bar.

Still scraping gunk off my pants.

Maybe it's a bar for lawyers?

Clay hadn't thought of that. He tapped out his reply. That would explain the slime. Of course, his grandfather, the man he respected most in the world, was a lawyer, so he was able to think and tell those jokes, or so he justified.

LOL.

Kelly Anne was no help. Going to stop and see Dylan Thompson.

That the boyfriend?

Yep.

Be careful.

This was a new twist. Baylee had never told him to be careful before.

For sure.

Got to go.

Clay took a slow cruise around the neighborhood before heading back towards downtown Port Essex. Botany Village was almost all the way back into town on the left. He drove past Crystal Landry's trailer, but there was no sign of life. Her double-wide backed up to the woods, giving some privacy out back anyway. There was only about ten feet between trailers on either side. Botany Avenue swung in a big U shape around the outside of the village, with smaller streets leading to smaller circles. Dylan Thompson was located smack in the middle.

In many of the lots, people were sitting outside in lawn chairs, many of them drinking and smoking, while a few kids played in small plastic pools, and others rode bikes up and down the streets of the trailer park. Sure enough, Dylan had plunked himself outside his trailer in a decrepit nylon beach chair. He had a full mop of curly hair sprouting from his head like a chia pet. He wore no shirt, just tight and torn jean shorts, all the better to see his emaciated body of skin and bones. Old acne scars dotted his face. Clay had seen pictures, but for the man, hard times seem to have been visited by even harder times.

"Dylan Thompson?" he asked as he got out of the Jeep.

"Who the fuck are you?"

"Clay Wolfe. I'm a private investigator."

"I told them a thousand times that I really found that worm in the cereal box. They got to pay up and make it right, no matter how many of you people they send out to try and convince me otherwise." Dylan puffed nervously on his cigarette in between liberal gulps of whatever was in the large orange plastic cup in his hand.

"Don't worry, I'm not the Capt'n Crunch police," Clay said. "I was hoping to ask you some questions about Kelly Anne Landry? And the death of your daughter, Ariel?"

"I already told the police all I know."

"Do you mind if I sit down?" Clay sat without waiting for an answer, carefully lowering his wiry frame into the tattered and faded fabric of the aluminum beach chair. "I just thought you might fill in a few details for me."

"Like what?"

"You said in your statement that you saw Kelly Anne Landry rub the residue from your heroin baggies on little Ariel's gums, is that correct?"

"Not my baggies. I don't do that shit."

"Okay, Dylan, not your baggies. But baggies that once held heroin?"

"Yeah, I suppose." Dylan took off his tortoise-shell glasses and wiped them on his shorts. "Who'd you say you was working for?"

"That doesn't matter. The only thing that matters is I'm not trying to get you in trouble."

"The fuck you're not. You're working for Kelly Anne, ain't you? She's trying to spin the blame onto me, that bitch."

Clay was truly starting to regret two things. The first was taking this case and the second was not wanting to ever shoot anybody ever again. Maybe he could make an exception and shoot this guy. Just this once. He was starting to think that Kelly Anne Landry and Dylan Thompson were a perfect match for each other.

"I just want to know who was selling you the heroin, Dylan. You give me a name, and I'll go away and leave you alone," Clay said. He took off his purple Oakley sunglasses and stared Dylan in the eye. "Just give me the name of the dealer."

"I told you I don't know any dealer. Kelly Anne was the one chasing the dragon, man. I don't know nothing."

Clay stood. "I think you're lying to me." He lifted his foot and flipped the lawn chair and Dylan over backwards. While the man squirmed to right himself, he stepped to the side and dropped his knee into Dylan's solar plexus, grabbed a handful of the bushy hair and dragged him flat.

"What the fuck?" Dylan gasped, trying to regain his breath.

Clay, with his knee still pinning the man to the ground, wrapped his left hand around Dylan's throat. "I don't like being lied to."

"Fuck you, man."

Clay slapped him. "Just give me a name." A few people had wandered over to see the spectacle.

"You can kill me, and it'd still be ten times better than what Curtis would do to me." Dylan was now openly crying between ragged gasps.

"Hey, buddy, get off of him." A heavy man with a too-tight T-shirt stepped forward loosely holding a baseball bat.

Clay removed his hands and stood, both palms facing the man. "No problem. I was just on my way." He stepped past him, climbed into his Jeep, and drove away. That was twice today he'd heard the name Curtis.

•   •   •   •   •

Baylee was putting together the bill for a local bank that had hired Clay to investigate an accusation from one of their customers. In this case, a hundred thousand dollars had disappeared from the man's savings account, and he had accused the bank of losing it to a hustler who had hacked his bank number and then had the money wired to an offshore account. The bank had hired Clay to look into whether the slip-up could have been the customer's fault, and not theirs.

On the third day of the case, Clay had hit pay dirt searching through the man's trash. This was quite legal, as once garbage was wheeled to the curb for pick-up, it was no longer protected as private property but was now part of the public domain. Paperwork showed that the man had given his brother-in-law access to the account, and further digging with Baylee's help had proven that his wife's brother was indeed the thief. She was certain that the bank would happily pay Clay's bill for $600 instead of the 100 big ones they thought they were going to have to cough up.

Baylee was aware that she was becoming quite smitten with her boss. At the same time, she didn't think it was such a good idea. There was, of course, the fact that he was her boss. But what really caused her trepidation was that he drank too much. Her father had been an alcoholic who had verbally abused her and her mother until the day he died of liver complications. Through the course of the abuse, she and her mother had become victims together, more best friends than mother and daughter. When Baylee was twelve, the prick died. She and her mother were already in a complicated relationship that was far from what a mother/daughter relationship should be.

They shared intimate details of the boys and men they slept with. They smoked and drank together. When Baylee got bad grades, it was the fault of the teachers. When she was suspended, it was the fault of the bullies. When the police found her with some weed, she and her mom both wondered what the big deal was. The break in their bond came her senior year when she found her mom having sex with her boyfriend. Not only was that inexcusable, it was just plain gross.

Baylee graduated high school and completed one year of an education degree at Central Maine Community College in Lewiston. It was too far to commute, and she didn't care enough to do it online. Besides, she'd met the love of her life. George McManus was a dream come true. He was nine years older, ran a forklift at the lumber yard, which meant he made decent money, and had a charming smile. He also delivered her the first orgasm of her life. Looks, money, and sexual prowess.

They'd dated for two years before getting married. They both wanted kids, trying hard for three years before discovering George had a very low sperm count. It was unlikely that she would ever become pregnant. It was around that time that their idyllic life began to sour. The great sex became less and less frequent before dropping off altogether. George started drinking more. Baylee could do nothing right. She dressed like a whore. Was fat. Left the house a mess. Couldn't cook. And then he started hitting her.

The long story short of her present situation was that she and Clay were both damaged goods and, long term, would be a train wreck together. But, heck, a brief daytime fantasy couldn't hurt, could it? The real reason to have originally answered this particular job application was that she thought it would be pretty cool to work her way up the ladder and become a P.I. She had been eight when she watched her first *Murder She Wrote*, and she was effectively hooked. A major disappointment for Baylee was when the network had not renewed the *Rizzoli & Isles* series a few years back, leaving her wanting more. She could be patient. She'd learned patience. But Baylee Baker knew what she wanted.

Baylee's reverie was interrupted by the door opening. A burst of elation coursed through her at the thought of seeing Clay's calming face. It was not. It was Curtis. Her dealer. At her place of work. He looked the part of a pharmaceutical salesman, dressed in a black suit with a light blue shirt and red striped tie. Hopefully Clay would not be back any time soon. This would be hard to explain.

"Baylee, you look fantastic today." His mouth creased into a broad smile that didn't reach his dark eyes, which were running down her body with a familiarity that made her skin crawl.

"What are you doing here?"

"Maybe I just wanted to see you," Curtis said.

"You shouldn't have come here."

"Ah, but I wanted to see the office of a private detective. It intrigues me what this man of yours does all day. Is he in?"

"Mr. Wolfe is not in at the moment."

"What exciting case is he working on?"

"His work is of a private nature." Listening to herself, even she thought the words pretentious and wooden.

"Ah, perhaps that is why they call him a private detective?" Curtis walked over and peered into the open door of Clay's office.

"What do you want?"

Curtis turned and took two steps to within a foot of where she sat. "I brought you something," he said.

Baylee fought back her anxiety. This was how it often began with George. A darkness cloaked in civility. A threat that loomed delivered in seemingly innocuous words. A bristling rage driving his sexual desire with a dangerous undertone of promised savagery.

"The extra doses you asked for?" Curtis held out a pill bottle. "It says Tylenol, but it's really Xanax."

Baylee reached a trembling hand up to take the bottle.

"Are you okay?" he asked. He did not release the pills. His free hand came up and touched her cheek. "You're clammy and shaking. Are you sick?" His fetid breath washed over her like sewage.

"I'm fine."

"Maybe we could get a drink later?"

"I, um, have plans."

"Another time, then." He let go of the bottle but did not withdraw his hand from her cheek. "Maybe I could stop by your house?"

The thought of this man in her house spiked her adrenaline glands into overdrive, and she began to shake. Anxiety over Clay's possible return to find this pill-pusher in the office was replaced by a sensation she rather enjoyed, a rush of the blood, a heightening of the senses, and a feeling of immortality. Fear was replaced by anger. She carefully flexed the muscles in her arms. An image of the Incredible Hulk raced through her mind.

When twelve-year-old Baylee Baker had walked past her father's casket, she had promised herself one thing: no man would ever dictate her emotions. She would not take abuse. From that point forward, she had controlled her relationships. It had been the betrayal of her mother, fucking her boyfriend, that had sent her into a temporary tailspin, allowing her to again be pulled into the emotional morass of a toxic male, but she'd eventually righted that situation. These were the thoughts that whisked through her mind.

"Get your fucking hand off me." Baylee slapped his hand free from her cheek and stood up face-to-face with the man, his disgusting breath washing over her. "The answer is no."

The beady eyes of Curtis turned harder and darker, if that was possible. "You shouldn't hit me."

"If you ever touch me again without my permission, I will rip you a new asshole. Get the fuck out of my face."

The rigid lines of Curtis' face suddenly eased. "You're pretty when you're angry," he said. "I am sorry if I offended you." He stepped back and away from her.

Baylee wondered if she had overreacted, the adrenaline subsiding in her as suddenly as it had built up.

"I'm sorry," she said. "I don't like to be touched."

"I understand," Curtis said with a smile. "I heard about that prick of a husband of yours." He walked to the door and opened it, pausing in the entrance. "Although, it would be a shame to let such a pretty face go to waste. You know how to get hold of me if you change your mind."

Chapter 8

STILL WEDNESDAY, JULY 1ST

Clay was finishing his second beer when Westy arrived at the Pelican Perch. It was three o'clock in the afternoon. He'd decided to grab a Reuben for lunch here, as they made a pretty kick-ass Russian dressing, which was the ingredient that tied the sandwich all together as far as Clay was concerned. He'd been finishing up when his phone had buzzed, Westy asking him if he was around.

The bartender put a Bud in front of Westy without him having to ask. Clay nodded that he'd have another as well. There were a few tourists at the tables and along the railing marveling at the view of Essex Harbor, but nobody else at the bar. Even though the Pelican Perch laid claim to the most picturesque seascape in Port Essex, it was a bit out of the hubbub of downtown. The local day drinkers went to the Seal Bar, while the regulars here didn't usually arrive until closer to 5:00.

"I was sitting here wondering," Clay said by way of greeting. "I got to thinking that there aren't any pelicans in Maine, making this here establishment an oddity in moniker."

"You probably shouldn't think and drink at the same time," Westy said.

"No, really, don't you find it strange that there is a place in Maine called the Pelican Perch?"

"Well, they do got that desert down in Freeport."

"But that at least resembles a desert."

"I guess this resembles a perch for pelicans, even if there aren't any representatives of that particular species here."

"Hmm. Perhaps wishful thinking on the owner's part."

"I heard something today when I was unloading my haul," Westy said. "Something that might interest you 'cuz it was about drugs and lobstermen."

"What'd you hear?"

Westy took a drink as he formalized his thoughts. He was a careful and organized man who hated to misspeak, make mistakes, or err in any way. "I was unloading my catch when I heard a couple fellows gossiping about Jake Lobbins. They said something about him getting addicted to Oxy after he hurt his back."

"Murph told me this morning he heard a rumor that the two guys who work for him have been flashing a lot of cash around."

"I wondered about it before, you know, running drugs through the pots."

"Never thought about it. You're the fisherman. How do they actually do it?"

"Could be just about anything. A couple years back they found a luxury yacht sunk up the river with tens of millions of dollars of drugs in the hull. Could be pleasure boats making the drops, or even container ships making the run between Portland and Halifax, hell even someone off a tanker. You get forty-five nautical miles out like Lobbins, there is little law, less enforcement, and pretty much anything goes. Like, maybe fifteen, twenty years ago when the Russians were buying pogies? I remember, there was a guy owned a junkyard out of Freeport. He was going out to meet the ships with used cars on the back of his boat. They'd just hoist 'em aboard, fix 'em up to sell once they got home. Who knows what the hell else goes on out there?"

"You're telling me off the coast of Maine could be full of pirates, kind of like off Somalia?" Clay grimaced. He thought that he'd left a lot of this mess behind in Boston, but here it was rearing its ugly head right here in Port Essex.

"Maybe not that bad, but there's definitely the potential for plenty of drugs flowing in from the Atlantic. It's like a sieve," Westy said.

"What about the Coast Guard?" Clay asked.

"Shit, man, they got two cutters and maybe fifteen people covering over a thousand NMs. They spend most of their time towing disabled boats and arresting drunks."

"Okay, I get it. If somebody wanted to smuggle drugs into the coast, it would be easy. Why go to the trouble of dropping them in the lobster traps? Why not just bring them right to shore?"

"You're the private detective, but offhand, I'd say that nobody is going to get suspicious of a lobsterman. Hell, he goes out and comes back every day. Like clockwork. That's not going to work for anybody else without raising red flags."

"Or, as you said, maybe the container ships going back and forth between Halifax and Portland are making the drop. They're running a steady regular route now, that Icelandic company, whatever their name is," Clay said. "Drop a small speed boat over the side and pull up a string or two from the exact GPS coordinates someone texts you well ahead of time. Lobbins comes along in the morning and pulls his trap. He comes chugging back into the harbor, and nobody even bats an eye."

"Until the two idiot cousins start flashing money around, anyway," Westy replied.

"I think it's time to have a talk with Jake Lobbins."

Westy looked at his phone. "He usually comes into the wharf around five, now that he's been doing the distance strings."

•   •   •   •   •

Curtis Volkov grimaced as he followed the truck down the road, having tracked Clay Wolfe and the fisherman buddy of his from the bar. He had a feeling he knew where they were going, and he was not wrong. When the truck poked its way into a space up the hill from the Knox Wharf, Curtis drove on past to the lobster shack parking lot before turning around to see what they were doing. The two men just sat in the front of the truck, waiting. Curtis knew that Lobbins usually came into the wharf about five o'clock. It was about quarter to. It took no real genius to know that they must be on to the man.

What to do? He had tried to call Lobbins, but there was no answer, his phone most certainly safely put away as he worked his way back into Essex Harbor. Would he check his phone before unloading his catch? Curtis doubted it, plus it was unwise at this point to leave a message that might become incriminating evidence. There was no way to intercept the man, to warn him. No matter how Curtis looked at it, Jake Lobbins had become a liability.

Curtis scanned the landscape, his eyes coming to rest on a small patch of trees this side of the bridge crossing over to Spruce Island. He pulled the Denali back onto the road and drove the short distance there. Just the other side of the bridge was a dirt road, and he took the right until he could pull off into cover on the side. He had an L.L.Bean fishing bag in the back seat, and he grabbed that, slinging it over his shoulder and working his way back to the copse of trees by the bridge. Luckily, there was nobody around, only the occasional car crossing the bridge and from which he was able to easily find cover.

The fishing bag held a McMillan 338 Tactical Rifle. He attached the Harris Swivel Bipod, the Night Force Mil Dot scope, and last but not least, an Elite Iron suppressor. This would not completely silence the weapon. But, absent a random passing pedestrian, Curtis doubted anybody would hear a thing. As he settled into a prone position, the scope immediately picked up Lobbins leaving the dock to walk to his truck, which was just past where Wolfe and his buddy had parked.

The past few years had been the best of Curtis' life. Sure, he had to rough people up once in a while, even kill a few of them. This was not a problem for him, and, as a matter of fact, he rather enjoyed it. The difference was that after shooting this schmuck, he'd go home and take a shower and go out and have a nice dinner. He'd sip a decent bottle of white wine. Maybe even meet a girl. If not, he knew a couple of broads in Port Essex who'd trade dollars for favors. It sure beat working for some paramilitary group crawling around some fucking desert and camping out under the stars and sweating his balls off during the day. This had been Curtis Volkov's life until he'd connected up with the boss, a man who'd rapidly grown a drug empire and was desperately in need of an enforcer to step in when muscle was called for.

The past few years had seen Curtis given a respect he'd never imagined in his life. Not for the grandson of a Russian who'd sold out to Hitler and the son of a rogue CIA double agent. Volkov was not his real name, but then again, he had never known his real name. All he knew was that he was not going to let this plush assignment slip through his fingers. Not for Jake Lobbins. Not for Clay fucking Wolfe.

•   •   •   •

Westy's truck was a regular there and fit in with the twenty or so other dark-colored pickups parked haphazardly around the wharf. It would seem that lobstermen were averse to walking, Clay surmised as he looked around, each vehicle crammed as close to the building and dock as possible. Lobster traps were piled in seeming disorder as well as the different colored buoys that identified each trap's owner. Fifty feet further up was the lobster shack with parking for ten cars, and eight picnic tables scattered along the cove.

The lobstermen who went out of Knox Cove had banded into a cooperative that called itself the Lobstermen in Knox Cove. This was silently snickered at by the locals who believed they'd unwittingly created the acronym of LIKC, not realizing how it might look in, say, a newspaper article. The members in turn, would argue that they'd done it on purpose as a bit of tomfoolery, as lobstermen were known for their foul mouths and practical joking. Either way, it brought them attention, and in turn led to a lobster shack doing a booming business in the summer months, as well as a solid wholesale business.

"That's his boat coming in now." Westy handed the binoculars to Clay. "The *Lob-Star*."

"I thought sailors used telescopes," Clay said as he took the field glasses.

"I think you mean spy glass or perhaps monocle."

Clay picked up the boat rounding the point and turning into the cove. "*Lob-Star*, what a great name." They'd been there for about a half-hour watching a steady wave of lobster boats pulling up to the wharf and unloading their catch for the day.

"What's your play?" Westy asked.

"I guess I'm just going to wing it," Clay said. "We could put him under surveillance, but that would take forever. I guess if he looks like he might be carrying drugs to his truck, I'll just approach him and ask him flat out."

"Excuse me, Jake, but is that a bag full of heroin you're carrying?" Westy cracked a smile, which was odd for him. "And do you mind answering a few questions?"

"Why not? I'm not the law. I don't even want to bust him. I don't think he's the dealer. He's just a mule, making some extra dough or satisfying his habit. I figure he's got two choices. He can talk to me and give me a name, or he can keep his mouth shut in which case I turn him over to the police."

They bantered back and forth while the *Lob-Star* unloaded its haul and then returned to its mooring. The two men who had been with Jake Lobbins got into a truck parked almost on the wharf, while Lobbins had to walk up past where Clay and Westy were parked. They knew this because his license plate also said Lob-Star. He was carrying a forest-green canvas laundry bag over his shoulder.

"I'm going to brace him," Clay said. "You got my back?"

"Yep."

Clay stepped out of the truck and in front of Lobbins, blocking his path. "Hey, Jake, can I have a word with you?" he asked.

Lobbins dropped the bag and punched Clay in the jaw. He staggered back in surprise at the reaction. He seemed to be rubbing people the wrong way lately. Lobbins stepped forward and swung a roundhouse blow that caught Clay in the side of the head and knocked him to the ground. The man was built like a brick shithouse, his arms solid muscle from hauling the heavy traps.

As Lobbins went to kick him, Clay drove his body forward into the anchor leg and knocked the man onto his back. They both rolled to their feet, but Clay was slightly faster and drove his fist into the man's chest. It was like punching a concrete wall. Lobbins wrapped Clay in a bear hug, lifting him from the ground like a paper doll. It felt like his ribs were cracking like matchsticks, and he couldn't breathe.

In desperation, Clay leaned his head back and crashed the top of his forehead into the man's nose, its cartilage breaking audibly, showering them both with blood. Lobbins let go of him and staggered backwards down the hill back towards the wharf. There was a roaring noise in Clay's head, and his adrenalin was pumping the blood through his body so quickly it made everything seem shadowy.

With a low animal growl, he went after Lobbins, swinging blow after blow at his head while the man tried to parry the punches while backpedaling down the hill. They reached the dock, and Lobbins grasped a lobster trap and swung the plastic-coated metal frame into Clay's side, knocking him to the ground.

Clay was dimly aware that a crowd of men had gathered around them, all cheering Lobbins on, calling for him to kick Clay's ass. One man kicked Clay as he went to stand up, and then the man went hurtling past him, propelled by Westy, off the dock and into the water.

"Let's keep this fair," Westy said.

Clay and Lobbins were circling each other, both bloodied and limping.

"I just want to talk to you," Clay said.

"I got nothing to say to you," Lobbins said.

"It's not you I'm after."

"Shut your mouth."

Lobbins rushed forward swinging haymakers like a windmill in a hurricane. Clay parried the first few, but then was struck in the ear, a high-pitched whine suddenly deafening him. He used the man's momentum and mass against him, grasping his shirt by the collar and pulling him forward over his extended leg and slamming him to the ground. Lobbins rolled over to his back and Clay leaped upon him, his forearm pressed into the man's neck.

All of a sudden, the fight seemed to drain out of Lobbins. His eyes went dull and his body went limp.

"I didn't mean for no baby to die," he whispered.

"I just want to talk, that's all," Clay said.

"I was going to lose my boat."

Clay pulled his arm from the man's neck and pushed himself backwards to his feet. He lowered his hand, a peace offering, and Jake Lobbins grasped it and allowed himself to be pulled to his feet.

"Let's make things right," Clay said.

"It's too late," Lobbins said. There were tears in his eyes.

"Help me get the real bad guys. Give me the name of the person you deliver to."

They were about two feet apart, whispering so as not to be heard by the men huddled around them who were suddenly confused, wondering what had happened, this brutal fight abruptly turning into some sort of bromance.

Lobbins suddenly seemed to stiffen, as if offended by something, and then took a step back with a surprised look on his face. Three red circles appeared on his white T-shirt and then somebody tackled Clay to the ground.

"Stay down," Westy said.

"What's happening?" Clay asked.

"Somebody just shot Lobbins."

Chapter 9

STILL WEDNESDAY, JULY 1ST

"We have a shooting on the Knox Wharf in Port Essex," Westy said into his cell phone. "One man down, shooter at large."

"I didn't hear any gunshots," Clay said.

"They must have used a suppressor."

"Are they gone?"

"Don't know. Don't want to find out."

Some minutes later, the sound of approaching sirens began to split the air. A police car pulled into the drive leading to the wharf and two officers got out. One was Donna.

"Unknown shooter," Westy called out. "One man down."

Donna and her partner began to canvas the perimeter with guns drawn. An ambulance pulled in, but nobody got out, not until the all-clear was given. "Male with GSWs" was all that dispatch knew so far. As with any call with gunshot wounds, they were staying clear until the area had been deemed safe.

The Police Lieutenant waved the all-clear and the two rescue personnel embarked from the ambulance. "What's the situation?" the woman asked.

Two more cop cars came in, and Donna went about giving orders to secure the scene. Westy was busy sharing with one of the officers what he knew.

"He was shot three times, I think," Clay said.

"Any other injuries?" the woman asked.

Clay knew that the Port Essex Ambulance Service worked in teams of two, one a paramedic, and one an EMT. She must be the paramedic, he surmised. There was also the driver.

"No, not as far as I know."

"Patient is breathing," the EMT said.

"Pulse?"

"Faint."

"Expose him," she ordered the EMT. He immediately went about cutting off Lobbins' clothes.

"Three wounds. One up high on the collarbone. One in the abdomen. The third just below the heart."

Clay spun his head around, trying to envision the scene. Where had the shooter been? Lobbins had been facing to the west. To the north were clusters of houses. A bit further up the hill and back towards town was his grandfather's house, the place he'd been living since returning to town over a year ago. Across Knox Cove to the west he had a clear vision of the Spruce Island Bridge, and just to the right was a small knoll covered by a copse of trees. That must be where the shooter had been.

"We need to get LifeFlight on the scene in Port Essex immediately." The paramedic was on the radio. "Let's get an occlusive dressing on the wounds and load him," the paramedic said to the EMT as she waited for a response. "Too messy. Doesn't look like we can get an IV going."

"Looks like you're going to have to meet at Mid Coast," the radio said.

"Not going to work. We need transportation ASAP."

"Sanford crew on way back from Boston and will meet you at Mid Coast."

"Lewiston? Bangor?'

"Lewiston down with mechanical issues. Bangor on delivery to Toronto."

"Got it."

"Should we drill him?" the EMT asked.

"We'll do it en route."

"Miles or Mid Coast?"

"LifeFlight meeting us at Mid Coast." This hospital was further but had a landing pad.

The strong smell of iron filled Clay's nostrils. He knew it would be days before the smell would completely leave him. It had been all too common working homicide in Boston.

"Get him on the gurney, and let's go," the paramedic said. "Wolfe, help get his arms."

Clay grabbed an arm, sliding his hand carefully under the now naked body of Jake Lobbins. He didn't recognize the paramedic, but she seemed to know who he was. They lifted the lobsterman onto the gurney.

Lobbins grunted.

"What's that?" Clay leaned closer. The man was staring at him with eyes hard with pain.

"Watch...police."

"What about the police?"

Lobbins began to shake and spittle streaked down his chin.

"Shit, we're coding here," the EMT said.

"Let's get on the goddamn road," the paramedic said.

"I'm coming with you," Clay said.

"Not happening," the paramedic said.

The three of them lifted the gurney and slid it into the back of the ambulance. The paramedic and EMT climbed into the back and slammed the doors. Within seconds the emergency response vehicle was off on the forty-minute journey to the Brunswick hospital.

"Clay?"

He turned to find Donna behind him in her uniform. "Yeah?"

"We need to get a statement."

It was hard being grilled by your lover, but it only got worse when the State Police Major Crime Unit arrived. Two detectives had had to drive all the way down from Augusta on the Wednesday before the Fourth of July instead of clocking out. One had plans for a barbecue with friends, and the other was missing his son's Cal Ripken game.

The fact that Clay had shown up, accosted the victim for being involved with smuggling heroin through his lobster traps, engaged in a bloody brawl with the man, and then stood two feet from him as he was shot and killed raised all sorts of red flags. It turned out that the canvas bag that Lobbins had been carrying was just some lobstering gear and a change of clothes.

Most of the lobstermen, leaping to faulty conclusions to make sense of what they thought they had seen, were sure he must have had some kind of gun and had passed on that thought to the cops. He told them everything as he remembered it, except the last part about the police. He wasn't actually sure what had been said. Did Lobbins want him to call the police? Be careful of the police? To not tell the police that he was a drug smuggler?

The K-9 unit showed up and were directed down the road to the spot Clay had guessed the bullets had come from. The Sheriff showed up. Every on- and off-duty policeman in Port Essex came by. The Lieutenant in charge of the MCU Central rattled off sharp commands. Marie Cloutier was the first on the scene from the media, but soon there were reporters and television crews from every station shouting for information.

It was three hours before Clay was allowed to leave, and that only with a promise to come into the station first thing in the morning to give an official statement of events. Clay walked down the shoreline before cutting up to the road to avoid the news crews. He expected to walk back to his Jeep at the Pelican Perch, but Westy was sitting in his truck waiting for him.

"Need a ride, buddy?"

"Not sure." Clay leaned in the window. "I thought you were supposed to have my back?"

"You mean the little squabble you had with Lobbins?" Westy asked. "I'm not going to fight your fights for you. Figured you had to win one sooner or later. Besides, he had about fifteen fellows itching to jump in if I did."

"He's got a pretty good punch."

Clay opened the door and clambered in, every part of his body aching. Donna had insisted he go to urgent care, but in the middle of a murder scene, she was unable to take him, as she was busy. He'd promised he would go. He lied.

"You did okay for yourself," Westy admitted. "He was a pretty big fellow."

"Was?"

"Yep. He died before they got him to the hospital. One of the problems of living way out on a peninsula, not that I think they would've had a chance even in an emergency room. He took three square."

"You see where the shots came from?"

"Nope. Same as you, I saw him stagger, and then realized what must've happened. I'd guess the shooter was undercover just to the right of the bridge.'"

"Yeah," Clay said. "I figure he was in that copse of trees on the knoll. What's that? Three hundred yards?"

"Yeah, I'd say about that."

"Pretty good shooting."

"Easy for anybody with any training," Westy said.

Clay wondered if Westy had ever killed anybody from truly long-distance. He guessed that he may have. Or was it only up close? The man had been a SEAL for eight years. Westy never spoke about that period of his life, but Clay had guessed from casual conversation that at least some of it had been in the Middle East.

"What'd you tell the police?"

"Didn't have anything to tell them."

Westy pulled the truck up behind Clay's Jeep. "You okay?"

"Yeah," Clay said. "You get home to your family. Thanks for waiting around for me."

Westy drove off. Clay thought about going into the Pelican Perch for a drink but couldn't handle the questions he was sure to face. Small-town Port Essex was certain to be abuzz with the news of the murder, and the fight between Clay and Lobbins that had taken place right before it. His phone buzzed. There were sixteen text messages.

One was from Baylee: You Okay?

Yeah. All good.

You want to come by and hash it out?

Got any whiskey?

Does Glenlivet count?

On my way.

Maria Cloutier had texted three times wanting an interview. Clay let her know that he'd meet her at the diner first thing in the morning, before going to give his official statement at the police station. There was a voicemail from his grandfather. He called him back to let him know that everything was okay, but he'd be in later. The rest of the messages he ignored.

Clay had to drive past the crime scene to get to Baylee's home on Spruce Island. The entire wharf had been lit with lights as dusk began to creep in. There were officers directing traffic. Media personnel wandered up and down the street trying to get the proper angle. The copse of trees on the knoll by the bridge had also been cordoned off and lit up. As Clay crossed over the bridge he looked back over his shoulder. It was like the circus was in town.

Baylee lived in a worn and modest three-bedroom ranch. It was cloaked in faded yellow vinyl siding. The front yard was neatly mowed and cared for with several flower beds. It was the back of the house that spilled down to the ocean that was the real prize, though. The water couldn't be seen at this time of the year through the trees, but Baylee had put in a crushed-stone path that lead to a two-person bench swing suspended by ropes that overlooked the rocky coastline.

It was to that spot that Baylee led him, bringing along two glasses, a fifth of scotch, and an ice bucket. They were joined by her basset hound, Flash. She lit several citronella torches to dissuade the few remaining black flies of the season and the early arriving mosquitoes. A gentle sea breeze was certain to help with that as well. From their vantage point, they could see the lit-up crime scene where Jake Lobbins had been shot and killed, but not the shooter's perch, which was blocked by a point of land.

Baylee wore a plaid blanket poncho and jeans with flip-flops on her feet and a baseball cap on her head. Clay had never seen her at home, only in a professional setting, and enjoyed this casual look. He also liked a woman who would drink scotch with him. The moon was working its way to full, but this was not distracting from the crispness of the stars on this perfectly cloudless night. Baylee poured them a couple of fingers each over two cubes of ice, and they sat side-by-side on the swing and didn't say a word until Clay was ready for a refill.

"He was about to tell me something when they shot him," he said.

"I guess somebody didn't want that to happen," Baylee replied. "What happened to your face? Seems like you added a few nicks and bruises to the ones you got the night you were stomped at Lucky Linda's."

"Lobbins and I got in a bit of a tussle before he got shot."

"Seems to me there are some pretty bad characters involved in this particular case."

"Shooting somebody—particularly with a sniper rifle—is a pretty big step up from a few punches," Clay agreed.

"You get killed, and I'm out of a job," Baylee said, elbowing him lightly in the side.

Clay laughed. "Don't worry. My will has you as the primary beneficiary of the business. Baylee Baker, Private Eye."

She turned her face to him, the moon caressing her bronze features. Clay would have loved to have met that Abenaki grandmother and was sure he would have found in her the beauty she'd passed on for two generations. "I think I'd rather keep you alive," she was saying, the little half-smile flitting across her mouth. "So, maybe it could be, Baker and Wolfe, Private Eyes?"

"Hmmm. If your name is first, then you bear all the responsibility, or so I've been told."

"I think I'd rather keep things the way they are, for the time being anyway, so why don't we keep you alive?" Baylee lay her head on his shoulder.

"That seems to me a good idea." Clay put his arm around her shoulders, each of them assuming that there was nothing more to the evening than a bit of mutual comfort. And there wasn't.

Chapter 10

THURSDAY, JULY 2ND

A cup of coffee just to make it to the shower seemed totally necessary the next morning. Clay had pried himself from bed, every muscle in his body aching, his face stuck to the sheet where his cheek had been rubbed raw in the altercation with Lobbins. He used two Keurig pods to fill a mug the size of a fishbowl and sat down at his computer to read the latest updates on the murder.

When Clay had quit working for the Boston police department the previous year and moved home to Port Essex, there had been more than one reason for his return. His concern with the health of his Grandpops had been a major reason, but he was also frustrated in his work as a homicide detective, disillusioned with his inability to mete out justice in a system that favored the rich, the mostly white, and almost always male.

When everybody knew that the real drug problems flourished on college campuses, he spent his time canvassing the ghettos and arresting men and women who couldn't afford to defend themselves in court. On more than one occasion, he'd been assigned a murder case that stemmed from drug use, while the Sackler family lived a life of lavish gluttony. Black men went to prison, and white men went to college.

Men battered their wives and girlfriends on a regular basis, but nobody wanted to press charges. Perhaps this was because when they did, the charges more often than not did not stick, and the man was set free. At the most, a slap on the wrist and an admonishment not to do it again were handed out, and the cycle repeated. And if you had money? You could get away with murder. The O.J.s of the world walked free.

Seven out of a 1,000 rapists are convicted of their crime. Seven. Boston alone had thousands of untested rape kits, just because the funds weren't there to follow up. As if no one cared. Unless the woman was wealthy or a celebrity. Before being promoted to homicide, Clay had arrested six men who were eventually convicted of rape, but three of them had been given zero prison time for their crime. Clay had read with horror the story of the du Pont heir, Robert H. Richards IV, who was convicted of raping his three-year-old daughter. The man was sentenced to eight years behind bars, but the judge suspended the sentence because he said the man 'wouldn't fare well in prison.'

So, it was safe to say that Clay had become jaded and cynical of a system that persecuted the poor and celebrated the rich, glorified the man and ignored the woman, and saw the law in terms of black versus white.

These job issues were coupled with his concern for his grandfather, who had grown old in Clay's absence. His mind was still keen, but his body had begun to fail him. It was only right that Clay had come home to aid the man who had taken him in when his parents were killed, the man who had raised him as his own.

His childhood room in Grandpops' house holding too many memories, Clay had instead taken over the studio apartment above the garage, giving both men some distance when they chose. He had his own entrance and mailbox. He still had to go into the main house to do his laundry, and he probably had dinner with his grandfather three or four times a week. Clay realized he hadn't checked in with the old man recently except to let him know that he was okay after last night's events.

The poster of Tom Brady still adorned his bedroom in the house, along with several *Sports Illustrated* pages of Carré Otis from the 2000 issue. He'd fallen in love the day he'd turned to the first page she was on. As a teen, he'd wanted to play quarterback in the NFL and marry Carré Otis. Instead, he'd ended up a cop and single, even if with a steady string of girlfriends who lasted anywhere from a few weeks to almost a year. He'd been sleeping with Donna for six months now, but was she really a girlfriend? He wasn't so sure.

Caffeinated, freshly showered, and feeling dapper in white cotton pants, a light blue Oxford, with a tie and a dusty rose waistcoat, Clay took the stairs down two at a time. His Grandpops was sitting on the porch of the main house. It was 6:30 in the morning, and Clay knew that Eugene Wolfe rarely rose before the south side of 10:00. The old guy must have been waiting for him.

Gene Wolfe had been a sharp-as-a-tack defense attorney in town for most of his life. The first part of his career had been taken up representing the wealthy elite from much of MidCoast Maine, but for the last ten years of his career he'd been doing pro bono defense for the poor and the indigent. This often involved men and women in trouble with drugs, which meant he was no tyro when it came to criminals and dope. He'd finally retired two years earlier at the age of eighty-two.

"Morning Clay," Gene said. "Come sit for a minute."

Clay had called him Grandpops up until the death of his parents. After that, he began calling him Gene. He didn't know why, and it never came up in the therapy sessions he'd had after the horrific crash.

"Hey, Gene," he said. "You're up early."

"Phone rang at 5:00 a.m. Some young fellow wanted to know if you were available. Said he was with the Portland newspaper."

"Sorry about that."

"I didn't unplug the damn thing until after the fifth call."

"Yeah, our phones will be ringing off the hook because of last night's tiff."

"Got time to tell me about it this morning?"

"I'm meeting with Maria Cloutier in about twenty minutes, and then I have to go do a formal interview with the police, so I'll have to give you the abbreviated version."

"That the young lady who writes for the *Register*?"

"That's her," Clay replied. Cloutier was at least forty-five. But he guessed that when you are eighty-four, just about everybody under sixty is a young sprite.

"So, spit it out."

"I was hired to find out who supplied heroin to that young mother, Kelly Anne Landry, who stands accused of killing her baby with heroin because she rubbed it on the little girl's gums. I had a lead that the heroin was coming in through Jake Lobbins' lobster pots. You might remember the name; he was a linebacker I played with, a few grades behind me. When I called him out on it, he went berserk and attacked me. After a bit of a tussle, he seemed like he wanted to come clean. Then somebody shot and killed him right in front of all of us. Apparently with a sniper rifle and at some distance, so likely a pro."

"Lobbins? Yeah, I remember him. Seemed like a good enough young lad. Was he truly smuggling dope?"

"Yep, I think so."

"You're not sure?"

"I didn't catch him in the act, and now I can't exactly ask him. I know the police will look into it, but I'm pretty sure he was, yeah."

"In his lobster traps." He shook his head. "Why would he go and do a darn fool thing like that?"

"Westy heard that he might have gotten addicted to Oxy. So, maybe to pay for his habit?"

Gene clasped his hands with his thumbs under his chin. Clay knew this sign. Whenever he was about to shake up the prosecution with a telling question or salient point in court, this was his tell that it was coming.

"Lobs was a good boy. Worked hard. Doesn't seem to be the sort to be running dope," Gene said.

"What's it matter now?"

"I suppose your next step is to find where the dope was coming from and where it was going?"

"I'm pretty much focused on the local dealer," Clay said.

"You don't care where it came from?"

"Probably Mexico or Asia. Drug cartels. Above my pay grade or ability to do anything about."

"What do you know about heroin?"

"It's addictive and makes you high."

"Opioids are a class of drugs that act on opioid receptors in the brain. Signals sent to these receptors can block pain and lead to feelings of euphoria. Morphine, heroin, oxycodone, and fentanyl—they're all in the same family."

Clay knew the basics of this from his internet search, but he knew that Gene was going somewhere with this. "Yeah, morphine and oxycodone are legal when prescribed by a doctor."

"But still highly addictive. Many people start out with these prescriptions for legitimate medical reasons, but then turn to heroin when the doctor cuts off their flow of morphine or oxycodone."

"So Lobbins probably started out with a legal opioid prescription, got hooked, then had to buy it from a dealer to get his fix. Then he started smuggling it to pay his sky-rocketing bills? He did tell me he was going to lose his boat, too."

Gene smiled. "Seems that it may have been on your mind as well."

"Yep."

"But you don't care where the dope was coming from, only who is dealing it locally?"

"Like I can do anything about drug cartels in Mexico?"

"It's the Chinese you have to worry about."

"The Chinese?"

"They are the world's biggest producers of fentanyl, the superman of opioids. A couple of grains of the stuff can kill you. Its medical use is for cases of pain so severe that Oxy isn't enough. Over the past five or six years dealers have been mixing it in with heroin—a better high, apparently, and a cheaper one, too, because of the price of fentanyl. More bang for the buck. It is fifty times more potent than heroin. But it has its side effects."

"Like killing people?"

Gene nodded. "My last year working in 2017, there were 70,000 overdose deaths in the United States. About 50,000 were opioids related. Over a five-year period, this went up almost 500%. This increase is linked directly to fentanyl."

"But fentanyl isn't derived from poppy plants like morphine and heroin?"

"It is manufactured. Tons of money in it. Very cheap investment, huge returns."

"And the Chinese sell it to Mexican drug cartels who mix it with heroin and then smuggle it into the U.S.?" Clay asked. "Or put it on ships that offload it into lobster traps to be picked up by lobster mules."

"Some of the time the Chinese ship it directly to the United States. Pharmaceutical companies can legally purchase it to reformulate into products like slow-release patches that they then package and distribute for medical use. The illegal shipments, well, their place of origin is almost untraceable because they transship it, making it possible to mail it directly to individuals for drug trafficking."

"It wouldn't take much to misplace a sack of the stuff," Clay said.

"A DEA agent once told me that two pounds of fentanyl can be used to manufacture a million pills worth $20 million. Pretty good payout for somebody of low morals."

"Like I said, above my pay grade. Crystal Landry gave me fifty bucks to find the local dealer. Pretty sure she meant who sold it to her. Not where it originated."

"Okay. For now," Gene said. "Just be careful. These people play for keeps."

"Yeah, I get that. So does Jake Lobbins, now, anyways."

It was a two-minute walk to the Port Diner, giving Clay time to prepare what he wanted to share with Cloutier. He'd met Cloutier almost two decades earlier, when she, freshly graduated from Wesleyan College, had interviewed him after the state championship football game. He'd then not seen her for some seventeen years until he returned to Port Essex, when she had done a brief story on him opening his private detective agency for the *Register*. Over the past year they'd developed a bit of a friendship, more the occasional lunch than anything else.

Her energy and nose for news were insatiable. If he wasn't careful, she'd wring every bit of information out of him, even down to what he vaguely suspected but only surmised. Over the years, she'd risen through the ranks at the daily newspaper. When the editor and owner of forty years had decided to retire, the possible death knell for the newspaper, Marie Cloutier had taken it over. For the past nine years she had been the heart and soul of the *Port Essex Daily Register*, and by extension, the heart and soul of Port Essex. She was inextricably linked to the pulse of the town. If there were any secrets to be told, she knew them.

"Sorry I'm late," Clay said, sliding into the booth across from Cloutier.

"You look like hell," she said.

"Thanks. It's been a rough couple of days."

The waitress came over and poured him a cup of coffee without asking. He'd only been back in town for about a year, but almost every day back had started here at the diner. Clay had been born in this place, and it seemed, been forgiven his time away as youthful exuberance, and was now accepted as a townie. It would take at least ten years for a person not born in Port Essex to be called a regular. If they were born out of state, well, they could just forget about it.

"You want to tell me what happened yesterday?" Cloutier asked. "I heard you and Jake Lobbins got in a fight right before he was shot."

"You know that drug case I was telling you about?"

"Sure," Cloutier said. "You're supposed to be finding out who supplied the heroin to Kelly Anne Landry that she used to kill her baby girl."

"Lobbins was the mule. The drugs were coming in through his lobster traps."

"Holy shit. Are you certain?"

"I had a couple of sources tell me that was the case. When I went out to the wharf to ask him about it, he flipped out."

The waitress came over with pad and pen. Clay ordered the potato skillet, and Cloutier got the pancakes.

"Through the lobster traps. Ingenious. Plus, that suggests some organization. The middle of the ocean's not exactly like some parking lot where you exchange goods for cash." Cloutier shook her head. "Lobbins didn't seem like a bad guy, the little bit I know of him. Was he doing it for the money?"

Clay pointed a cocked finger at her. "Bingo," he said. "That's what I need to know."

"Aren't you the private detective?"

"I'm bringing you an exclusive on the story of the decade in Port Essex, and you want to quibble?"

"Any luck finding out who the local dealer is?"

"I had a chat with Dylan Thompson yesterday, and he dropped the name of Curtis. You know anybody by that name?"

Cloutier cocked her head sideways. "Nope."

"I'm going to go put the squeeze on Dylan later and see what I can find out."

"How about where the drugs are coming from?"

"We'll leave that to the police and the Coast Guard, or the DEA, FBI or CIA, or whoever is responsible for running the drug cartels down."

"You think it's the Mexicans?"

"Don't have any idea," Clay said. "But I'm not interested in finding out."

"Why not?"

"Maybe I want to stay alive."

"Sounds reasonable," Cloutier said. "But my father used to tell me that you don't kill a snake by cutting off its tail."

"Lot less chance of getting bit if you stay away from the head, though."

Their breakfast arrived, and they bent to the task of eating. Clay sprinkled Tabasco liberally over the top of his potato and egg mixture.

"You still dating that woman who owns the Tremblay block?" Clay asked around the last bite of bacon.

"Denise? Yeah, we're still seeing each other," Cloutier said.

"Allen Daigle has his legal office there. I was wondering if you could ask her what kind of tenant he is. Does he pay his bills on time? That sort of thing."

"What's this have to do with?"

Clay looked left and right. "His wife thinks he's cheating on her."

"What's it matter if he pays his bills on time?"

"I think he's got something going on, but a hunch tells me it's not sex."

"That all you going to tell me?"

The two detectives with MCU spent two hours interrogating Clay. They were highly suspicious of his story of heroin being smuggled through the lobster traps, but they agreed to have the cousins picked up for questioning. The long and short was that Clay knew very little about what had happened and why. Finally, they turned him loose. As he was leaving the station, he ran into Donna coming in.

"Anything new?" he asked.

"Not really, or that I could tell you, anyway" she said just a bit shortly. "I have to go in and file my report so I can go home and get some sleep." Her face softened, and she made to reach out and touch his arm before stopping herself. "Why don't you come by after 5:00 and wake me up? We can fill each other in," she said.

"You been up all night?"

"Yep. Forensics just packed it up."

"Heard Lobbins died on the way to the hospital."

Donna nodded, then looked around. "Let's talk later, okay? Wake me up. I plan on sleeping naked. You know where the key is."

Chapter 11

STILL THURSDAY, JULY 2ND

Clay knocked on the door of the trailer. Crystal opened the door wearing a T-shirt that said 'Bachelor Monday Bitches'.

"Mr. Wolfe, good to see you." She opened the door wide and let him in. Kelly Anne was sitting on the couch with two young children. Clay figured that she must have gotten them out of foster care somehow. Her eyes were bleary, whether from the night before or the present, it was tough to tell.

"I remember you," she said. "You're the asshole my mama hired to find the heroin dealer," she said.

"That would be me," Clay agreed. "Maybe you want to just give me a name, and we'll be done with it?"

"I don't have no more money for you right now," Crystal said. "Kelly Anne, she lost her job while in jail, and I've had to be helping her and the kids out."

"Why are you protecting a drug dealer?" Clay sat down opposite of Kelly Anne. "Why don't you just give up the name."

"First of all," Kelly Anne said with a cagey look on her face. "I'm not saying I know any drug dealers. But, if did, it certainly wouldn't be in my best interest to go around blabbing his name, now would it. Especially if the man is a well-respected professional from town."

That was certainly new information, Clay thought. "You and Dylan both said something about Curtis. Is that the dealer's name?

First name? Last name?"

"Don't know what you're talking about."

"You got somewhere we can talk in private?" The older of the two children seemed to be taking an active interest in the conversation.

"I got nothing to say to you," Kelly Anne said.

"You want to stay here, you tell the man something," Crystal said.

"I'm not saying shit," Kelly Anne said.

"Then get your ass out of my home," Crystal said.

"What? You're kicking me out? Well, fuck you! I was just leaving anyway." Kelly Anne grabbed a ratty purse from the table and left, slamming the door behind her.

The two kids, ages about four and seven, watched silently. Their faces were impassive. This was not unusual behavior in their lives. Crystal sat down on the seat vacated by Kelly Anne.

"She tell you anything new?" Clay asked Crystal.

"Nah, she's always been a stubborn cuss, that one. She came out of jail clean, but I think she's back on the hard candy. Looked like she might even be shooting the vein in her arm. Think I saw a bit of bruising there."

"Is she looking for work?"

"You saw her. Ain't nobody gonna hire a junkie, even in this booming economy. I thought if she got put away, that jail might straighten her out. Looks like she's going to walk away with just a slap on the wrist and an invitation to shoot up." Crystal's eyes were ringed with too much aqua-colored makeup, but otherwise she looked better than the first day Clay had seen her. He looked around, seeing a neat and tidy space, if small. He could smell something cooking in the oven, and it smelled damn good.

"You say you got a boyfriend who's a lobsterman?"

"Maybe." Crystal eyed him distrustfully. "I heard you was involved with Jake getting shot and killed."

"I was there, but I didn't do the shooting," Clay said.

"People said the two of you were scrapping?"

"Yeah, but we were all done by then. He was just about to talk to me, I think."

"About what?"

"I think he was running the heroin through his traps," Clay said.

"Son of a bitch! You mean boats were dropping them in his pots, and he was picking them up? Who was he delivering to?"

"I don't know." Clay shrugged. "But I'm betting that's who killed him."

Crystal jumped up and walked over to the window. "Fuck me. You mean they killed him to keep him from talking to you?"

"I don't know that." He looked at her, considering what he was about to say, then asked, "What do you know about a guy named Curtis? Seems like he has something to do with all the drugs coming through town."

She drew in a breath at the name and shook her head. "You know what, Mr. Wolfe? I think I want you to drop the case. You can keep the fifty bucks."

Clay cursed silently to himself. He should've kept his yap shut. "I can't do that, Crystal. A baby is dead. A man is dead. In my town. For what? So people can get high? So that somebody can make a few dollars? No, I'm going to see this one through. I'd appreciate your help, but you don't need to pay me." Clay took out his money clip from his pocket and peeled a fifty from it. "Here. I don't want it."

"You don't need to return that money."

"Buy the kids some food. Some toys. Whatever." Clay walked out the door and climbed into his Jeep.

He drove to the inner circle where Dylan Thompson's trailer was located, but there was nobody there. He hated to sit in the office, but it was sometimes necessary, and so that is where he went to catch up on a few other things.

Don came in with the news that he'd caught the workman comp guy on camera mowing his lawn. Not exactly taking the vacation time and money to go party in Las Vegas, but definitely less injured than he claimed. If he could drive a lawnmower, he could drive a crane. Clay told him to write up the report and submit it so that they could report back to BIW.

Don agreed to start tailing Allen Daigle the next day. Clay had done some light stalking and discovered that the name of the woman that Daigle had been with the day before was Gabriella Richardson, thirty-eight, married to Harold. He gave this information to Don as well.

At five, Baylee poked her head in the door. "I'm heading out. You want me to lock up?"

"Wow. 5:00 already? I'll walk out with you." Clay shut down the computer, turned off the light, and joined her at the door. "You got plans this evening?" he asked.

"I'm getting a drink with Tammy down to the Pelican Perch. Want to join us?"

"No, but thanks. I have somebody I have to see."

Baylee shot him a sideways glance. "No worries."

"Baylee?" Clay touched her elbow. "Thanks for talking last night. I just needed somebody I could be myself with."

"And who had scotch," she said with a smile.

"You want a ride?" he asked.

"I got my car."

"You're never going to find parking down there. The Fourth doth approach. Downtown is already a madhouse."

"You're probably right, but I can just walk. You best get to whoever it is you're going to see." Baylee set off walking the few blocks to the Pelican Perch.

Clay watched her walk away until she rounded a corner, and then got in the Jeep to navigate the crowded roadways across town to Donna's. His thoughts dwelled upon Baylee as he drove to his lover's house. What made her tick? He'd heard a few stories that suggested a wild youth, a young marriage, and of course, a pattern of abuse that had eventually led to her being acquitted for shooting and killing her husband. This suggested the circumstances had been severe and the evidence that her life was in danger overt.

Baylee had at least three tattoos that Clay knew of, but he guessed there were more, concealed by her clothing, and he wondered what they might be and where. He sometimes saw her sitting at her desk with a faraway look in her eyes, her lips twisted in some inner pain. He wondered what she was thinking. Was it the torment of her husband's physical and mental abuse? Perhaps it was thoughts of her estranged mother, a woman about whom Clay had never heard her speak a word.

Donna's cruiser was parked in the driveway. Clay pulled the key from underneath the stone turtle statue in the front flower bed. It was not the most secretive of hiding places, but the woman was a cop, after all. He let himself into the house and walked down the hallway to her bedroom. The house was entirely devoid of any sort of clutter, and for the first time Clay realized there were no pictures of family. Did Donna have any family, he wondered?

She was, as promised, naked. A white sheet was partially wrapped around her, but plenty of skin was exposed to prove she'd been good to her word. Clay took a moment to appreciate her fit and toned body, ample breasts, and sculpted bottom.

Clay caught sight of himself in the mirror and barely recognized himself. His blue-green eyes, or the right one anyway, was ringed with a similar color bruise, and his goatee, usually trimmed to look mildly neglected, had actually turned a bit wild on his chin. He knew that women found him attractive, especially his eyes, but he wasn't sure why. At least he was well-dressed.

He carefully removed his clothes and laid them over the back of the chair. He took one last glance in the mirror, noting his toned shoulders and rock-hard abs, but then his eyes trailed down to his thin legs that would barely support a stork, and he shook his head.

He slid into bed, leaving his introspection behind. Donna sighed and turned her back to him, and he lightly trailed his fingers up and down, allowing his fingernails to gently graze her skin. After a bit, he slid his right arm around her so that his hand was resting gently on her breast and began kneading her left buttock with his other hand. She arched her back in appreciation, and he continued this massage for several minutes before his hand trickled its way around to her front and his fingers began their teasing play from belly button to upper thighs. She began to moan *sotto voce,* and he leaned in and nibbled on her ear.

She reached her hand behind and grasped him, and then suddenly rolled over and pulled herself astride him with a fierce look in her eyes and began to grind. It was hard and fast, and minutes later she tumbled off of him, and they both lay gasping.

"Better than any alarm clock," she said.

"Although I do come with a snooze feature," he replied.

"Does that mean you're going to ring the bell again?"

"Ha, maybe later. We could go out and get some dinner together."

"Can't. I got to get back to work. Your fault."

"Any leads on who did the shooting?" he asked.

"Not that I'm going to share with a private detective poking his nose in where it doesn't belong," she said, her tone a bit curt to someone to whom she'd just made love.

"How about the heroin in the lobster traps?"

"I need to talk to you about this case." She stood up and pulled on her panties. "I think you need to drop it."

"Drop it? What for? If it wasn't for me, you wouldn't know how the drugs were getting into town."

"First of all, there is no proof of that," she said.

"Why did Lobbins attack me?"

"I don't know, maybe you rubbed him the wrong way?"

"He was a mule. I know it." Clay stood up and grabbed his boxers. He was angry but had to admit that she looked stunning facing him in nothing but light-blue panties accentuating the blue in her eyes.

"Jake Lobbins was a lobsterman. His record is absolutely clean."

"Port Essex is drowning in illegal drugs from heroin to street Oxy, and what have the police done about it?"

"Are you saying we're not doing our job?" she asked.

"I'm saying perhaps you could use a little help."

"Help? Like you butting your nose in and getting a man killed?"

"If he wasn't a mule, then why was he murdered?"

She put her bra on and then pulled on her uniform pants. She still looked mighty good that way, he had to admit.

"Maybe Lobbins wasn't the target," she said.

"What? You think the shooter was trying to kill me?" he asked.

"You've been out there stirring things up." She began buttoning her shirt. "These are dangerous people you're messing with."

"I'm not some guy who took an online course to be a private investigator and then hung out his shingle," he said. "I'm a former homicide detective from Boston. I can take of myself."

"Chief Knight wants you to back off," she said. "Drop the case."

.   .   .   .   .

As Baylee got closer to the Pelican Perch, she could feel the anxiety blowing in like storm clouds threatening the serenity of the day. The fear that this angst would incapacitate her and leave her a writhing mess in front of all these people made it so much worse. Her palms began to sweat, and she could hear her heart hammering in her chest. This was the first time since killing her husband that she had ventured out into public for the purpose of pleasure.

She sat down on a bench, the other side occupied by an older man with a shabby jacket and a pipe. Five things I can see, she thought. Man. Pipe. Car. Seagull. Store. Four things I can hear. Talking. Car, is that allowed? Breathing. Door slamming. Three things I can feel. My chest. The sun on my face. My ring. Two things I can smell. Barbecue. My sweat. One thing I can taste. Fear.

Om gum ganapatayei namah. Om gum ganapatayei namah. Om gum ganapatayei namah. Baylee repeated over and over, giving salutations to the remover of obstacles. Just as backup, she slid a Xanax out of her purse and chased it down with some water. After a minute, the numbness began to spread through her body, calming the storm. While the day was no longer sunny, the danger of a tropical storm had passed.

Baylee climbed the steps up to the third-floor Pelican Perch bar. She hadn't been here since George. They'd had some good times here. Then they'd had some bad times here. Now he was dead.

She knew that Clay liked this bar. In fact, he'd invited her several times to join him. Although everything in her had wanted to say yes, her mind had screamed 'what if you have a panic attack?' What if she froze and started shaking and couldn't control herself? What if Clay realized he couldn't have some crazy woman working for him and let her go? What would she do for work? What if she never saw him again?

It seemed a good idea to do a trial run. When Clay had walked out with her from work, she'd thought it necessary to invite him to join her and Tammy. Inside, her nerves had rebelled. Baylee had only ever had one full-blown panic attack, an episode that ended with her calling an ambulance because she thought she was dying. One was more than enough. At the same time, some part of her had been enthused by the prospect of him saying yes.

"Hey, Tammy." Baylee walked up behind her at the bar. There was no empty stool.

"Baylee," Tammy swiveled, stood, and hugged her. "This guy was just sitting here until you arrived." She cast a hairy stare at the man to her left.

"That's fine, I can stand," Baylee said.

"Get," Tammy said to the man.

"Can I get your phone number?" he asked.

"Get." The man got.

Tammy had straight blonde hair, a freckled face, and mischievous, dancing eyes. "Sit down, and let's get you something to sip on."

"White Claw," Baylee said to the bartender as she sat in the recently vacated seat.

"Is this invisible?" Tammy held out her left hand.

"What?"

"Looks like a fucking wedding ring to me, right?" Tammy looked over at where the man recently hitting on her had moved on to a fresh target. "I am so sick of feeling like I can't even go out without some raging teenage hormone in a pasty adult body trying to woo me with slick lines like 'aside from being sexy, what do you do for a living?'"

"What part do you have a problem with? That you're married, that he's gross, or that his pick-up lines are cheesy?"

"Door number two, Monty." Tammy was a belly laugher with a case of snorts thrown in, loud and unapologetic.

Baylee grinned. "How is Josh?"

"We're not here to talk about husbands," Tammy said. "Ugh, sorry about that."

"All good. I couldn't agree with you more. Let's leave husbands off the table."

"Tell me what it's like to be single and sexy as hell." Tammy said.

"Talk about cheesy pick-up lines," Baylee replied, then sighed. "Not much to tell."

"Oh, come on, don't leave a married broad hanging. How about that fine-looking man you work for? Clay Wolfe? Just his name makes me tingly."

Baylee covered her blush with a swallow of White Claw. "He's a little too refined for me," she said.

"He is a bit of a dandy," Tammy agreed. "But he is fine looking with eyes to kill for and a tight body. Mm-mm. Tasty."

"I think he's seeing somebody."

"Of course he is. We're not meant to keep our young nubile bodies to ourselves. That's why we have to hook *you* up."

"Hook me up? Who are you? Tinder?"

Tammy snorted and slapped the bar top. "I do like to swipe right, and then left, up and down, and then in a circle, if you know what I mean."

"Do I know what you mean? You just described my dating life in a nutshell."

"Speaking of smooth like a nutshell, I just shaved myself bare."

"You best keep your voice down if you don't want the guy behind you slobbering on your back," Baylee said.

Tammy turned and glared at a man intently studying the bottles behind the bar.

"I heard your man was somehow involved in that shooting yesterday," Tammy said.

"He's not my man." Baylee finished her drink. "But, yeah, he was down at the wharf. Said he was only about two feet from the guy when he was shot. Could've been him."

"What was it all about? I heard the two of them were in a fight."

Baylee leaned closer. She loved her friend but did not trust her in the slightest to keep her mouth shut. "Clay has been doing some investigative work on whether or not Lobbins' wife was cheating on him."

"Aren't they separated?"

"Yeah, but why?"

"You don't think it was Jenny who shot him?" Tammy's eyes got really big, and her lips narrowed into a perfect 'O.'

Baylee shrugged. They went on to talk about people they knew who were cheating, old friends from school, Tammy's two kids, and just about everything that could be covered in ninety minutes and three drinks.

Chapter 12

FRIDAY, JULY 3RD

The phone buzzed, and Clay picked it off his desk. He'd been in the office for a couple of hours already. It was not quite 8:00 in the morning. It was a text from Marie Cloutier.

Lobbins had back surgery last year. Rumor has it he got addicted to Oxy.

Moving heroin to pay his Oxy bill?

Clay texted back.

Maybe. Some people replace Oxy with heroin. Easier to get. More potent, especially the new kind with fentanyl. He also ran up some big health bills. No insurance. Dropped his Obamacare as soon as he was allowed. He probably still blames the liberals.

Cloutier was most certainly a liberal, by way of Wesleyan College. Clay grinned and pecked out a reply.

Them liberals are worse than varmints. So, he has an expensive addiction and high health care bills and doesn't want to lose his boat. Who would know these things?

Just about anybody.

Clay sipped his coffee. He leaned back and put his feet up on the desk. He felt pretty good. For the first time in a few days he wasn't hung over and hadn't been beat-up the previous evening, either. Things were looking up. He'd probably have to go down to the Knox Wharf and ask around among the lobstermen, but he had a feeling he wouldn't be very welcome there, not after a fight that ended with one of their own being killed.

Lobstermen, Clay mused, were like street gangs except instead of colors and territories, they had wharves and were ready to die for that symbol of their tribe. Usually the warfare was carried out against other lobstermen who were suspected of raiding their traps or cutting their lines. This easily spilled over to include other fishermen aboard boats, oyster farmers, and even those digging clams in the flats. If there was anything that united all these disparate elements together, it was a threat from a landlubber. Westy had told him a story about a young lobsterman who'd just gotten his license to fish 300 traps and made the mistake of putting a string or two too close to the traps of another, long-established boat. It was the fall, and the youngster pulled up the string a day later to find each trap filled with the severed body parts of a deer. Including the head. Maybe he could get Westy to do his dirty work for him.

Clay grabbed his phone and texted Westy.

Hey, can you ask around about any strangers Lobbins was hanging around with lately?

He expected no reply, knowing the man was out on the water and often out of any service area.

The phone buzzed in his hand, making him think that Westy had actually replied, but it was Cloutier.

In regard to that other matter? Allen Daigle has actually inquired of Denise if the building is for sale. Seems to have plenty of money. It sounds like his legal business is booming.

K. Clay texted back.

The outer door opened. Clay unwound from his desk and went to the door. It was Baylee arriving for work.

"Morning, Baylee," he said.

"Don't you look dapper this morning," she said. "Or maybe you just went a night without getting punched?"

"It was a close call, but I did manage not to get whacked." Clay was not really joking, as he'd thought Donna had been going to hit him for not staying out of police business. "And you are a vision of loveliness, but let's get a gander without those dark glasses."

"What are you saying?" Baylee lowered her sunglasses down the gentle slope of her nose.

"It's not what I'm saying. It's what you said. Last I knew, you were heading out for drinks with Tammy Belanger."

"We had two, and then I had to get home," Baylee said. "Okay, maybe three." She hoped that Xanax glaze wasn't too obvious.

Clay raised an eyebrow.

"I had to get home to feed Flash," she said. "Besides, it's not me who drinks too much." Perhaps too much Xanax, she thought, but not alcohol.

"I was home asleep by nine," Clay said.

"Rugged couple of days, huh?"

"For sure," he said. "Got plans for tonight?"

"Tonight?"

"Fireworks over Essex Harbor? Not to be missed."

"I'll probably have a glass of wine, sit in my swing, and coddle Flash who hates loud noises," Baylee said.

"Why don't you and Flash come over to my place? Gene is going to make some snacks, and Westy and his wife will probably come over. We can sit on the porch and ooh and ahh together."

"That sounds wrong," she said. "As a matter of fact, I believe this might constitute workplace harassment."

Clay flushed. "At the fireworks," he said.

"Are you sure there will be fireworks?" she asked.

He started to reply, stopped, opened his mouth, and then shut it tight.

"Hmm, cat got your tongue?" she asked.

"Now who's talking dirty?"

She started to reply, stopped, opened her mouth, and then shut it tight.

And then they both laughed.

"Sure, boss, sounds like fun. What time?" she asked.

"Seven work for you?"

"Yep. Oh, that reminds me. Tammy said that Dylan Thompson has been digging bloodworms over in the mud flats the last couple of weeks."

Clay brought up the tide chart on his phone. "Low tide was 4:00 this morning. I bet he's home sleeping by now."

"Or at the Side Bar having a couple," Baylee said.

The Side Bar was indeed where Clay found Dylan. He was at the bar with a beer and a shot glass in front of him. He had a red, white, and blue bandana collecting his curly mop of hair, and mud still speckled his arms from the morning's work.

"Bloody Mary," Clay said. "And whatever he's drinking."

The bartender nodded. It was just past 9:00 in the morning. Clay was reminded of the time he had gone to Scotland and walked into a bar at a similar hour with two friends. They must have arrived just as a factory shift had gotten out, because the place was packed. When he and his friends had walked in with their backpacks on, the bar had gone eerily silent. It had reminded him of a scene from *American Werewolf in London* at the time. There were seven other people in the bar this morning, each of them engrossed in the drink in front of them.

The bartender poured a Michelob Ultra in a glass, set it in front of Dylan, and then added a shot of Jägermeister. "Vodka preference?" he asked Clay.

"Absolute."

The bartender sloshed half a glass of the clear liquid and topped it with a premix. "Olives?"

"Please."

He popped a couple of olives in and set it down before going back to his crossword puzzle at the other end of the short bar.

"What the fuck you want?" Dylan asked once he'd taken a gulp of the beer.

"Just getting a drink and being friendly."

"I told you I don't know nothin'." He nudged the shot glass, and the amber-brown liquid shifted like molten lava.

Clay waited for the bartender to go to a table by the door to deliver two beers to a couple of guys who still wore their thigh high boots from the clam flats. "I just need a last name for Curtis," he said.

"Curtis who? What the fuck you talking about?" Dylan looked nervously over his shoulder as he spoke.

"He doesn't need to know where I got the name."

"I don't know no Curtis."

"Of course, if I have to, I can spread the news that Dylan Thompson told me the local drug pusher was a fellow by the name of Curtis. See how that goes down."

"C'mon, man, don't be doing anything stupid."

"Then tell me his last name."

Dylan slammed the Jägermeister down the hatch. "I don't know it," he said.

Clay nodded for the bartender to pour another shot. He had a feeling that he held Dylan's attention only as long as there was alcohol in front of him. If that dried up, there would be nothing to keep the man from getting up and walking out.

"Okay," Clay said. "Where can I find him?"

"I only met him once, and he came to me."

"Give me a break, Dylan. I'm not here to bust you for using drugs, but I know for a fact that you're pretty into the White Horse."

"Yeah, so?"

"So, you must know how to find him when you want to score."

"You don't buy from Curtis. He's the guy who pays you a visit when you fuck up." Dylan downed the shot, finished the beer, and stood up to leave.

Clay stood and blocked the man's exit. "Don't make me hang you out to dry."

"Volkov," Dylan said under his breath. "Now get the fuck out of my way."

On the short drive back to the office, Clay's phone rang. It was Niles Harrington. He was wondering if Clay could meet him at the Seal Bar.

Clay had started his day reading an email update from Niles with the information he'd requested, consisting of contact information for his son, Asher, forty-three, and daughter, Charlotte, thirty-eight. Asher had three kids, ages seventeen, fourteen, and twelve. They were most likely too young to be suspects. Charlotte had never married or given birth. He'd meant to call them, but then the text message from Marie Cloutier had interrupted him, and the arrival of Baylee had driven the missing Shade from his mind.

Scott McKenny had not yet provided the information on his two employees, but that was okay, as it gave Clay an excuse to pay the man a visit. There was something he wasn't sharing, whether it was about the *Fourth Shade* or something else, Clay wasn't quite sure, but the caretaker was definitely withholding information, if not outright lying.

These thoughts carried him to the Seal Bar, wondering if Niles Harrington was going to be upset that he hadn't actually done anything about looking for the *Fourth Shade* yet.

Clay spotted Niles sitting at a table in the corner overlooking the harbor. He pointed at him to the hostess and walked on past, but then he noticed Murphy was at the bar with the regulars and veered in that direction.

"Hey Murph, can I ask you a quick question?"

Murphy looked around, and then let his gaze encompass the square bar and the men who sat at it. "Take your time, I'm not going anywhere."

"Yeah, I'm meeting somebody, and he's waiting for me over in the dining area. He had a statue stolen from his house. It's a man about two-feet high. He calls it the *Fourth Shade*. You heard about anything like that?"

"I thought there were just Three Shades?" Murphy asked.

Clay shook his head. The man never ceased to surprise him. A former clam digger who spent his entire day in bars, but he'd seemingly read Dante. "Long story, but yeah, it looks like the other three."

"Worth a lot of money?"

"Yep."

"Nobody is going to try and move something like that local. It's probably in New York City as we speak, or even Paris," Murphy said.

"Yeah, you're probably right. Keep your ears open, though. I think there had to be local involvement in the theft, and that sort of thing is hard to keep quiet around here."

"Will do."

"Oh, one other thing," Clay said. "Do you know a fellow by the name of Curtis Volkov?"

Murphy rolled it off his tongue. "What sort of name is Volkov?"

"Russian, I think."

"Can't say that I do. Guess that answer won't get me a free drink."

"Ask around, will you? You find him for me, and I'll cover a week of bar tabs. I got to go. You got my number, right?"

"Sure do," Murphy said. "It's embedded in that fancy new phone of mine. If I can ever remember to keep the damned thing turned on."

Clay crossed over into the dining area. There was no partition to separate it from the bar. There was a glass of brown liquor waiting for him, and he suspected it was most likely Bowmore. He hoped the drinks weren't coming out of his pay.

"Clay, glad you could make it."

"Hello, Niles. I was heading in this direction when you called, if not to this exact spot."

"Saw you talking to that lad at the bar."

"He's the sponge for all the gossip in town. I was asking him if he'd heard anything about your statue."

"Had he?"

"No, but he'll keep his ears open. As soon as somebody brags to a buddy, he'll hear about it and let me know."

"Is that your plan of action? Wait?" Niles' smile vanished from his face.

"No, not at all. I plan on interviewing your immediate family and your caretaker's employees to see what might turn up."

"You haven't done that yet?"

"No, not yet. Sorry. I've been caught up in another case, but I'll get right on it."

"That have anything to do with the shooting the other night? I heard you were right in the thick of things."

"Might've," Clay said.

Niles looked as if he wanted to pry, but after a minute, merely said, "I wanted to ask you privately if you thought McKenny was acting strange the other day when you were asking him questions."

"Yeah. I'd say he was definitely holding something back," Clay agreed. "I was thinking of paying him a visit this afternoon. He's not working at your house today, is he?"

"No. You have his cell number, don't you?"

"For sure. I'll hunt him down. Most people start kicking off work early today and firing up the barbecues. Maybe I'll find him at home."

Chapter 13

STILL FRIDAY, JULY 3RD

Clay had just left a message for Scott McKenny to call him back when his phone buzzed with a text from Westy.

Can't make tonight. Little one got a cold. Raincheck.

Clay put down the phone and thought about what to text back.

You sure? Got Baylee coming as well. Gene will be disappointed.

Ahh. A date. Nice.

Need you to be there.

No can do, Kemosabe.

Can you meet for a beer?

Tomorrow. 4. Pelican Perch.

K.

Clay looked back through the messages and added a last comment.

Not a date.

* * *

Baylee closed the office at 3:00 and went home. It was a holiday weekend, after all, but closing in the mid-afternoon on a Friday in the summer was not abnormal. Besides, she had a few errands to run and preparations to make for the evening.

The first stop was at Hedone, a women's clothing store down on Commercial Way. It had been quite some time since she'd bought herself something nice to wear. She was in luck and it was still open. After forty-five minutes of deliberation she went with a sleeveless, bright-yellow sundress with a collar and four buttons leading down from the neck to the waist. Light-pink carnations traipsed their way across the material. Her only misgiving was that it wasn't red, white, and blue for the celebration of Independence Day, but hey, those weren't her best colors. Or anyone's, come to think of it, she reflected.

Clay had told her that she need not bring anything, but she couldn't very well show up empty-handed. She stopped by the market and picked up a bottle of Francis Ford Coppola's Cabernet Sauvignon and a twelve-year Glenlivet. Not cheap, she thought, but she knew that it would be appreciated.

Her phone buzzed with a text from Tammy.

Me and Josh going to Pelican Perch for fireworks if you want to join.

Baylee grinned as she thought out her reply. Going to Clay's house for dinner & Fireworks.

STFU.

Of course, Tammy would overreact, but why Shut The Freak Up? She pecked out a reply. With his Grandpops and Weston and Faith.

Meet me for a drink.

Baylee looked at the time. Can't. Have to go home and get ready.

I want to hear all about.

Baylee grinned and sent her reply. She then dropped the phone on the seat and drove home. A bath was in order. Maybe a glass of wine. She was going to try to avoid a Xanax.

·   ·   ·   ·

Eugene Wolfe was sitting on the front porch when Baylee pulled into the narrow drive at ten minutes past 7:00. She helped Flash out, and the two of them crossed over the small front-yard and up the steps. Lugging a bottle in either hand added to her self-consciousness. Flash had no such reservations or anxieties but bounded up the steps and jumped onto Gene's lap with his large Basset Hound paws up on his chest.

"Well, hello there," Gene said. "You must be the Flash I've heard about. Those sure are some ears you got hanging from your head. More like palm fronds than ears, I'd say."

"Hello, Gene," Baylee said.

"Baylee, hello. Glad you could make it."

He stood up, a friendly twinkle to his blue eyes, and, jostling Flash off his lap, greeted her with a kiss on the cheek, the sort of thing that was frowned upon these days. She didn't mind. There was nothing creepy in the kind smile that peeked out from behind a pointed silver-beard.

"I brought something to drink." She held out the bottles.

"The good stuff," he said. "We usually consume Dewar's for cocktails and drink boxed wine with dinner." And indeed, there was a rolling cocktail cart with these choices, as well as bottles of vodka and rum, which looked slightly dusty. "Can I pour you something?"

"I guess I'd take a snifter of the scotch with a couple of ice cubes."

"Glenlivet it is for the both of us." Gene already had the bottle opened up. "Clay is in the kitchen, and I bet he'd love one. Would you mind taking it in?"

Baylee went in through the front door, its low height one sign that the house had been around since the mid-17th century. She'd been there several times before, mostly before Clay had returned home from Boston.

That had been in the aftermath of her shooting her husband. It had been Gene Wolfe who'd connected her with an organization that defended domestic abuse victims charged when they retaliated. Free of charge. Suffering from the devastating depression of having killed somebody she once loved, ignorant of the legal ramifications, and without the proverbial pot to piss in, Baylee had been looking at twenty years in prison if not for the help of Gene Wolfe.

Clay was in the kitchen stirring something in a bowl. "I brought you a scotch," she said.

"Ahh, thank you. I was holding off until your arrival. Thought it would be bad form to get soused before you got here." He had started his morning off with a Bloody Mary, had a midday Bowmore, and might have tippled a few more since, but all in all, he was on his best behavior.

"Can I help with anything?" Baylee asked.

"Do you mind keeping Gene company while I finish up in here? I should be out in fifteen minutes."

"Thought he was doing the appetizers?"

"Talked him out of it. Between you and me, his knees are starting to go."

"What are you making?"

"Sliders and wings. Hope you like them okay?"

"Vegan sliders and wings?" she asked.

He paused, and then laughed. "You're not vegan. As a matter of fact, you might be the opposite of a vegan. I don't think I've ever seen you eat vegetables or fruits since I've known you."

"Yeah, I'm a steak and cheese kind of girl," she said. "Sliders and wings sound great."

"Westy and Faith had to back out. Sick kid."

"That's too bad." Baylee liked watching Clay in the kitchen cooking, but she followed his request. "I'll be on the porch."

Flash had wormed her way up onto the outdoor sofa alongside Gene, who was energetically scratching her belly while she lay on her back and paddled her feet in appreciation. The first sip of scotch seemed to go straight to her head, relaxing her, making her happy she'd not taken any Xanax that day. It also served to loosen her tongue.

"Clay grew up in this house?" Baylee sat on a cushioned armchair that rocked gently back and forth.

"Since he was eight."

"And you raised him?"

"Yep."

"If you don't mind me asking, what happened to his parents? I heard they died in an accident, but that's all I know."

Gene poured himself a bit more scotch. "Clay's dad was my son," he said. "Went away to college and then decided to follow in his father's footsteps and got a law degree from Quinnipiac in Connecticut. He returned home with a girlfriend." Gene took a sip of scotch, reflecting that it had been some time since he'd been down this particular stretch of Memory Lane.

"What was his name? Clay's dad? Your son?"

"Malcom. But everybody called him Mack. We had 200 people at the wedding. Everybody said it was a match made in heaven." Gene cleared his throat. "Mack had joined my law practice by this point. Soon after he became a partner, Clay was born. There was a complication with the birth, and Sally wasn't able to have any more children. That's why he doesn't have any brothers or sisters."

"Did they live close by?"

"Second house on the right," Gene nodded in that direction. "Molly, my wife, watched Clay during the week until he went off to school, and then she was there to get him off the bus most days. Sally, she worked part-time, four days a week, and Mack and me were up to our necks in cases back then."

"Your wife, Molly, died in the car crash as well?"

Gene nodded in the faint light of the porch. "Mack and Sally took Molly to the Christmas lights at the Botanical Gardens. You know the ones I'm talking about?"

Baylee nodded that she did. She noticed her glass empty and poured herself another finger with no ice.

"Clay didn't want to go, and that was all the excuse I needed to stay home and keep an eye on the boy. You know, you've seen one set of lights, you've seen them all."

"They're pretty spectacular," Baylee said.

Gene grunted and tossed down some more scotch. "They planned to stop and have dinner on the way back. The waitress at Captain

Jack's remembers them coming in but swears she didn't serve Mack more than two beers. You know, that was back before everything was on video surveillance of some sort or another."

Baylee had only been to Captain Jack's a few times, but she knew it to be a brew pub with a lively atmosphere and good beer. It was about ten miles out of town across the bridge on the next peninsula to the north.

"The next morning their car was found partially submerged in the Atlantic Ocean off of Route 91. You know where the road makes the big turn as it sweeps out over the cliffs? There's a turnoff right there for people to stop and enjoy the view? That's where they pulled the car out the next morning."

"Mack was the driver?" Baylee asked the perhaps painful question without thought, then put a hand to her mouth.

Gene nodded. "That he was. The three of them were still strapped into their seat belts. They must've been knocked unconscious going down over the rocks."

"There were no witnesses?"

"Not that came forward."

"Skid marks?"

"Nope. Speed limit out there is fifty, but there is a slow curve sign. For all intents and purposes, they just drove right off the road, down the rocks, and into the ocean."

"Any theories?"

"Mack tested positive for cocaine." Gene idly scratched Flash's belly. "I'd wondered about it. Probably should've known it was going on. Stress of too many hours in a thriving law practice. Young child at home. He was burning the candle at both ends. I should have seen the signs."

"That's terrible," Baylee said. "What a horrible thing. I'm so sorry."

"All because I didn't want to go see Christmas lights," Gene said so quietly that Baylee wasn't sure she heard him correctly.

Baylee took a sip of scotch and ruminated on how she and Clay were both essentially orphans. Technically, her mother was alive. In reality, the woman was dead to her and forever would be. Her father had died of alcohol abuse. Clay's parents had died due to his dad's drug abuse. It bothered her how much Clay drank, too. She also knew that it affected her more because of her bad memories of her own father, the mean, messy, and bad drunk that he was. She wondered if Clay would judge her more harshly if he knew she was—and here she sighed inwardly—addicted, yes, addicted to Xanax. How could he not?

At that moment the screen door opened, and Clay stepped out. "Food is ready. Do we want to eat out here or inside?"

Chapter 14

STILL FRIDAY, JULY 3RD

Dylan Thompson was sitting outside his trailer trying to get drunk enough to not want a heroin fix. That wasn't really working so well, as the lowered inhibition just made him more likely to indulge. On the plus side, in a largely incapacitated state, he was quite simply too drunk to get it together to score some junk. It'd been two days since his last fix. Two days of restlessness and lack of sleep. He'd been shitting a gooey tar, more like pissing out of his asshole. His muscles and bones ached. Tonight, he was going to drink until he passed out just to get some rest.

The fireworks provided a minor diversion for him. He had a handle of Allen's Coffee Brandy, a bowl full of ice cubes, and a large plastic cup with a flamingo on it. He'd been drinking steadily since coming off the flats digging for bloodworms this morning, hadn't even bothered to clean up. His hair shot out in every direction like snakes trying to escape a barrel. A thin sheen of sweat covered his face.

Who did that fucking Clay Wolfe think he was, sniffing around and trying to get him in trouble? He probably shouldn't have given up Volkov's name, but it was the only way to get that private investigator off his back. Besides, how would it ever come back on him?

The grand finale exploded into the black night sky with a ferocious eruption of color and noise. Dylan had always liked fireworks. The colors. The patterns. The precision of a finely orchestrated show. It was once his dream to become a certified pyrotechnical operator. Pretty stupid that you had to pay to take classes just to get a job, but he guessed that it would be better than digging bloodworms.

Just as the last of the finale fluttered into darkness, Dylan glimpsed the silhouette of a figure towing something behind him coming down the street in his direction. Probably just one of the neighbors returning from the fireworks show early, Dylan thought, but there was an eeriness to the scene, like that creepy Pennywise from that Stephan King movie *It*. He shook his head and muttered "damn" under his breath. Was it heroin withdrawal or the coffee brandy that was fucking with his head?

The guy walking did not have the shaggy red hair of Pennywise. As a matter of fact, he had no hair whatsoever. It was Curtis Volkov pulling a wagon. That was almost as off-putting as if it had been Pennywise. He was in his customary dark suit, thin red tie, and soft-blue shirt. His shoes gleamed in the moonlight, as did his head.

"Curtis," Dylan said, his voice overly loud and forceful with the courage of the coffee brandy. "Whatcha doin' here?"

"Hello, Dylan." Curtis walked right up to where he was sitting in the tattered lawn chair.

"What's in the wagon?"

Curtis stepped aside. "A little thank you for keeping your mouth shut when that Clay Wolfe fellow came nosing around." The wagon was one of those large, plastic garden haulers large enough to fit a load of manure or a barrel of yard waste. In this case, it was filled with fireworks.

Dylan stumbled to his feet. "Damn, man, those are 500-gram cakes. You got enough firepower to start WWIII." He picked a box from the cart and tried to read what it said, one part of his mind wondering how the man knew he had talked to Clay.

"All yours," Curtis said.

"You serious?"

"We take care of our customers."

Dylan wondered if he had any junk on him. But, no, he was quitting. Maybe just a taste? "Well, fuck, thanks, man. Let's set some of these bad boys off."

Curtis looked at his watch. "Curfew for these things is 10 p.m. Best wait until tomorrow night, the real 4th of July."

"Maybe just one?"

"I didn't buy you these just to get you in trouble with the police. Help me carry them inside."

It took a few minutes, and Dylan was seriously huffing and puffing. But he was smiling as he looked around, his already cluttered trailer housing a collection of fireworks that would make him the envy of the entire park the next night.

"You want some coffee brandy, man?" Dylan sprawled out on his couch as Curtis stood in the midst of a collection of fireworks that had most certainly put a dent in Big Al's inventory.

"Nah, I've got to be going. But I have one more present for you." He pulled a syringe out of his pocket and held it up.

Dylan's mouth went dry. "I, uh, usually smoke it."

"This is the black tar stuff. Can't really smoke it. I got you a good hit loaded right up."

Dylan wanted to say no. He actually thought he did say no, but before he knew it, he was fumbling the needle into his arm and sending the sticky liquid hurtling into his system. "Fuck, yeah," he said. "Them Mexicans know how to grow them some poppies."

"Again, we appreciate your keeping your mouth shut," Curtis said. "This is the least we can do."

Dylan's eyes were glazing over. He had a twisted half-smile on his face with just a trickle of saliva leaking from one corner. "No problem, man." His head lolled back, and his eyes closed, and then fluttered open. "Everything is cool, man."

Curtis Volkov waited another minute until Dylan's breathing had slowed to shallow, ragged breaths. He took out a cigar, smelled it, snipped the end off, and lit it. Then he leaned over and pulled the fuse out of one of the 500-gram cakes labeled *Death from Above*. He lit the fuse and walked out the door smoking his cigar. He was almost to his car when the first explosion occurred, and then the detonations came so rapid fire that it was impossible to distinguish between them. He looked over his shoulder and grinned. It looked like hell was trying to tear its way to the surface using Dylan Thompson's trailer as an entrance.

Chapter 15

SATURDAY, JULY 4TH

A thudding at the door awoke Clay from a sound sleep. He looked at his phone. It was 6 a.m. on a Saturday. On the 4th of July. He hadn't stayed up overly late or had too much to drink, although the stiff nightcap after Baylee had left had probably been unnecessary. The evening had been nice, even if overhearing his grandpop's story about the death of his parents had squeezed his heart a bit tight.

His newest slider recipe had been a success, the trick being to mix mayonnaise, mustard, and ketchup into the hamburger before forming the small patties. This made them nice and juicy, and chopped onions and mushrooms added flavor, all topped by regular old American cheese and a pickle.

The fireworks had been brilliant, if not much appreciated by Flash, who spent the ordeal curled tightly in Baylee's lap. It had been nice to spend some time with Baylee outside of work. Clay found an ease in talking with her that he had with few people, if any.

"Police, open up."

Clay surmised this was not a visitor he could ignore. He pulled on a pair of shorts and a T-shirt and opened the door.

"Clay Wolfe?" There was a police officer at the door and another one back at the top of the stairs to his small deck.

"That's me."

"I am Officer Rinaldi, and that is Officer Laurent. Do you mind if we ask you a few questions?"

"What's this about?"

"Do you mind if we come in?"

"As long as I can put some coffee on." Clay stepped back from the door. His apartment was one room for the kitchen, dining, and living, with a separate bedroom and bathroom. "Have a seat," he said as he fired up the Keurig.

"How do you know Dylan Thompson?"

"Is that what this is about? Did that puke try to pin something on me?"

"Please answer the question."

"I can't say that I know him. I've run into him twice, and we had words both times."

"About what?"

"Him being a piece of shit junkie, mostly. What did he accuse me of?"

"Dylan Thompson is dead, Mr. Wolfe."

·　　·　　·　　·

Somebody was hammering on Baylee's door. It was 8:00 in the morning. She had been up hours before the sun. The phone had rung several times. She didn't want to see anybody. There were demons writhing in her thoughts. The door opened.

"I know you didn't get lucky last night. Your car is in the driveway."

Tammy walked in and found Baylee sitting with her back against the sofa of her living room. She had her arms folded around her knees and was rocking back and forth. Her foot was tapping on the floor. Her eyes were red, and her lush hair was a tangled mess. She was seemingly oblivious to the stream of tears running down her cheeks in such profusion that the blouse over her chest was damp.

"How'd you get in?" Baylee asked.

"Hello to you, too," Tammy said.

"Hi, Tammy."

"What's wrong? Was that pig-fucker mean to you last night?"

Baylee shook her head. "Nothing."

"If he left you like this, I am going to gut him like a marlin."

"He didn't do anything, okay. He was a perfect gentleman, and we had a fine evening."

"What's up, then?"

"I just don't feel good. I got a cold, or something." Baylee suddenly got a panicked look on her face. "Did you lock the door behind you?"

"What? No."

Baylee jumped up and ran to the door. "Goddammit it, Tammy."

"What's going on?"

"What do you mean?" Baylee came back and sat in an armchair. Flash came over and lay on her feet.

"Why's the door need to be locked?"

"Locked? What do you mean?"

"What aren't you telling me?"

Baylee began crying. "I killed him; you know. I loved him, and I killed him. Do you think I'll kill every man I love? Will there ever be another man to love? Who would ever love me? What is the fucking point?"

Tammy came over and sat on the arm of the cushioned chair. She put her arm around Baylee. "It's okay," she said into her ear. "What are you on?"

"What do you mean?" Baylee's voice had grown bleary. "Nothing."

"I'm a fucking nurse, Baylee. What are you on?"

"Nothing, that's the problem," she laughed nervously. "But I was on Xanax. For my nerves, you know. Just to calm me down, ever since, well, you know."

"You quit? Cold turkey?"

"Yes, ma'am." Baylee laughed again.

"How much were you taking?"

"I don't know." Baylee let her head fall back on the cushions, so she was staring straight up at the ceiling with her eyes closed. "Depends on the day, you know. Two, maybe three milligrams."

"Where were you getting that kind of dose?" Tammy shook her arm. "Shit, girl, that's enough to put a horse out. Never mind. When did you last take any?"

"Thursday, right before I met you at the Perch. Let me sleep a little bit."

"You can't just go cold turkey," Tammy said. "Not if you were doing those kinds of doses. You could go into convulsions. Heck, you can even die. Do you have any left?"

"I'm not taking any. I'm not going to be a druggie."

"You got to wean yourself off that stuff. I see it every day. It fucks you up good. Let me help you back off of it slowly."

Baylee nodded at the kitchen. "My pills are there on the island. Next to a glass of water. I've been…contemplating my options."

Tammy went in the kitchen. There was a bottle spilled open on the island. Next to it was one of those X-Acto knives. It was razor-sharp and lethal looking. She took a one milligram pill and cut it in half with the blade, looked at the tool, then wrapped it in paper towels and put it in her pocket. Tammy picked up the half-pill and the glass of water and returned to the living room.

"Here, girl, take this," she said.

"I don't want him to hate me," Baylee said.

"He won't."

"I need to get clean."

"It has to follow a process, love. We'll get you there."

·   ·   ·   ·

It was just after noon before Clay got a chance to get to Scott McKenny's house. He lived in a neighborhood of about forty houses, mostly capes and colonials, with a few ranches thrown in, perhaps showing the various stages of the development. The street in front of Scott's modest cape was filled with cars, suggesting that either he or one of the neighbors was hosting a get-together.

When there was no answer at the door, Clay walked around to the back, hearing an increasing din as he got closer. There was no fence or gate to navigate, and he found himself on the edge of a crowd of about twenty-five people. Horseshoes and beanbags were both being tossed. People stood and sat in clusters, the loudness of their voices suggesting that the alcohol consumption had started well before noon on this Independence Day.

There were two rectangular folding tables across the back of the yard with covered dishes on them. A low fire burned under an eight-foot-long metal tub on one side of the yard, which Clay surmised held lobsters and other shellfish. On the other edge of the lawn, various coolers, recycle bins, and trash cans filled with ice and drinks of all sorts were lined up.

"What do you think you're doing here?" Scott McKenny stood at his side with a can of Budweiser in his hand.

"I seemed to have lost my invite."

"Didn't send you one."

"I don't see Niles here, either. You forget him, too?"

"I didn't…enough about your goddamn invite." His voice was rising in anger, his eyes narrowing.

It wasn't that Scott's eyes had started out small, Clay observed. More that slowly, over the years, they'd become engulfed by the rest of his face. The man stood with that wide stance of the heavy man who is belligerent and thinks he knows best on any subject.

"Pour me a whiskey on the house and give me my five minutes."

"Then you will leave?"

"Yep. No fuss, no muss," Clay said.

They went inside to what was a very orderly house, even if most of the items looked like Mrs. McKenny had purchased them from the discount bins at Walmart.

"What do you want?" Scott asked.

"A whiskey sure would be good right about now," Clay replied.

Scott pulled a bottle of Jim Beam off the refrigerator shelf and poured a finger into a glass. Clay narrowed his eyes and looked at him, and he poured a bit more. "Ice?" he asked.

"Two cubes would be great."

"I'm in the middle of a party here," Scott said, handing him the glass. "Drink up, and get out of my house."

"Why haven't you answered my text messages or phone calls?" Clay was aware that he sounded a bit like a jilted lover.

"It's the goddamn 4th of July weekend."

"Okay, how about we try something else?" Clay took a drink of the Jim Beam. Certainly not Bowmore, or even Glenlivet, but it had a nice mellow burn. "Why did you lie to me?"

"What are you talking about?"

"First of all, saying that you don't let your employees into Mr. Harrington's house."

"I didn't lie about that." Scott's eyes did their tell-tale flicker.

"Not even to use the bathroom? Can't imagine that the neighbors would like to look over from their mansions and see Billy Ray squatting next to the hot tub and pinching a loaf. Plus, who's going to clean it up? Do you have poop bags on the job site?"

"Okay, so maybe I let them in if they need the facilities."

"Are you always there?"

"Absolutely." His eyes fluttered over to the door.

Clay decided to let that one go. He decided to go for broke with a wild guess, but one that had been niggling at him since researching the Harrington offspring. "Why didn't you tell Mr. Harrington that his daughter, Charlotte, came to the house recently without him knowing?"

"What? How'd you know that?"

Clay finished his bourbon whiskey. He held his glass underneath the ice maker, throwing the extra cube that spit out into the sink, and then poured another healthy drink from the bottle. He said nothing.

"Look, you don't need to be telling Mr. Harrington about that," Scott said.

"If I can clear her of having stolen the *Fourth Shade*, well then, I don't see any reason I would need to tell him. But you need to be straight with me so I can do that."

"She likes to bring her new boyfriends here to show off," Scott said. "About once a year. Different man every time. At first, she begged me not to tell her daddy, that he would be so mad, and I agreed. After a few times, I guess it was too late to tell him."

"I've seen pictures. Charlotte Harrington is a very beautiful woman," Clay said. Scott's eyes flickered to the doorway, but Clay guessed that this time it was to make sure that his wife wasn't there. "I would guess that she can be very persuasive."

"That she can be."

"And your suggestion that she liked to show off suggests you don't think she has much of her own money?"

"I don't know about that."

Clay nodded. "As a matter of fact, she might feel entitled to help herself to a family heirloom?"

"Honest, Mr. Wolfe, I give her the code and a key. And that's all I know. She's his own goddamn daughter. Why would she steal from him?"

It was a good point, Clay thought. Why, indeed?

Clay mused about the conversation as he drove back towards the Pelican Perch where he was meeting Westy at 4:00. It seemed possible that Charlotte Harrington was at the very least an increasingly appealing candidate in the theft of the *Fourth Shade*. It was obvious that Scott McKenny and his employees had had access as well, but Clay didn't think it was likely that they would have recognized the statue's value. The question was, how to check up on her? He knew she lived in Los Angeles. Did he need to book a flight to the West Coast? Wicked inconvenient when he was enmeshed in this drug running case. Perhaps he'd bitten off more than he could chew.

The streets and sidewalks of Port Essex suggested that few people had left since the parade this morning at 10:00 a.m. Clay, fresh from being grilled by the police, had sat on his deck overlooking the parade route with a cup of coffee in his hand. It seemed that the death of Dylan Thompson was being chalked up to stupidity. The man had either been drunk or high and mistakenly blown up a cache of fireworks stored in his trailer. It was possible that he was sober, but nobody, not even the cops, believed that. He was too well known in town. Of course, Clay's information that he'd bought the man a few beers and shots over twelve hours before his death suggested alcohol.

There was not enough left of the body for any kind of definitive proof. The two cops indicated there was little chance of computed tomographic analysis finding any biological fluids to substantiate drugs or alcohol in the system. Initial reports had not shown any blunt force trauma: the man had simply burned to a crisp in an enormous fireworks explosion.

Where had Dylan gotten all the fireworks? The man had a heroin addiction and lived on what money he could make digging bloodworms. From what the cops had said, there had to have been a thousand bucks' worth of fireworks to cause the explosion and ensuing incineration that had occurred. Where had the money come from? Who would buy him such a gift? Or was it an elaborate—and seasonally appropriate—plan to cover up a murder?

The tourists had been pushed from the downtown and invaded the sanctity of the Pelican Perch. Clay had to work his way past a line on the stairs waiting for a table, elbow his way through a crowd of people four-deep at the bar, also waiting for tables, before sliding into the empty stool next to Westy. There was a beer waiting for him.

"Stowaway," Westy said. "Probably warm but figured it would save your seat for you."

"The beauty of a good beer is that you can drink it warm," Clay replied. "That Budweiser in your hand gets warm, it tastes like shit."

"Cold is better on a hot day. Trick is to not let it get warm."

Clay took a sip and had to agree, so he soldiered through and finished half the beer. The sooner he got through it, the sooner a cold one would arrive. "You hear about Thompson?" he asked.

"Dipshit junkie," Westy said. "Blowing himself up in the middle of a fireworks display is about the best thing that could have happened to him."

"I saw him yesterday morning. Bought him a couple of drinks up to the Side Bar, actually."

Westy turned his block-sized head like some piece of heavy machinery to level his gray eyes at Clay. "Yeah? What about? That baby-murder thing?"

"You got it. When I talked to him first a few days back, we got into a bit of a tussle. After, he let slip out a first name that seemed like it might be connected with who's behind the heroin in town. Curtis. Crystal seemed to know that name. And not in the good sense of knowing, either. She lives at Botany Place, too."

"Could be a last name."

Clay tilted his head slightly. "Hadn't thought of that. Well, anyway, at the time I was unable to follow up, so I hunted him down at the Side Bar yesterday morning to see if I could get a last name."

"And?"

"The man seemed scared, real scared, but he whispered the name 'Volkov' to me as he left. Curtis Volkov. Heard of him?"

"Nope. What's he look like?"

"Didn't get that. Figured with a name like that I could track him down, but the computer didn't turn up a thing. There's a UFC fighter named Alexander Volkov. Nicknamed Drago."

"Like the Russian in *Rocky IV*?"

"Guess so. Don't think it pertains, though."

"No, not at all," Westy said. "Interesting, though."

"I should probably get Baylee on it. She's better at getting the 'net to yield up its secrets than I am."

"You thinking there's a connection?"

"Between what?" Clay asked.

"You talking to Dylan Thompson and him being dead."

"The thought had crossed my mind."

Westy waved the empty bottle at the bartender, and Clay raised his empty glass as well. "Probably shouldn't be seen talking to you," Westy said.

"Why's that?"

"Lobbins. Thompson. I'm seeing a pattern here."

Clay looked around the crowd. Was somebody watching him right now, he wondered? Was somebody following his every move? Was it that guy over by the railing looking like he had nothing better to do than just stand alone and stare off into space?

"It does seem to be a bit much of a coincidence," he said.

"Who knew about Lobbins before he was shot? That you were onto him, I mean?"

"Murphy turned me onto it." Clay sat staring at the back wall where the restrooms were located. "And you."

"Who knew about you wanting to question Thompson?"

"Crystal Landry. Kelly Anne. His whole trailer park. People at the Side Bar. Baylee. You. Probably half the town."

"Did anybody know he'd given up a name? Curtis Volkov?"

"Murphy and you. Looks like you are the two prime suspects," Clay said.

"Well, I was right next to you when Lobbins was shot, so it must be that old Irishman."

Clay raised his glass. "Case solved."

"How was your date?"

"It wasn't a date."

"About time you found a nice girl and settled down." Westy stared straight ahead as he spoke.

"You're starting to sound like the women that Gene brings around the house."

"That old dog is still courting the widows, is he?"

"Seeing more action than me."

"You got your mystery woman," Westy said.

"I think that might be over. She wants me to back off my investigation into the drug trade in Port Essex. None too happy with me that I wouldn't comply."

"A woman worried about you is not the end of a relationship."

It is if she is the police, and you're tainting her investigation, Clay thought, but instead said, "Yeah, I think our problems run a bit deeper than that."

Chapter 16

SUNDAY, JULY 5TH

Private Investigative Report
Date: 7/5/20
To: Clay Wolfe
From: Donald Brooks
Subject name: Allen Daigle
File Number: x-3232
Investigation Type: Domestic Services
Date Assigned: 7/2/20

Subject Information
Name: Allen Daigle
DOB: 3/10/76   Height: 5'10"   Weight: 205
Address: 18 Perkins Lane, Port Essex, ME 04888
Phone: (207) 362-9128
Special Features: Wears glasses, mole under chin on right side

• **Investigation Summary**
Friday, July 3: I began my surveillance at 5:00 a.m. The subject, Allen Daigle, came out of his home on Perkins Lane, number 18, at approximately 6:00 a.m. He went to his office on Commercial Way and was not seen again until noontime when he came back out. I followed him as he visited the Seal

Bar where he spoke with a man but did not have a drink or food. The identity of the man is unknown. He then went into the Works on outer Commercial Street but was back out in under five minutes without a bag. This pattern of meeting with single men and women was repeated at four more locations. In total, there were five men and two women, and he never talked longer than ten minutes. He picked up food from the Cabot Street Deli and was back at the office by 1:00. At 5:00 p.m., he came out of the office and got into his BMW. He then visited eight houses and the Side Bar. The addresses are in the detailed report. He had dinner with a woman at the Knox Cove Grill. They both arrived and left separately. At 9:00, the subject went back to the Side Bar and had two drinks. He was home by 10:00.

Clay breezed through the details of Saturday. Daigle did not go to work but did visit seven more people. He went to dinner with his wife and was home by 9:00. Clay grazed over the description of Daigle's residence, car, and the detailed report to see what recommendations Don was making about further surveilling the man.

• Recommendations

It is my conclusion from two days of surveillance that Allen Daigle is not having an affair but is involved in some sort of shady practice. There is video of most of his meetings and it appears some sort of exchange is taking place. If I was a betting man, which I am, I would lay heavy money that Allen Daigle is dealing drugs of some sort.

Clay put his feet up on his desk. He'd come into the office by 8:00 on this Sunday morning, and Don had already emailed this report at 6:17 a.m. Don was off today, saying something about going down to Portland to catch a Sea Dogs' game with his two boys. At the time, Clay hadn't thought twice about agreeing to leave Allen Daigle unobserved for the day. Sunday was not a very common day for cheating on your spouse, after all, but how about dealing drugs?

From the report it was pretty clear that Daigle was selling something, most likely drugs, but it might be as innocent as marijuana. Even though it was slowly becoming legalized throughout most of the state, a ban on sales had been enacted here in Port Essex.

He called Marie Cloutier to let her know that it looked like Daigle might be selling drugs. This was a heads-up to her as a reporter, but also in that her girlfriend was the landlord for a potential dealer. He also knew that she would share with him the results of whatever sleuthing she did. She had no new information but promised to get right on researching Daigle further. He thought about calling Baylee to see if she could do some research on Curtis Volkov but decided against it as it was Sunday.

It wasn't like he was being paid to take on the local drug trade, Clay thought, so it didn't really matter who got the praise for bringing the criminals to justice and putting a halt to the flow of narcotics into Port Essex. With a sigh he texted Donna. **Where are you?**

Work.

Cup of coffee?

Pretty busy.

I got something for you.

Is it my birthday?

I think I know major dealer in town.

Meet you at Koasek Park in 20. Back lot.

K.

Clay waited for a minute to see if there were any further texts. He had a suspicion that he and Donna were over. If they had ever started. If brief hookups constituted a relationship. He'd been blaming her for the lack of intimacy to their heated couplings, for she never wanted anything more than sex. To be truthful, he was equally to blame. Clay had never been in a relationship that lasted more than a year, and most had been significantly shorter than that.

More than one girlfriend had told him that losing his parents as a child had given him major attachment issues. This was usually said in tears and much less cordially. Donna had been the perfect match for somebody who enjoyed sex without any attachments. Perhaps he should put some effort into this relationship? It wasn't going anywhere, but did everything have to go somewhere?

The phone buzzed in his hand jarring him out of his reverie. It was Niles Harrington. "Clay Wolfe," he said in greeting.

"Clay, Niles here. Thought I'd check in with you on the *Fourth Shade*. Has there been any progress?"

"Actually, I was about to give you a call. Can we get together sometime today?"

"I'm having a bit of a get-together at my house starting at noon today. How about you come by, and I'll carve out a few minutes to speak with you."

"Sounds good. I'll come by about 12:30." The line went dead.

Clay wondered how one went about telling a man that the prime suspect in the theft of his precious property was his very own daughter? At least once he handed Daigle over to the police, he would be able to concentrate on finding the *Fourth Shade*.

Koasek Park was 100 acres of land with several walking trails located just at the tip of the harbor. There were two parking lots. The larger, just off the Harbor Road, was often filled with tourists thinking that a two-mile hike might make up for seven Margaritas they'd sunk the night before. The back lot was often empty, except at night when teenagers went out there to drink, smoke, and have sex. Clay's first time had actually been in that parking lot when he was sixteen. Betty Lou was two years older, liked sex, and had been more than happy to introduce him to the world of carnal delights for the next three months.

Donna was in her own car but in uniform. She got out as he pulled in and walked over to his window. She was damn sexy, Clay thought, with her hair tied back, the blue officer attire matching her eyes, and the duty belt with baton, radio, handcuffs, taser, and of course, pistol.

"Let's take a walk," she said. Clay got out and they took a path into the woods, but then she veered off trail. "There's a nice spot with a little stream over this way."

A breeze was blowing, keeping the mosquitoes and black flies at bay. The tops of the pines swayed with the motion of the air. Donna led them to a glade hidden by bushes and fir trees next to a bubbling creek. She took off the duty belt and set it next to her as she sat down.

"I've had my man Don following somebody because his wife thought he was having an affair," Clay said, sitting down next to her. "It appears that the guy isn't cheating but rather, he's dealing."

"You sure of this?" Donna leaned back on one elbow and stuck a long piece of grass in her mouth.

"Pretty sure. He's a lawyer in town but meets with a variety of people during his lunch hour and after work, and some sort of exchange is made. I've got video of it in the car, as well as the report."

Donna nodded. "I'll handle it myself," she said. "Who is it?"

"Allen Daigle. Has a practice on Commercial Way."

"Yeah, I know him. Seems like a decent enough guy. Never would've guessed."

"Me neither," Clay said. "Just got lucky. Bad luck for him that his wife hired us to find out whether or not he was cheating on her."

"I'll get right on it first thing tomorrow morning," Donna said. She began unbuttoning the front of her shirt. "Would you like to collect your reward now?" she asked.

Clay mentally shrugged. Why not?

The small get-together that Niles Harrington was having required valets to park the cars down the road in an empty field. There were about twenty round tables that each sat eight people scattered across the back yard overlooking the Atlantic Ocean. Near a hot tub, a band playing Jimmy Buffet music was set up, the current song being "Cheeseburger in Paradise." At least everybody was dressed semi-casual, and not in tuxes and gowns.

"Get something to eat and drink," Niles said as he greeted him. "I'll come find you in twenty minutes or so, and we can have that talk."

Clay went to the buffet table and got a few oysters, a lobster claw, and a couple of steak tips. The bartender refused to accept a gratuity. He didn't really want to socialize with the elites of Port Essex who spent anywhere from a weekend to two months there, so he took his plate and drink down to the water and sat on a rock watching the waves crash onto shore.

He supposed his next stop should be to visit Crystal Landry to let her know that he'd uncovered the local drug dealer and turned the case over to the police. It would be odd to go to her mobile home in the trailer park after being here, Clay thought, the two opposite poles of Port Essex society. From the filthy rich to the dirt poor in just a few miles. Somehow, he felt at loose ends, waiting. It was up to the police now to put together a case and make the arrest.

"Pretty view, isn't it?" Niles sat down across from Clay. "Sometimes seals come by and sun themselves on these very rocks."

"It doesn't suck," Clay said.

"You managed to get some food?"

"Yes. It was excellent."

"You have an update for me?"

Clay contemplated the last sip of brown liquor in his glass. "How close are you with your daughter?"

"Charlotte?" Niles raised an eyebrow. "We haven't spoken in two years."

"Did you know she comes and stays in your house here periodically throughout the winters?"

"She hasn't been here in five years."

"Scott McKenny says otherwise."

Niles stood up and took a few steps towards the water, his back to Clay and the party. "I did not know that. Did McKenny happen to say why he kept this secret from me?"

"He insinuated that she pleaded with him the first time to give her the code, and he took pity on her. After that he wasn't able to stop. My take was that she may have used her feminine wiles to get his cooperation."

"She was always a manipulative bitch," Niles said. "Takes after her mother."

"She was here a few months back. Would she take the *Fourth Shade*?"

"You mean steal from her own father?"

"Yes. I suppose that's what I'm asking."

"I don't know. Maybe. I guess she might feel that she is entitled to it. When she sided with her mother in the divorce, I cut her off financially. She's an artist, which is another word for unemployed." Niles turned around and walked back and sat down again. "I suppose that's why I hired you."

"Can't you ask her?"

"I told you, we don't talk."

"What do you want me to do?"

"Find out if she is the thief."

"She lives in Los Angeles."

Chapter 17

STILL SUNDAY, JULY 5TH

Four hours later Clay was boarding a private jet at the Brunswick Executive Airport. Of course, Niles Harrington would have his own jet, Clay thought with a wry grin. He was breathing in rarefied air now, rubbing elbows with the rich, famous, and elite. The month before, Clay had done some bodyguard work for a rapper he'd never heard of. The man had done a show in the new outdoor venue in Portland and decided to visit Port Essex. He'd hired Clay to oversee his protection for the three days he'd been in town. The man had seven hangers-on that were all packing, so Clay wasn't sure what his purpose was, but the gig had been a glimpse into the lavish lifestyles of celebrities.

Where did Niles Harrington's money come from, Clay wondered? He'd Googled the man and realized that the Harrington family money went back several generations. They, as most truly wealthy people, seemed to have their fingers in every piece of the pie out there. He decided to get Baylee and Cloutier digging into his background as they both were much more astute with technology than he was. He'd call them in the morning. For now, he settled back, asked for a Bowmore on ice, and tried to make sense of things.

By luck rather than skill he'd uncovered the local drug dealer in Port Essex and turned what he knew about Daigle over to the police. Whereas he should have been happy, the whole thing had left a bad taste in his mouth, like he'd walked away leaving the job half-finished. Who had killed Lobbins? And Thompson? That "accident" was just so convenient. But Clay had not been hired to uncover these truths, only to find whoever had sold the drugs that led to the death of poor little Ariel Landry.

Not that the mother, Kelly Anne, showed the least care. The only person out there that seemed to give a shit about the death of the little baby girl was the grandmother, Crystal, and she'd fired Clay from the case. Why? Most likely she was just scared. He made a note to sit down with Crystal on his return and try to make amends.

It was time to move forward with the current case, finding the *Fourth Shade*. He was intrigued by the bones of the case, which had all the elements of an Agatha Christie mystery. A sculpture stolen by the Nazis during World War II and then filched by a GI during the liberation of Europe and smuggled back to the United States where it had spent the last seventy years sitting on a shelf in Port Essex, Maine. This piece of art created by one of the most famous sculptors ever had then mysteriously disappeared. It would be almost a let-down if it turned out to be merely a burglary by an estranged and spoiled daughter. The fact that he was being well-paid and was currently on a private jet sipping scotch on his way to L.A. was just icing on the cake.

He'd called Charlotte Harrington and set up an appointment to meet with her the following afternoon at her studio. He'd claimed to be the representative of a private art collector interested in her work. Niles had told him that she was narcissistic, and thus overpriced her work, rarely selling anything. He spent the next six hours on the plane browsing her website and researching her medium.

Her work appeared to fall under the category of pop art. Charlotte created large oil paintings of realistic subjects and attached inflatables to give them a three-dimensional appearance. The colors were vivid and loud. While it was intriguing, Clay did not understand any of it. Her work made him think of the recent banana taped to a wall that had sold for $120,000. *Tsk, tsk*, he admonished himself. He had to at least appear interested in purchasing some of her work.

Clay woke the next morning at around 11:00. He'd taken the saying of when in L.A., do as the natives would do, arriving at the London Hotel in West Hollywood the previous evening at about ten, immediately hitting the Sunset Strip. He was hoping that Niles Harrington wouldn't flinch at covering his bar tab from the previous evening. With his room alone running over $700 a night, he doubted that the man had many concerns about money.

He'd missed the complimentary breakfast and so went down to the Boxwood Restaurant for lunch, wolfing down a plate of pork belly and Maine scallops. Afterwards, he went up to the rooftop pool for a swim, then showered and touched up his scruff, preparing to meet with Charlotte. Her studio was only a half mile from the London, so Clay decided to walk it. He made it 100 yards at best in the oppressive heat before hailing a taxi. There hadn't been much need to download the Uber App in Port Essex, but he imagined that day was coming.

It turned out that Charlotte was part of an artists' cooperative in a building that housed eight individual studios. The edifice, just a block off Sunset Boulevard, was a square, two-story structure with yellow walls and purple doors. There were four doors on each floor. She was number 5, on the top, right side of the building.

The woman sitting in a chair on the balcony painting was not what Clay expected from his social media stalking and what he knew of the entitled heir of Niles Harrington. She was petite, a slender waif of a figure who couldn't weigh more than ninety pounds. A rainbow-colored Fedora was perched jauntily upon blonde curls with one streak of green meandering its way from front to back under the hat brim. Her skin suggested she could be twenty-two, even though he knew her to be thirty-eight. A lavender blouse fit tightly and matched her eyeshadow.

"Charlotte Harrington?" he asked.

"Call me Charly," she replied. "Are you that man who called about my work?"

"Clay Wolfe," he said. He'd dabbled with the idea of creating an alias, but for what purpose? Surely the woman didn't know him.

"You're the one interested in my art?"

"Yes. My employer is interested in adding to his collection."

"And why did your *employer* not come himself? Or herself? I understand that this sort of thing is done for fabulously expensive works of art, but I don't have anything priced over $10,000."

There were seven or eight other people on the balcony, none of them within her space, but several within earshot. "Can we speak in private?"

Charly stood and beckoned him to follow her inside. She locked the door behind them and flipped a sign to "closed." Apparently, a fringe benefit of being an artist was you made your own hours based upon your whims. She pointed to an armchair next to a canvas that was the size of double doors with a cartoonish clown painted on it. There was an inflatable balloon flower bursting from his lapel, his orange hair was yet another inflatable, as was his bulbous red nose. She pulled a wooden chair across from his and sat down.

"What is it you want, Mr. Wolfe?"

Clay pursed his lips. His plan of just outright asking had seemed better in his head than it did right now in her presence. "My employer," he cleared his throat, "has it under good authority that you might be selling a very valuable sculpture."

"I don't sculpt, Mr. Wolfe. I create pop art. Almost exclusively oil and inflatables."

"It is not your work, but rather, the work of the Parisian master, Rodin."

"What the hell are you talking about? Oh." Frustration turned to realization turned to confusion. "Who is your employer, Mr. Wolfe?"

"I am not at liberty to say."

"My father? Niles Harrington?"

Clay simply sat stone-faced.

"He really did it, didn't he?"

"Who really did what?"

Charly laughed and shook her head Clay found her quite… stimulating. "No, Mr. Wolfe, if you want anything from me you are going to have to start sharing first."

As Kenny Rogers had sung, Clay thought, you needed to know when to hold them and when to fold them. "If I'm going to call you Charly, you have to call me Clay."

"Where are you from, Clay?"

"Port Essex."

"And my father hired you?"

"Yes."

"Why?" The look in her eyes suggested she knew but did not want to say.

"The *Fourth Shade* was stolen."

"And that bastard thought it was me?"

Clay shrugged. "Scott McKenny let on how you have been secretly visiting the house over the past few winters. You had knowledge of the statue's value, you're estranged from your father, and you had opportunity."

"Scott McKenny? That weasel? If I were you, I'd concentrate my search on him."

"Did you visit the house back in January?"

"Yeah, sure. Maine is beautiful in the winter."

"Were you by yourself?"

"None of your business."

"Was the *Fourth Shade* there?"

Charly stared over his shoulder. Her eyes were the murky blue of the lagoon in Iceland he'd visited a few years back.

"Yes, I think so," she said.

"But you didn't take it?"

"No. I'm not a thief."

"When did you last speak with your father?"

"Just over two years ago."

"What happened?"

"None of your damn business."

"Tell me about your father."

It was Charly's turned to be stone-faced. "What do you want to know?"

"Why don't you speak with him?"

"I don't agree with his moral philosophy of life."

"And what is his moral philosophy of life?"

"That he has none." Charly laughed, a hollow burst of air.

"Is that why he and your mother got divorced?"

"Again, none of your damn business."

"Does your father give you money?"

"I wouldn't touch his dirty money with a ten-foot pole."

"But you would stay in his house?"

"That was my grandfather's house before it was his," Charly said. "And it was not bought with Big Pharma money."

"What did you mean when you said, 'he really did it'?" Clay's gut instinct was that she had not taken the *Fourth Shade*, which made this trip to the West Coast a waste of time. Or was it? He'd never been to L.A. before, much less Hollywood.

"Would you care to get a drink?" Charly stood abruptly, her diminutive figure standing over him. "*I* sure would."

"Sure."

Clay thought this might be a fine way to extract more information from Charly Harrington, or so he told himself. Somewhere in the recesses of his conscious, he knew that there was an attraction, a sexual vibe between them, a magnetic pull that he was all too familiar with, one that he had thus far in life been powerless to resist.

She had a turquoise-colored Mini Cooper convertible that she drove dangerously fast. Clay would've been happy to go around the corner, but she insisted they go to "the Hut." It was about ten miles.

On the plus side, he got to see the Hollywood Hills and Laurel Canyon, places he'd only heard of in movies and read about in books.

There were seventy-eight drinks listed in the Grog Log. Charly insisted they share a Coconut Reentry, which had seven ounces of rum and came to the table ablaze. She showed him her name on the wall, on a calligraphy scroll titled *Loyal Order of the Drooling Bastard*, signifying that she had consumed all seventy-eight drinks in the Grog Log in the course of one year.

Charly spoke sparingly of the divorce that had led to her estrangement with her father. She had not seen the man in years. While she did secretly visit the house in Maine, she had not taken the *Fourth Shade*, nor, as an artist herself, would she want to be an accomplice of any sort to the theft of a treasure, particularly one with such sordid roots.

Later they drove back to West Hollywood and shared an Artichoke Cashew pizza at the SoHo House and drank several glasses of wine. The heat of the day had cooled, and they sat out on its exclusive, member-only rooftop terrace with tree limbs twisting around them, drinking wine, taking in the view, and talking about everything but the *Fourth Shade*. Clay was not normally attracted to petite women. He'd been known to say that he didn't find a boyish figure attractive, but there was something animated and alive about Charly that excited him.

After a cognac, they descended from the rooftop, made the wise choice to leave the car, and walked back to his hotel, where they tumbled into bed together. Charly was still there in the morning, and Clay spent another day with her.

When he insisted that he must return to Maine on Wednesday, he found that Niles Harrington's private jet was on a trip, and it was only after much haggling that it returned to pick him up Wednesday night. So, no, California had not been a wasted trip, as far as pleasure and enjoyment were concerned, but it had been unsuccessful in terms of resolving the missing *Fourth Shade*.

Clay kissed Charly in front of the private jet office, their lips lingering, knowing that they would most likely never see each other again. It had been a delicious few days, but now they both had to return to their lives.

"When I first met you," Clay said, his hand cupping her cheek, "you said 'he finally did it'. What did you mean by that?"

"Does it matter?" she asked, her lips poised and her eyes wide.

"It might help clear you of suspicion."

Charly bit her top lip. "Scott McKenny emailed me asking if I knew any art dealers that didn't ask too many questions. I wondered if he'd stolen something from my father, but to tell you the truth, I didn't care all that much. I still don't care that much."

"Did you give him a name?"

"I told you I'm not a thief, and I don't consort with thieves either."

Chapter 18

THURSDAY, JULY 9TH

Clay discovered that it was much easier to sleep on a private jet than on a commercial airline, and thus walked into the office at just before 9 a.m. on Thursday with a spry step. He'd stopped home and showered and shaved. It had been a good couple of days, and while Charly had convinced him she'd not stolen the *Fourth Shade*, he had a couple of solid leads to follow up on.

"Look who made it back from the City of Angels," Baylee said. Today was her first day completely free of Xanax, and she felt great, thanks to Tammy who'd led her through the process. She could see the sparkle back in her eyes this morning, a sparkle that had been missing for some time now.

"It's certainly no city of angels," Clay said. "But to my worn peepers, you certainly appear to be an angel on this fine morning." And it was true, Clay thought with a wry grin. The sight of Baylee and conversing with her were more stimulating than the carnal delights of the past few days with Charly Harrington. Or Donna for that matter. Why was that, he wondered?

"That sounds very wrong," she said. "I might have to revive that sexual misconduct complaint."

"File it with HR." Clay walked over as if to lean over and hug her but then just sat on the corner of her desk instead. "But really, you look fantastic this morning. Did you do something new with your hair?"

"Nope. Nothing new here." Except a tingle caressing her body from his compliment, she thought. "So, did Charlotte have the *Fourth Shade?*"

"No, no she didn't. As a matter of fact, she redirected suspicion back at McKenny."

"How so?"

"She said that he recently contacted her asking if she had any connections with art dealers who knew how to keep their mouth shut."

"That's pretty tidy, isn't it?"

"What do you mean?"

"I guess if I stole something from my employer, you in this case, I wouldn't ask your daughter how to sell it."

"I don't have a daughter."

"You know what I mean."

"Charly and her father haven't spoken in years."

"Charly?" The sparkle in Baylee's eyes became a harder glint.

"Yeah, that's what she goes by." Clay looked down at the floor. "I think McKenny felt comfortable in going to her as she's not on speaking terms with Niles, and also because of his complicity in her staying secretly at the house, one hand washing the other and all that."

"All because...Charly...told you?"

"Yeah, I guess." Clay stood and walked over to the door to look down at the street.

"You're the private dick," Baylee said. "I guess you gotta trust your instincts. I'm just a receptionist."

"Any drug arrests while I was gone?"

"Not that I heard of. Was there supposed to be?"

"Don filed his report with me Sunday before I left for California. It was pretty clear that Allen Daigle was not cheating on his wife, but rather, might be dealing drugs."

"Heroin?"

"Not sure. I turned it over to the police to handle."

"And that's it?"

"What do you mean?" Clay went and sat in one of the four armchairs in the reception area.

"You've closed your investigation into the drug traffic in Port Essex?"

"I supposed it depends on what the police turn up when they apprehend Daigle."

"If they apprehend Daigle."

"I pretty much gave them Daigle gift-wrapped with a nice bow."

"Okay, let's say they get the goods on the man and arrest him. How does that change anything?"

"You're saying somebody else will step up and replace him?" Clay leaned back and closed his eyes. "There's always going to be drugs. We can't stop that. We have to accept that we're just a tiny harbor in the ocean. We can try to keep the shallows safe, but we have no control over what happens in the deep waters where the big fish predators swim." Even as he said it, he realized how faux-profound it sounded.

Thankfully, the phone rang, and Baylee picked up the receiver. "Clay Wolfe, Private Investigator." There may have been a touch of sarcasm. "No, I am all set." Clay stood up and went to his office. As he went through the door, he heard Baylee say just a wee bit insistently, "I don't need any more."

He called Donna's cell phone, but it went to the answering machine. He texted her. What's up with Daigle?

Clay spent the next couple of hours putting together his report for Niles Harrington. He'd spent a good deal of the man's money, not even taking into account jet fuel, and realized that he had very little to show for it. He omitted from the report that he'd had sex with the man's daughter, four times—but who's counting? He really should sit down face-to-face with him, but he needed to have something showing more significant progress to present before doing that, so he emailed the report instead.

It was time to dig into Scott McKenny and see what he could turn up. He had too much on his plate to follow the guy around and watch his house, so he texted Don. Got a new case for you. Interested?

The reply was almost instant. When?

Starting immediately.

Sure. You at the office?

Yep.

On my way. 10 min.

K.

Still no reply from Donna. He'd texted her several times from California and gotten no reply. Was she ghosting him, he wondered? Fair enough if she was, but it was not like her to completely ignore him. She hadn't even replied when he texted that he was going to California for a couple of days.

Once Don had come and gone after getting briefed on his McKenny assignment, Clay decided it was time to be proactive. First, he would visit Donna to find out where the Allen Daigle investigation stood, and then he would check in with Crystal. Baylee was preoccupied on the computer, a frown of worry creasing her features. She waved him off when he asked if everything was okay.

Donna's Ford Mustang was in her driveway with the top down. After he had rung the bell and banged on the door several times, she finally appeared in a white T-shirt and shorts, her hair tousled, her mouth twisted in annoyance.

"What?" she asked through the screen door.

"Can I come in?" Clay asked.

"The sun was up when I went to bed."

"I've been trying to get in touch with you."

"I've been busy."

"What's going on with Allen Daigle?"

"Nothing."

"Nothing? Why not?"

"He went on vacation."

"What?"

"Monday morning, he and his wife drove to Boston and took a flight to Punta Cana. They are booked at a resort there through the weekend."

"Did he know you were on to him?"

"He's had the trip booked for a few weeks. I think it's just a vacation." Donna yawned. "When he returns, we'll put him under surveillance and scoop him up once we have hard evidence against him."

"How come you haven't been replying to my messages?"

She shrugged. "You said you were going to California. Figured I'd wait until you got back. I'm going back to bed." She cracked the door open. "Care to join me?"

"I can't." The tousled look was certainly enticing, but Clay found he had no interest. "Got an appointment."

"Suit yourself." Donna closed the door.

Clay found Crystal Landry on the job at the laundromat. She wore her customary jean skirt with a white belt made of lace circles. Her tube top today was yellow and her eye-shadow green. She was chewing gum energetically trying to make it to the next smoke break, or so he assumed.

"Whatcha want?" she asked.

"Crystal." Clay looked at the two customers currently sitting half asleep waiting for their laundry. "I wanted to update you on the case."

"Ain't no case. I let you go."

"Don't you want to know who was responsible for the drugs that killed your granddaughter?"

"That was a pipe dream. Ain't gonna happen."

"I found the person responsible and have turned him over to the police." Why did this woman always push his buttons? Make him sound so pompous sometimes?

Crystal paused in her folding and looked at him. "I got to finish up this WDF order and then I'm done for the day. How about I meet you over at the Side Bar? You can buy me a drink." She winked at him.

The Side Bar was only about a hundred yards up the street, but Clay drove anyway. It wasn't until he was walking in the door that he figured out that WDF must stand for wash, dry, and fold. The bartender nodded at him when he entered. Until a week ago he'd never been in the place, and now he was being treated as a regular. It was just past 4:00 in the afternoon, but seven or eight solitary figures sat huddled over drinks.

He'd just taken his first sip of Gentleman Jack on the rocks when Crystal came in and sat next to him at the bar. A drink appeared instantly in front of her.

"What's so important? You just trying to find ways to see me?" Crystal asked, again with a big wink.

"I just want to let you know that I found the local drug dealer and turned the case over to the police. The man responsible for your granddaughter's death."

"My fucking heroin-addicted daughter is the responsible one," Crystal said. "Which probably means it's my fault for fucking her up."

"I wouldn't be too hard on yourself."

"So, what patsy did you locate?"

"Patsy?"

"You said local dealer. You didn't get any of the real kingpins, now, did you?"

"Kingpins?"

"Mr. Wolfe, do you have any idea what you have got yourself in the middle of?" Crystal placed her empty glass down and another full one appeared in front of her.

"What do you know that you're not telling me?"

"Who'd you turn over to the police? That fucking lawyer, Daigle?"

"There has been no arrest as the police are investigating the matter, so I'd rather not say." Clay drained his own glass and raised it to the bartender for another.

"I heard you got in a fight with Lobbins right before he was killed."

"He was the one bringing drugs in through his lobster traps. I confronted him. He was shot."

"One of." She looked away and snorted, shaking her head.

"What?"

Crystal laughed a dry cackle. "You have no fucking idea, do you?"

"Why don't you tell me?"

"And get myself killed?"

"Why'd you hire me, Crystal?"

"I didn't fucking know then what I know now."

"What do you know, Crystal?"

"You need to let this go, is all I'm saying."

"Why?"

Crystal sighed and took a drink.

"What's got you so scared?" he asked more insistently.

"You're gonna get killed is what's going on."

"At least tell me why I have to walk away. Please."

Crystal slammed down the empty glass. "Why can't you just be done with it?" she asked plaintively.

"Be done with what?"

"The whole shitshow," Crystal said. "Port Essex is the port of entry for heroin for most of New England. Lobbins and Daigle are the tips of the iceberg. That's what I'm trying to tell you. I was pissed off and hired you before I knew how bad this fucking thing was. You best back off, or you're going to find yourself dead."

Clay just stared at her. Port Essex? His town? "I can take care of myself," he finally said.

"The enforcer is one mean motherfucker, or so I've been told."

"If you know so much, why did you hire me?"

"I found some stuff out. Stuff that can't be unfound."

"Stop feeding me a line of shit, Crystal."

Crystal pinched the bridge of her nose and sighed. "I told you my boyfriend is a lobsterman. Well, he hears things. Jake wasn't the only one smuggling drugs in the pots. There's a bunch of them."

"And he's just sharing this with you now?"

"I found the heroin in his stuff a few days back. When I asked him about it, he didn't want to talk but I told him I was going to take it to the police. Did he know that shit killed my grandbaby, I asked him? Was probably killing my daughter as we spoke? He told me he was being forced to sell it by some bigwig. Had something over him."

"And the big boss is some guy named Curtis Volkov?"

"Where'd you hear that? You want to forget that name right now."

"What's the big deal about some two-bit dirtbag. It's like he's some Voldemort."

"You read about the fellow that went missing a few weeks back? Ted Jones? People say he owed Daigle money. When Curtis showed up to collect, Ted made the mistake of saying you can't get blood out of a turnip. You know what that motherfucker did?" Crystal didn't give him a chance to answer. "He told Ted that might be true, but he could get blood out of him. He gutted him like a deer. He hung him from a tree by his arms, put a kiddie pool underneath him, cut his junk off, and then sliced him open from his asshole to his chest and let him bleed out."

"If this Ted guy is missing, how is it that you know what happened to him?"

Crystal looked at the bartender who appeared to be studiously ignoring them but had been drying the same glass for some time now. She leaned closer to Clay and whispered in his ear. "He's making my boyfriend run drugs through his pots. Dale, he tried to stop, and Curtis told him that was how he was going to end up if he didn't shape the fuck up. Showed him pictures on his phone, too."

"Looks like somebody needs to have a chat with Mr. Volkov," Clay said.

This reminded him that he'd meant to have Baylee see what she could find on him. Don's finding proof that Daigle was dealing and then having to go to L.A. in search of the *Fourth Shade* had distracted him. If you could call Charly a distraction.

"You got anybody you care about?"

"What's that?" Clay was jolted from his thoughts.

"You fuck with these people, and they'll kill everybody you care about *and then* kill you."

Clay's thoughts went to Grandpops, Baylee, and briefly to Westy. He discounted Westy, as nobody in their right mind would mess with him. It flitted across his mind that Donna was not on the list. She was a cop, after all, and could also take care of herself. Even though he was—or had been—sleeping with her, he wasn't sure she'd count as somebody he cared about.

He asked for the bill and was shocked that it was only $12. He looked closer. Crystal had been drinking ginger ale. He thought she'd been holding her liquor pretty well. Clay tossed his credit card over to the bartender who was still drying the same glass. He best check in with Grandpops and Baylee. If what Crystal Landry said was true, he'd stirred up one helluva hornet's nest. He probably should *not* have Baylee research Curtis Volkov.

Chapter 19

STILL THURSDAY, JULY 9TH

Baylee shut down the computer, grabbed her purse, turned off the lights, and locked the door to the office as she left. She was feeling a bit queasy, probably the lingering effects of being completely off the Xanax, and thus decided to go straight home. Flash would be happy to see her.

It wasn't like she needed anything at the store. She doubted that she'd eat more than an apple and some crackers and cheese for dinner. She looked forward to the time when her appetite returned, because she did enjoy eating. As she got into the car, her phone buzzed.

It was a text from Tammy. You doing ok?

All good. Home for a quiet night.

Need me to come over?

Nope. Maybe get a drink tomorrow?

YES!

When she was halfway home her phone buzzed in her purse again, and she made a mental note to check the message when she got home. It was probably just Tammy again. If she had to guess, Tammy was probably sending her the eggplant and the peace emoji, suggesting that tomorrow might be the day to hook up after a year of abstinence.

Baylee had zero desire for a huey, as Tammy called it. The idea of bringing a stranger home and getting naked with him gave her the chills. She knew that Tammy was just trying to help, but she wished she'd leave it. If anything, Baylee was ready to be courted properly, she thought with a smile. Meet for coffee. Have dinner. Go for ice cream. See a movie. Maybe a kiss after the third date. And not with just anybody.

She crossed over the bridge to Spruce Island and looked to the left where Knox Wharf was and thought about Jake Lobbins being killed as he had stood two feet from Clay Wolfe. The thought of how close to death Clay had come made her insides tighten and her lips dry. She was glad that he had wrapped up the drug case and handed it over to the police. Searching for a missing statue seemed inherently safer.

A few hundred yards from her home was a pull-over with a black SUV parked. There was a trail that led down to a fishing spot, and it was not unusual for a vehicle to be parked there, she thought, though the SUV seemed a bit too fancy and shiny for the regular locals who mostly drove old beat-up trucks. Probably some tourist family in a rental who'd discovered the trail on Yelp or some site and thought a 400-foot walk was all the exercise they needed prior to going and ordering lobster and steamers.

Black clouds threatening a storm came rolling in from the northeast as she pulled into her driveway. The cool air gusting off the ocean carried a chill that made her shiver as she got out of the car. Flash might have to wait for his walk, she thought. The door was unlocked, which was strange, because she was usually very good about locking it. She paused momentarily on the threshold, and then the rain came pelting from the sky driven by 20 mph winds, and she slid inside with a shiver.

Flash was not there to greet her, which was also strange.

•   •   •   •

Clay thought about calling but it was only five minutes to home. He pulled into the driveway with a squeal of tires and thought that perhaps he was being overly dramatic. He jogged up the front steps and gave a quick rap on the door before pulling it open and going inside. Gene was sitting in the living room watching the five o'clock news with a scotch in his hand.

"Who put the hustle in your bustle?" Gene asked.

"Just checking in," Clay said.

"Sit down. Stay a spell."

Clay sat in the armchair kitty-corner to his grandpops. "Everything good here?"

"Why wouldn't it be?"

Clay rolled his tongue over his teeth forming his thoughts. He knew there was no use or purpose to lying or downplaying his fears. "I think the drug operation in Port Essex might be a bit larger than I thought."

"Meaning what?"

"Meaning we're talking bigger players than local dealers."

"Get to the point, Clay."

"I've heard that Port Essex is the point of entry for much of the drugs—heroin and fentanyl, anyway—up and down the East Coast. That means they're being backed by real money. Maybe the cartels. The Chinese? I don't know who, but people who can afford to buy serious muscle to back their play."

"And you digging around has put your life in danger?"

"Not just my life. Your life."

Gene nodded. "I know." He reached under the pillow next to him and pulled out a compact pistol barely larger than his hand.

Of course, the old geezer had been ahead of him on this one, Clay thought. He pulled out his phone and texted Baylee. Call me.

"What do you know?" Gene asked.

"Crystal Landry tells me there is an entire network smuggling drugs through lobster pots. I have the name of the muscle. Curtis Volkov. She said he's an animal. Likes to kill people slow and then use the threat of that violence to scare others into compliance."

"And he knows you've been digging around?"

"For sure. I'm thinking he's the one who shot Lobbins because I was onto him. Might have taken out Dylan Thompson as well."

"Where are you at with your investigation? Any new leads?"

"I had Don following a lawyer in town. Allen Daigle?" Clay looked at Gene who nodded that he knew the man. "Looks like the guy's income was being bolstered by selling drugs locally. I turned him over to the police." Clay looked at his phone. There'd been no reply. **Where are you?** he typed.

"Are you done with the thing, then?"

"I thought so."

"Do the bad guys know that?"

"I don't know."

"Did the police arrest Daigle?"

"Not yet. He went on vacation. They're waiting for him to get back."

"Who'd you take it to?"

"Donna."

"You want me to check in with the Chief on this?" Gene played canasta with the chief of police and two others every Tuesday evening.

"Yeah, that'd be great. In the meantime, keep that pocket piece handy and lock the doors. I need to go check on Baylee. She's not answering my texts."

Clay made sure all the doors were locked and then went out and up his stairs. His Glock 23 was in a lockbox in his closet. He'd only carried it twice since retiring from Boston PD, both times when he was working as a bodyguard. He slid the magazine in, racked the slide, and grabbed a spare magazine.

•   •   •   •

Curtis was sitting on her sofa. "What are you doing in my house?" Baylee asked.

"You missed our appointment yesterday," he answered.

"I texted you that I quit." Baylee looked around for Flash. No sign of him or Ollie.

Curtis shrugged. "I guess I needed closure."

"Closure? What is this, fucking Oprah?" Baylee went and sat at the desk in the corner of the room. Her pistol was loaded and in the top drawer, which was locked.

"I thought we had something more than a buyer/seller relationship."

Baylee kept her face impassive, but a shiver of disgust rippled up her spine. "What company did you say you worked for?" she asked.

"I didn't."

"Where's my dog?"

"Maybe you could make us dinner? Put on something nice? We could light some candles and listen to the storm?"

Baylee's ex-husband had always acted and spoken with that same eerie calmness right before he would abuse her. "I need you to leave." She pulled out her phone.

Curtis stood, took two steps, and smashed it from her hand with a swiftness and violence that shocked her. "What...what do you want?"

He now towered over her sitting form, exuding a simmering rage. His features were darker than the storm clouds outside. "I want you to like me," he said.

"I don't know you."

"Why don't you slip into something comfortable, and we'll get to know each other."

"Let me give you back the last of the Xanax," Baylee said. "I don't want to be tempted by them anymore. And then I'll change."

She picked a small box from her desk and removed a key, fit it into the drawer keyhole, turned, and slid it open. She grasped the pistol with her right hand as she felt his hand cup the back of her head and then lights exploded as he slammed her head into the desktop. The gun slipped from her hand and onto the floor.

"That was not smart," he said.

With his hand firmly gripping her hair, Curtis raised her to a standing position, the room reeling around her, blood running from her nose down over her chin and dripping onto the floor.

"Do you not like me because of Clay Wolfe?" he asked.

Baylee jammed her thumb at his face, but he turned his head, and she left a ragged scratch across his cheek instead of gouging out his eyeball.

He punched her with a left jab to the forehead as if hitting a speed bag, and her neck snapped backwards then recoiled as the hand entwined in her hair jerked her forward.

"Let me tell you something about Clay Wolfe," he said.

Though her head was spinning, this was not her first rodeo. Baylee knew full well that playing passive did not work. She brought her knee up into his groin, and she took grim pleasure from his cringe of pain and the indrawn gasp, which at least gave her respite from his terrible breath. Unfortunately, the hurt she had inflicted was not enough for his grip on her to loosen.

Curtis flung her by her hair across the room and over the coffee table. Everything was swirling in her scrambled mind, and she couldn't seem to remember how she ended up sprawled on the floor.

"The man doesn't know how to mind his own business. He needs to learn," he said.

He kicked her in the side, and Baylee found herself gasping for air. She had to keep her wits about her, she thought, trying to make sense of the situation with her addled mind. Where was the gun? She felt the hand in her hair again and was pulled up to face the guy she only knew as Curtis. He cupped the back of her head and kissed her brutally on the mouth.

"I heard you like it rough," he said, holding her again at arm's distance. Her blood was on his chin, streaking his lips.

She spit on him and knocked at the arm holding her, but his grasp was like iron. The man was much stronger than George had been. Baylee dug the nails of both her hands into his bicep, causing him to let her go, but before she could move, he slapped her across the face, sending her tumbling through the room. She saw the gun lying by the desk and scrambled on all fours to reach it, but he kicked her in the ribs, and she found herself on her back looking at the ceiling.

Baylee must have drifted off temporarily, because Curtis was now straddling her body as she struggled back to consciousness, his hand again wrapped into her hair pulling her head from the floor, his rancid breath like smelling salts, driving away the cobwebs.

"You think you're better than me, don't you?" he asked.

Baylee tried to reply but no sound could escape her mangled lips. Then they both heard the sound of a car pulling into the driveway.

"Maybe Clay Fucking Wolfe will finally get the message," Curtis said, drawing back his fist.

Then, everything went black for Baylee Baker.

Chapter 20

Clay knocked. No answer. He knocked again. No answer. He looked back around. There was her car in the driveway. The only other vehicle was his Jeep. Clay thought about clambering into the bushes to look through the window. He could see a faint glow of light illuminating the inside, offsetting the ominous presence of the dark clouds that had so far held off the downpour that seemed imminent.

He tried the doorknob. It turned in his hand. He cracked the door.

"Baylee?"

No answer. He pulled his Glock out of the holster, feeling silly. She was probably in the bathroom. Or napping? Or taking Flash for a walk. What would she think when he burst into her house holding a gun? Hadn't the woman been through enough with that asshole of a husband? This thought gave Clay pause. What if he stepped through the door, and she shot him thinking he was an intruder?

"Baylee?" he called louder.

And then Flash howled from somewhere back in the house, and he knew that his instincts were correct.

"Baylee?" Clay pushed the door fully open and stepped into the entrance with the pistol in both hands sweeping the room. The entrance brought him into the living room. His eyes followed the Glock as it swept the room, noting the overturned coffee table, the smashed lamp, and then the inert figure on the floor.

"Baylee?" He sidled over to her, keeping the Glock trained on the archway to the hallway. He could see the kitchen across the way. Flash howled again.

Clay knelt down next to Baylee who was splayed on the floor, one arm flung back at an awkward angle. "Baylee?" He reached out a hand and placed his index and middle finger against her carotid artery next to her windpipe. There was a strong pulse. He had to clear the house first before going any further. He couldn't help her if he was dead.

The kitchen was empty, the door to the backyard slightly cracked. The door to Baylee's room was open, and he stepped in with pistol raised. His eyes took in the four-poster bed with white lacy material draped around matching the curtains on the windows. Clay pulled open the bi-fold closet doors with one hand. It was crowded with clothes and shoes, but no bad guys.

There were two guest rooms. The first held Flash and Ollie, the basset hound galloping out and past Clay with ears flopping. The cat came gingerly through the door much more reluctantly, then shot out of sight. The second spare room had an easel with a watercolor and a bunch of paints but was otherwise empty. Clay had no idea that Baylee even painted. What did he really know about his receptionist?

Back in the living room, Flash was licking Baylee's face, and as Clay approached them, she opened her eyes, panic rippling outward and fear springing forward.

"Where is he?" she asked. She tried to sit up but groaned as she put weight on the crooked arm.

Clay put his Glock back in the holster and sank to his knees next to her. "It's okay. There's nobody here. Just me and Flash." He pulled out his phone.

"Who are you calling?"

"911. Ambulance. Police."

"Wait. Help me up."

"Your arm is broken. Probably your nose. Who knows what else? We shouldn't move you."

"Just wait, would you? I think I just dislocated my shoulder. It's not uncommon."

Not uncommon when your husband is smashing you around, Clay thought grimly. "That's why we need a paramedic."

"Help me pull my arm down," she said in a voice so filled with pain that it brooked no argument.

Clay pushed Flash away and grasped her arm gently and pulled it down by her side. She slid it outward at an angle from her body and turned her palm upward. "Grab my wrist and pull."

He gave a gentle tug.

"Put your right hand on my chest and pull, dammit," she said.

He didn't want to put his hand on her shoulder, so the only option was on her breast. As a cop he'd performed basic medical treatment on several occasions, but never on somebody he knew. Clay took a deep breath and pulled her arm away from the shoulder. There was a small click and Baylee gasped.

"You can take your hand off my breast now," she said.

He did so, but slowly, his fingers tingling. Clay argued to no avail to call an ambulance, but at least she let him drive her to urgent care once they'd cleaned the blood from her face. She held a damp cloth to her mashed lip as they drove.

Flash was in back, upon Baylee's insistence, and Ollie had been fed.

"I have to call the police," Clay said.

"And tell them what?"

"That a man tried to kill you to get me to back off investigating drugs in Port Essex."

"What?"

"This has to do with the heroin case."

"No. No, it doesn't," Baylee said in a low voice.

"I'm sorry," Clay said. "I didn't expect it to pull you in."

"I know the guy," Baylee said.

"You know the man who beat you up?"

"Yeah, he's been selling me Xanax."

Clay turned to look at her as he gave up on passing the car trolling along in front of him. This was a new twist, he thought. Xanax? Wasn't that some sort of depression medicine? Baylee gave no sign that she was depressed, but he only saw her in the office. She had been in an abusive relationship. She had killed her husband. She lived alone. Again, that troubling thought, what did he really know about her?

"I kind of got addicted to it after I…after George," Baylee said as she stared out the side window of the Jeep.

"Can't you get a prescription for Xanax?"

"Sure. That's what got me started. But then my shrink wanted to wean me off of it, and I wasn't ready to give it up."

"How'd you find somebody to sell it to you?"

"There was a girl I used to run with before I settled down with George. We used to get in trouble together, back in the day. We keep up once in a while, and I asked her if she knew where I could get some pills. She's still running in that race, if you know what I mean. She said she'd look into it, and the next day Curtis called me."

Clay slammed on the brakes. "Curtis?"

Baylee rubbed her recently dislocated shoulder where the seatbelt had locked up on her. "What the heck?"

"Did you say the dude selling you Xanax is named Curtis? The guy who beat you up?"

"Yeah, so what? You know him?"

"You know where you can find him?"

"No, he always contacts me. He said he's a salesman, and his route takes him through Port Essex once a week, but I'm starting to think that's bullshit."

Clay gave into the pressure of the honking horns behind them and started driving forward. Had he really never mentioned the name Curtis to Baylee, he wondered? If he had, perhaps the man would be behind bars now instead of still out there somewhere. They most certainly could have avoided Baylee being almost killed.

"Why'd he beat you up?" he asked.

"Because I quit buying from him. I got off the stuff."

"A salesman beat you severely because you quit buying Xanax from him?"

"I think he likes me."

"Helluva way to show it. What? Are we back in seventh grade where boys pull the hair of the girls they like?"

"He kissed me." Baylee visibly shuddered.

"I need to talk to this man."

"He came onto me in my own house. And when I rebuffed him, he got kind of violent. All right. Fucking violent, like he might have killed me without even meaning to. Like I felt with George. I did try to pull a gun on him," she said.

"Dylan Thompson told me that a man named Curtis Volkov is behind the entire drug operation in Port Essex," he said. "Crystal Landry just told me today that Port Essex is the point of ingress for most of the heroin in New England. She also told me that her boyfriend is being forced to be a mule through his lobster traps by Curtis who apparently cut a man up and bled him dry to punish him for being unable to pay for his habit. I'm guessing that Volkov is the one who killed Jake Lobbins. Maybe Dylan Thompson."

"Curtis? Six feet? Shaved head? Beady eyes? Bad breath?"

"I don't know," Clay said. "I couldn't get a description out of either Dylan or Crystal. They're terrified of him, almost like he's the bogeyman."

"They can't be the same guy. It must be just a coincidence of names."

Clay turned into the parking lot of the urgent care center. "Two guys named Curtis who deal drugs and go around killing and hurting people in Port Essex? I don't think so."

Clay called Donna while Baylee was getting five stitches in her lip, a sling for her arm and shoulder, and the diagnosis that her nose was not broken. She turned down the offer of a prescription for oxycodone and was checking out when Donna came in with two patrol officers. The two cops took Baylee into a private room to get a statement while

Clay and Donna went to get a cup of coffee.

"You need to get the state police on this," Clay said as they settled into chairs in the small cafeteria.

"For what?" Donna asked. "Why don't you tell me what you know?"

"Some guy beat up my receptionist. Do you need more?"

"You know the state police don't get involved in your common assault and battery cases," she said.

"I think it's the guy behind the drugs in Port Essex."

"I thought Alan Daigle was the one behind the drugs in town. Which is it?"

Clay sighed. "I have it on good authority that our town is portal to most of the heroin, and some other drugs as well, in New England." Even as he said it, he knew what question was coming next.

"Who is your source?"

Clay wondered if Crystal Landry could be considered good authority. "I believe that the man who beat Baylee up is also the one who killed Lobbins. The state police are running that one, right?"

"And why do you think that?"

"I was told that the man's name is Curtis Volkov. That's the name Baylee gave me when I asked her who beat her up. Or the first name, anyway."

"I need more to go on," Donna said.

"Do you have forensics over at Baylee's house now?"

"Yes. They just got started."

"Baylee said the guy kissed her on the mouth."

"The doctor swabbed her mouth."

"That should get a DNA match."

"In anywhere from three to six months," Donna said.

"What?"

"We have rape cases backed up longer than that. Assault? It's a long line."

"This guy is funneling drugs through Port Essex to all of New England and is responsible for at least one murder," Clay said.

"So you say." She shrugged, and he wondered briefly at her hesitation. "I'll run his name through the system, but I wouldn't hold my breath."

"Can you keep an eye on my...on Gene's house? I'm going to bring Baylee back there, and I'm worried that this guy is going to come after them when I'm not around."

Donna stepped in close. "Is there something more to Baylee Baker that I should know?" she asked.

"What?"

"Are you sleeping with her?"

"No. She works for me. I've put her life in danger, and now I intend to protect it. That's the sum of it." He was well aware of the pheromones of her natural scent and tried to step back but found himself rooted to the spot.

"Are you getting tired of our arrangement?" Donna's musk swirled around Clay.

"Hey, Lieu, we're done interviewing the vic," a patrol officer said coming into the room. "Should we cut her loose?"

"Let me talk to her first," Donna said.

"Sure thing, Lieu."

"I'll put your house on a drive-by list," Donna said to Clay as she walked out with the patrol officer. "Miss Baker will be all yours in about ten minutes," she said, turning to give him a last look that would curdle milk.

"I'll be fine to go home," Baylee said to Clay as they clambered back into the Jeep. Flash was quite energetic in welcoming her back, nuzzling the back of Baylee's neck and making low whining noises.

"You're going to stay with Gene until this blows over. Besides, forensics is going to be combing your place half the night. I'll take you over in the morning to get some things."

"I don't want to be a bother."

"How do you feel?"

"Like I got hit by a truck." Baylee grinned through her stitched lip. "Starting to think I should've taken them up on drugging me."

"You turned down pain medication?" Clay turned his head to her as he pulled the Jeep onto the road.

"Yeah. I don't want to go down that road again."

"You're not to blame for what happened."

"For getting addicted to Xanax? Sure I am. Who else should I blame? George? He's dead."

"You went through a lot."

"Maybe so, but that doesn't make it right."

Clay thought about how he liked to dull the edges of his pain with liquor. "No, I suppose it doesn't. We do the best we can."

They rode the rest of the way to Clay's house in silence. When he parked in the driveway, neither one of them made any move to get out. The clouds had rolled through, their promise of unrelenting downpours an empty one, and the stars filled the sky, glittering hard against the blackness of the night.

"Maybe I should step away from this case," Clay finally said.

Baylee looked at him, their eyes meeting and locking. "You said something to me a little bit back. You were trying to make me feel better about killing my husband. I've been thinking about it. More so over the past few hours."

"Yeah? What?"

"Some motherfuckers need to die," she said.

Chapter 21

FRIDAY, JULY 10TH

Clay slept in the living room on the couch with his Glock slid underneath close at hand. Baylee was put up in the guest room. It was still dark out when a tap on the door woke him. Clay reached down and grasped the pistol before rising and approaching the front door.

Westy was on the porch in his fishing gear. It was just before dawn, yellow streaks blossoming into the sky out over the Atlantic.

"Heard you had some problems," he said.

Clay opened the door wide. "Come on in."

"Did some dude really kick the shit out of Baylee?" Westy entered the house and sat down in one of the armchairs.

"Yep. He was sending me a message. At least, I'm pretty sure I was the intended recipient."

"Same guy who killed Lobbins?"

"I would think so."

"She okay?"

"Dislocated shoulder. A few stitches in her lip. Bunch of bruises. Sounds like she held her own, maybe learned a few things fighting off that husband." Clay shrugged. "She's sleeping upstairs."

"You think he might come after her again?"

"Not really. If he had wanted to kill her, he could have. Like I said, he was just sending me a message to back off."

"You got any leads on the guy?"

"Name is Curtis Volkov. Rumor has it the heroin traffic through Port Essex is more of a highway than a back road. Sounds like he's the muscle for the operation."

"What's going on with Daigle?" Westy pulled his KA-Bar knife from its sheath on his belt and began absently twirling the seven-inch blade. He'd shown it to Clay once, explaining that it'd been given to him upon graduating from SEAL training.

"I turned everything I knew about him and what he was doing over to the police. Seems he went on vacation."

"Think he'll come back?"

"Does it really matter?" Clay asked.

"What do you mean?"

Clay went to the front window and stood with his back to Westy. "As long as he's gone, I mean, what does it matter if he comes back to face the music?"

"You don't really believe that garbage," Westy said. "People have to pay for their crimes. Especially piece-of-shit heroin dealers."

"Yeah, I know." Clay turned and faced Westy. "But I'm starting to think that doesn't really resolve the issue, now, does it?" It wasn't really a question.

"Oh, we'll find the fucking Russian," Westy said. "He'll get what's coming to him."

Clay wondered if Westy had carried out operations against Russians while he was a SEAL. Weren't they our allies now? He wasn't sure who the enemy was supposed to be. "Baylee said he has no accent."

"What's that mean?"

"Sounds like he might be an American with a Russian name. Sort of like Beck is German but you're a U.S. citizen."

"He's a sick fuck, is what he is."

Clay nodded to concede the point. "He's just another tool," he said.

"Another tool? What are you sayin' here?"

"Crystal Landry tells me there's a whole stable of lobstermen smuggling heroin through their pots. Whoever is behind this is supplying most of New England. So I kinda doubt our lawyer friend is the kingpin of the operation."

"And it's coming right through our town?" Westy sheathed his knife and stood up. "So who's behind it?"

"That's the million-dollar question."

"Mexican cartels? The Chinese? The name Volkov points towards the Russians."

"Couldn't tell you." Clay frowned. "All we got for leads is Daigle, who is on vacation, and Curtis Volkov, who doesn't seem to exist."

"So, we either hunt down Daigle on his supposed vacation or set a trap for Volkov?" Westy asked.

"We?"

"I don't much like men who beat up women."

It took ten minutes for Clay to convince Westy to go out on the fishing boat as normal that day, but afterwards, to ask around—very quietly—to see if his acquaintances had noticed any suspicious activity in the lobstering communities. Memories were not short, and men were still held responsible for their father's past sins.

Clay made a pot of coffee, and once it had percolated, took a mug of the steaming brew out onto the front porch. A picture on the sideboard next to the porch door had caught his eye of his mom and dad, Clay, a toddler standing shyly in front of them, taken on this very porch. It had been some time since he'd thought about his parents. His mind drifted back to the day he'd discovered he was an orphan. Gene had answered the door that morning to a man in a brown uniform and another in a blue uniform. It wasn't until years later that he realized one was a sheriff and one was a Port Essex police officer, both men who knew Gene well and had taken on the burden of breaking the terrible news—that his wife, son, and daughter-in-law had died in a freak car accident.

Clay had been in the living room watching *Inspector Gadget* when the men in brown and blue had come to the door. He didn't know until later that Grandpops had been out half the night scouring the roads between the Botanical Gardens and Port Essex trying to find a trace of his family and had just returned at first light to be close to the phone in case it rang. He didn't know that a neighbor had slept on this very couch to keep a watch on the young boy sleeping upstairs. It was only when Clay turned sixteen that Gene sat him down and answered every one of his questions. All he remembered at the time was that Grandpops sagged in the middle and had to be helped to a chair by the men he understood to be cops, like Inspector Gadget, but much more somber and serious.

Of course, Gene didn't have to tell Clay that his father, Mack Wolfe, had been found with an unhealthy amount of cocaine in his blood. That information he learned soon after he returned to school from two older boys on the playground, not that he even knew what that meant at the time. In his mind, cocaine took on the transformative power that anger had on the Hulk, turning the harmless Dr. Banner into the raging green monster. Clay had become more than a little obsessed by science fiction movies and books, trying to find the creature called cocaine. When he finally realized his mistake, and that cocaine was a drug and not an alien, he'd been momentarily comforted.

After a bit, that comfort turned to anger, for he came to blame his father for the poor choice he'd made. How could his father have favored this drug over his own family, he wondered? That was when Gene had sat Clay down and talked the whole thing out, right after Clay had been brought home by the police for underage drinking, two days after he turned sixteen.

The four-hour conversation hadn't made things right again, not by a long sight, but with the chance to express his anger had come Clay's first glimpses of the adult world, one filled with the weaknesses that men and women fight against. Gene made him understand that Mack had loved his son, loved his wife, loved his mother, but had come under the thrall of the powerful drug. Sometimes, sadly, unlike in movies and comics, for people in the real world of mortality and consequences, there were no second chances. It had been an accident, even if one borne of addiction. It was then that Clay decided that he wanted to be a policeman, the mature manifestation of this desire morphing into the ambition to be a homicide detective.

Now, as Clay sat sipping his coffee on the porch of Grandpops' house, he wondered that perhaps he'd subconsciously transferred his anger at the cocaine that led to death of his family to a more tangible enemy—actual living, breathing, murderers. Who were the animals that distributed this deathly poison to so many weak souls? He'd been shocked when Gene told him that there had been over 70,000 overdose deaths in the U.S. in 2017, the most recent year statistics had been posted. Three hundred and fifty-four of them in Maine alone— more than twice the number of people who'd died in road deaths.

As the sun rose over his hometown of Port Essex on the beautiful coast of Maine, it was hard to believe that this idyllic village was the gateway for drugs sold all across New England. How many people, he wondered, had died from heroin or other illicit drugs that had passed right through the place with all of the serenity of a Winslow Homer watercolor? It had to be stopped. Kelly Anne Landry was a symptom of the problem, her daughter collateral damage. Allen Daigle was a by-product of greed. Curtis Volkov was evil incarnate. They were all tools of the Angel of Darkness who hid behind these foot soldiers and a wall of money, profiting off the weakness of man while seemingly oblivious to the pain and suffering inflicted.

"Beautiful morning." Gene Wolfe pushed through the screen door and walked carefully over to the wicker chair next to Clay, who noticed that he was no longer using a cane.

"That it is," Clay said. "You sure picked a good home to enjoy the sunrise."

"Fifty-five years now."

"A lot of good folks live here."

Gene gave him a long look over the rim of his coffee cup. "I suppose so."

"Kind of felt like Port Essex was an undiscovered gem hidden away in some secret paradise." Clay was staring out now over the downtown buildings and streets that were starting to come to life on this Friday morning.

"It's a beautiful town filled with good people."

"How do you figure this evil got in?"

Gene took a long time to answer that, but finally cleared his throat and gave voice to his carefully collected thoughts. "When Molly and I moved here back in 1965, it wasn't much more than a fishing village," he said. "There was only a smattering of houses up here on the hill and half the buildings down on Commercial Way. We bought this place, and I hung out a shingle down between two fish houses."

Gene paused again, long enough for Clay to consider prodding him along, or maybe getting another cup of coffee. But he knew better then to hurry his grandpops in a story and he certainly didn't want to break the train of thought, so he settled back and waited while watching as two men trundled kegs into the Seal Bar from a parked truck blocking half of the main drag.

"Boys were starting to come back from Vietnam then, younger than me in many cases," Gene continued, "Young men with faraway eyes filled with haunted images that none of us civilians could even begin to understand at that point, not that we can now, but we at least have a glimmer of the horrors they witnessed. And at least we know enough about PTSD to recognize it as a mental health condition to be treated rather than shamed. That was the first time I heard anything about drugs, soldiers having used whatever they could get their hands on to dull the pain. Marijuana at first, but then there were other things. LSD. Acid. Mushrooms. The soldiers did it to forget. The young people did it to protest. The rest of us wash it away with liquor."

"There have always been drugs of one form or another," Clay said.

"Yep. Since the beginning of time. Opioids are just today's tobacco, big business purposely getting people addicted for their own financial gain, though."

"Big business?"

"Sure. Big Pharma knows full well the addictive powers of what they're selling, but they downplay it. Push it on the high school soccer girl who tears a tendon without any thought of how this will affect the rest of her life."

"What do we do about it?"

"I guess the line has to be drawn somewhere. What's the harm in a scotch at night? Not much, I suppose, but abusing it causes almost 90,000 deaths a year. Not much harm in a bit of marijuana but tripping on hallucinogens got way out of control. When that abated, crack cocaine began to rear its ugly head." Gene couldn't help but look up to the north, the site of the accident that had robbed them both of so much, and the vision of the curved roadway with the rocks below along the ocean filled each of their minds.

"So there's no point in fighting this particular war?" Clay finally asked in a thick voice.

"Just the opposite, my boy. You have to fight it every single day. You got to get up in the morning and be ready. When you think about that next drink at night, you got to fight it within yourself. Sure, drugs are bad, but 90,000 people died of alcohol related causes last year. Think about that as you hide your pain in a bottle or fill the tedium of life with brown liquor."

How did this become about me, Clay wondered? "Are you telling me to fix myself and let the rest go?"

"Not at all. I'm saying the devil is both inside and outside and all around. You got to address Beelzebub inside your own head before you can attack him outside."

"I got to heal first?"

"You aren't ever going to be healed, son. You just have to grasp that you're hurting."

That sure was a lot to take in, Clay thought, but then he couldn't deny that these same thoughts had slowly been waking from hibernation in the recesses of his consciousness. "So, you think I should drop my pursuit of drug trafficking in Port Essex?"

"If you want your ass kicked to the curb." Gene stood up and walked back into the house.

Clay sat there musing on the past, present, and future until his phone buzzed. It was a text from Marie Cloutier.

Police have no comment on Daigle. I have three people who have backed up that he IS the one selling heroin. Thinking of running story Monday with what I have.

Clay replied without thinking any further. Story has gotten much bigger than Daigle.

Want to share?

Breakfast at the diner?

20 minutes.

K.

Not enough time for a shower, Clay thought, but he sure could use some fresh clothes. He stuck his head in the door. Gene was sitting on the sofa reading a book. "You got that pocket pistol still?" Clay asked.

Gene patted his right pocket and nodded.

"Can you keep your eyes peeled until Baylee wakes? She's got herself a real gun to keep the both of you safe."

"What are you going to be doing?" Gene asked.

"Keeping my ass from getting kicked to the curb."

Chapter 22

STILL FRIDAY, JULY 10TH

Cloutier was waiting for him out front on a bench fashioned from an old red wagon. The fact that she hadn't gone inside and ordered food hinted at the fact that Clay had piqued her interest. This notion was bolstered by the first words out of her mouth.

"Are you telling me Daigle is just a minnow?" she asked.

Clay looked around. "No names," he said. It was then he realized he might be putting her in danger by just being seen with him.

"What's going on?"

Clay glanced into the busy diner. "Let's go for a walk instead of eating."

"I'm hungry."

"Baylee got severely beaten up last night. Most likely because she works for me."

"I can eat later." Cloutier stood and began walking away from town. "Is she okay? What the hell happened?"

Clay matched her stride. "Baylee was attacked in her home by a man named Curtis Volkov. Crystal Landry, the grandmother of the baby who died, told me that he's the muscle for an operation that is flooding northern New England with drugs via Port Essex. Sounds like heroin, Oxy, and maybe some other things are being dropped in lobster pots out at sea, picked up by the lobstermen, and brought into town to be turned over to this Volkov guy. If it's happening in little old Port Essex, you can sure as shit bet it's happening in other harbors as well."

"More than just Jake Lobbins here?"

"Yes. I don't know how many, but at least a handful by the sounds of it."

"And this Curtis Volkov is the one who killed Lobbins?"

"I would guess," Clay said. "And probably Dylan Thompson."

"The addict who went up in a blaze of fireworks?"

"The very same."

Cloutier nodded at a bench on the side of the road. They'd circled their way down to the outskirts of Commercial Way where there was a small park, quiet at this hour except for a couple of dog walkers. "Can we sit?" Her face was red, and she was huffing.

"Absolutely," he agreed, realizing they'd been walking faster and faster as they talked, enervated by the implications of those words for their own safety. This secluded park was a much better choice for privacy than walking the sidewalks.

"I thought Thompson's death was an accident?" She sat down with a groan.

"The dude pissed away any money he made digging bloodworms on heroin, but suddenly has fireworks worth over a thousand bucks in his trailer? Right after having been seen talking with me?"

"The thought flashed through my mind as well," Cloutier said. "Bloodworms, huh? Not a real lucrative job."

"It seems the harder the task, the less the pay." Clay joined her in sitting.

"Okay, so you're telling me that Daigle works for Volkov? The real story is that Volkov is running a huge drug operation and has killed at least two people, three if you count little Ariel Landry on the fatality list."

"No," Clay said, shaking his head. "Volkov is the muscle. Perhaps Daigle reports to him, but they both work for somebody else."

"Who are you thinking? A Mexican cartel? What's the big one?

The Blood Alliance or something like that?"

Clay could see her already writing the story in her head. The Blood Alliance comes to Port Essex, Maine. "Could be," he said.

"What? You don't think so? You think it's the Chinese?"

Clay took a deep breath, then turned to her, holding out his hands palms up as if asking for patience. "A few days back some guy named Niles Harrington came up to me at the Pelican Perch and hired me to find a missing statue for him. Called it the *Fourth Shade*. Said it was a Rodin original his grandfather found in a Nazi treasure trove at the end of World War II. He brought it back with him, and it has been in the family ever since."

"What the fuck are you talking about now?" Cloutier asked with a pained look.

"Bear with me," Clay said. "Anyway, he shows up for his summer holiday in Maine and discovers the *Fourth Shade* missing. Stolen, presumably. The only one with access is his caretaker. Scott McKenny. Know him?"

"Don't think so. He must not be very newsworthy."

"When I talk to McKenny, he tells me that Harrington's estranged daughter comes to stay every winter. That she conned him into giving her a key and the alarm code more than once, and Harrington knows nothing about this."

"Hold on," Cloutier said. "Back it up a moment. Did you say this Harrington fellow was wealthy?"

"His name is Niles. Of course he's wealthy."

"How wealthy?"

"He's got perhaps the nicest house across the harbor on the point."

Cloutier whistled. "How much is this Rodin statue, what'd you call it? The *Fourth Shade*? How much is it worth?"

Clay shrugged. "Hard to say. It's stolen goods. Ten million? Priceless? Maybe it doesn't even exist."

"What do you mean, it might not even exist? And what does this have to do with drug trafficking in Port Essex?"

"I'm getting there if you'd just slow your roll."

"I'm a reporter. That's what I do."

"Well, just zip it for two minutes. When I tell Harrington what McKenny told me, he insists that I go out to L.A. to investigate his daughter to see if she really stole the thing."

"I suppose when you say L.A., you're not talking about Lewiston/ Auburn?" Cloutier looked at Clay and clapped her hand over her mouth, and then made a production out of locking it shut and throwing away the key.

"He sends me out in his private jet. She turns out to be a perfectly nice young lady who doesn't like her father at all. She's an artist. Could be that she felt entitled to the *Fourth Shade* and took it, sold it, and is lying to me, but I believe her." Clay flushed slightly. "It came up in conversation that she doesn't want any of her father's dirty money."

"Dirty money?"

"She was okay with staying in the home here in Port Essex because it was built long before her father invested heavily in Big Pharma. It turns out that Niles Harrington is the majority owner of a company that makes Oxy rip offs, amongst other things."

"And? Your point is?"

"Maybe Harrington is behind the heroin trafficking in Port Essex."

Cloutier snorted. "That's rich. And you come to that conclusion how?"

"Down in Boston we used to say there was no such thing as a coincidence. If two things crossed paths, well then, they were related."

"The dude is probably a billionaire with a profitable, *legal*, pharmaceutical business. Why would he become a drug trafficker?"

"I don't know, it's just a theory right now."

"Okay, so let's play along for a minute. If he's the bad guy that you've been hired to find, why does he come out of the woodwork and hire you? Why not just stay anonymous?"

"You know how they always say criminals return to the scene of the crime? Well, it's true. Maybe this is like that. He just can't help himself." Clay watched a man come into the park. He was bald. But then a little girl came running over to him and grabbed his hand. It was not Volkov. "And maybe he thought it would be easier to keep tabs on me that way?"

"Perhaps him hiring you to find the *Fourth Shade* was just a wild goose chase to disrupt your investigation into the drug trafficking in town. Perhaps you were getting a little too close for comfort to something." Cloutier stood up and looked like she was ready to go back to the Register office and start writing the story, then took a deep breath and sat down. "Yeah, send the dumbass PI out to L.A. to go see his daughter."

"The *Fourth Shade* did exist and did disappear during World War II. Charly seemed to support the story that it really was in the possession of her father, so I guess it's most likely true. Maybe he just put it in the closet, and it's not missing, though."

"Who's Charly?"

"The daughter."

"Lemme guess. She pretty?" Clay looked down at his shoes. "You fucked her? *You fucked her?* More than once? OMG. You got played. Talk about coincidence, that's just too fucking rich."

"What I'm asking is you hold off the story for a few days while I try to track some things down. If you expose Daigle, Harrington and Volkov might just go down to Brunswick and get on his private jet and fly back to Houston."

"I thought you turned Daigle over to the police?"

"I did. But then he and his wife went on vacation. They're investigating him and plan to arrest him when he gets back, I believe. If we can hold off until then, it would be great."

"When does Daigle get back?"

"Tomorrow."

"Okay. You can have until then. But I'm running with whatever I got on Monday."

*   *

Clay was in the middle of calling hotels and asking for Curtis Volkov when Baylee walked into the office at five minutes before 9:00. He never would have guessed that quaint little Port Essex had seventeen hotels and that didn't even include bed and breakfasts and the like.

"What are you doing here?" he asked her.

"Good morning to you as well," she replied.

"Sorry. Good morning. What are you doing here?"

"Last I knew I worked here?" she asked with a raised eyebrow and that shy half-smile of hers.

"I mean, you should be home in bed resting."

"I believe my home is still a crime scene. Looking for strands of hair or something like that. I probably should point out to the police that Curtis is bald, and they can skip that step."

"You should be home in my bedroom resting," Clay said.

"Oh, you'd like that, me just lounging around in bed waiting for you, now wouldn't you?"

Clay felt that he'd done his fair share of blushing this morning, and it wasn't yet 9:00. "You know what I mean. In my childhood bedroom in Gene's house… The point is *resting*."

"Speaking of your childhood bedroom, who is that chick on the poster in the bathing suit made of shoelaces? She looks pretty rested."

"Obviously you're feeling better. How's the shoulder?"

Baylee wrinkled her nose. "A bit sore. But it's going to be sore there or here, so might as well help out in tracking down that mofo. That's the plan, right? Find Curtis and turn him over to the police? Or do we get to shoot him?"

"I'm surprised Gene let you out the door."

"He was asleep on the living room couch when I left. I put a note on his chest telling him where I was."

"Are the police really still at your house?"

Baylee laughed. "I don't know. They've got a police sketch artist coming to the station at noon and want me to come by then. I figured I'd ask about the house while I'm there. You getting tired of having me around already?"

"Not at all. As a matter of fact, I'm not letting you return home until we put this thing to rest. I just thought we could swing by and pick up a few of your things once they're out of there."

"I'll stop by when the police are done with me if they say it's okay," Baylee said.

Clay shook his head. "Not alone. I'll go with you. Just text me when you're done, and I'll come get you."

"Sure thing, boss. What's on tap for today?"

"I was in the middle of calling hotels and motels in the area looking for Curtis Volkov when you came in. If you take that over, I can go pay Crystal Landry a visit and see if I can get any more out of her."

"Sure thing. Did you run his name through Background Checker?"

"Yep. What'd you tell the police, anyway?" Clay asked.

Baylee looked down at her feet. "I didn't tell them."

"Tell them what?"

"I didn't tell them that I knew Curtis. That I was buying Xanax from him."

Clay nodded. "I'll check in with my source at the PD...." He paused, then frowned. "Unless that particular well has dried up."

Baylee glanced at him, a sly look on her face. "Does that source have anything to do with your mysterious meetings?"

"Tell me again what Curtis looks like."

Baylee sighed. "Six feet. Shaven head that looks like a bullet sitting on large broad shoulders. Dark, beady eyes. And his breath smells like he eats rat shit for breakfast. Can't miss him."

"Okay," Clay stood up to leave, and then paused. "Hey, you want to see what you can dig up on Niles Harrington?"

"The dude who hired you to find the *Fourth Shade*?"

"That's the one."

"What am I looking for?"

"I don't know. Anything suspicious. I want to know if he is who he says he is."

"You got it, boss."

Clay figured that Crystal Landry would be at the laundromat by then. It was only a two-minute drive. His mind was filled with swirling thoughts about Volkov, Harrington, and Daigle. He had a mental checklist in his head, but it was slightly disordered. The pieces were not quite fitting together. He needed to have a private conversation with Donna but feared the confrontation. She was apparently pretty hard set on having him off the case.

Baylee had seemed like a wounded bird this morning, her arm like a wing in its sling. The discoloration under her eyes from being punched in the face. The soft brown of those eyes as she teased him gently made something melt inside, and any desire to speak with Donna about anything left his head completely. He knew he needed to formally end the relationship, if you could call it that, with her. Of course, then it was out the door with any more inside info from the cops' investigation. His quest to find and jail the man who had beaten Baylee up and left her mangled on the floor was making him confront all sorts of things he'd prefer not to.

Another woman was folding clothes in the laundromat. She told Clay she'd been called in because Crystal hadn't shown for work today. Clay hoped that it had nothing to do with his conversation with her the day before. As he climbed back into his Jeep, Clay cursed silently and richly. First Lobbins, then Dylan, and now, maybe, Crystal.

Clay crossed his fingers that he'd find the woman at home, perhaps sick, perhaps just playing hooky, but it was not to be. Not only was she not there, her trailer was gone. Just like that. Clay went to the park office and asked about it, but the man at the desk was rather unhelpful. The day before a crew had shown up with a big rig. The paperwork and permits were in order. They unhooked the electric and plumbing, ripped the slats off the sides, jacked it up, attached the wheels, backed the truck up to hook it up, and drove off. The whole thing had taken them less than six hours. Pretty damn efficient, they were, the guy at the desk said. LJ's Mobilehome Transport. Signed by one Danny Hart. There was a phone number, and Clay called it, being sent straight to voicemail, a gruff voice that just said the company name and to leave a message.

While Crystal was having drinks with Clay at the Side Bar and filling him in on the extent of the drug trafficking in Port Essex, her mobile home had been uprooted and shipped off to God knows where. Clay hoped that she'd gotten away safely, but he sincerely doubted it.

Crystal Landry had vanished into the ether along with her trailer.

Chapter 23

STILL FRIDAY, JULY 10TH

Clay texted Baylee asking if she could look into LJ's Mobilehome Transport. An internet search on his phone showed no website. As he was about to drive off, it buzzed with a call. "Murph. How's it going?" he said.

"I'm fair to middlin' Clay, how about yourself?"

"Well, to tell you the truth, not so good. My client, Crystal Landry, who only paid me fifty bucks, and then fired me, has disappeared, house and all."

"House and all?"

"Yep. She's missing and so is her trailer."

"Maybe she went to Oz?"

"Yeah, and maybe some sick son-of-a-bitch put her down a rabbit hole. Speaking of despicable human beings, you got anything on Volkov for me?"

"That's why I'm calling. I'm sitting next to a guy at Lucky Linda's. He has some interesting information to share. Can you stop by?"

"Be there in five minutes."

He actually made it in four.

Murphy was sitting at a table in the corner with a fellow in rough clothing, unshaven for several days, his hair tousled.

"Clay Wolfe, this is Tommy Flanders."

Clay shook the man's hand, surprised to find it soft, and pulled up a chair. "Good to meet you."

"Tommy here, he was complaining to me that his son got himself in with the wrong outfit and can't seem to fix it," Murphy said. "His boy is a lobsterman out of Eider's Wharf."

"Is that right?" Clay asked. He looked at Tommy. "Perhaps I can help out."

"I could use a drink." The man was pale and shaking, whether from alcohol abuse or fear, it was hard to tell.

Clay waved at a waitress. "A couple of Jameson's for these fellows and a cranberry juice with a splash of ginger ale for me."

Murphy raised an eyebrow but didn't say anything. Clay decided the man looked more like Dobby from the Harry Potter series than a leprechaun. Once the drinks had been brought, Clay turned back to Tommy.

"If you give me something good, I'll put $50 worth of credit on your tab."

The man squirmed. "Only fifty?"

"Don't you want your son out of danger's way? I'll take care of that as well."

"He won't get arrested?"

"I'll do my best."

Tommy knocked back half his whiskey, wiped his mouth, and seemed to come to a decision. Clay noticed that his nails were well manicured. There was no wedding ring.

"Okay. What do you want to know?"

"Let's start with your boy's name."

"Jerry. Jerry Flanders."

Tom and Jerry, Clay thought, trying his best to keep from smiling. "And he's a lobsterman?"

"Yessir."

"And he fishes out of Eider's Wharf?"

"Yep."

The man finished his liquor, and Clay held up a single finger for the waitress to bring one more. Murphy hadn't touched his yet. The waitress had the same rough look as Crystal Landry, and Clay deliberated whether to ask her if she knew the missing woman or not. One thing at a time, he thought, although wasn't everything tied in to that one thing?

"Made it a double to save me from walking," she said setting the glass down on the table.

"You know a lady by the name of Crystal Landry?" Clay asked.

"Maybe. Who's asking?"

"You seen her around lately?"

"Last I knew she was hanging out mostly at the Side Bar."

"When's the last time you saw her?"

The waitress looked up in the air, whether to think or in exasperation, it was hard to tell. "At least a week ago. Came in here and wanted to borrow some money."

"How was she acting? Anything out of the ordinary?"

"Real twitchy, even more than normal. I figure she's back on the Mexican Mud."

"Mexican Mud?"

"Yeah, that was back when she was doing it a few years back. Used to be that brown Mexican shit all around here, but now it's all white powder mixed in with fentanyl. Stuff will kill you quicker than a shark attack." The waitress walked off to another table where a man was furiously waving an empty glass.

Clay turned back to Tommy Flanders. "Your son is smuggling heroin through his lobster pots?"

"They're making him. He's not a bad man, but he got himself doing the occasional smack. When he got behind on some payments, well, he agreed to do a pick-up and delivery. After that first time, they wouldn't let him off. Said they'd turn him over to the police."

"So, how does it work?"

Tommy shook his head. "Don't really know. All I know is every Friday, Jerry picks up his pots with more than lobsters. Then he delivers the packages to some guy named Curtis. He's a mean motherfucker."

"Friday?" Clay did some mental calculations. "Today is Friday."

Tommy gave him a look as if to say Clay was not too swift. "Yep."

"And your boy makes the delivery today?"

"Yep."

"What time?"

"Three o'clock."

Clay looked at his phone. It was 11:00. "Where?"

Tommy looked around nervously and leaned forward over the small table. "You know Messier's gravel pit?" When Clay nodded, he continued, "That's the spot. Three o'clock. Today."

Clay rubbed his chin with his thumb trying to envision the old gravel pit. They used to have fires there when they were kids and they'd drink and smoke, and some of them probably did a whole lot more. He didn't think high schoolers hung out there anymore. It was a different time. Used to be that people didn't care as much if some teenagers wanted to go off and get drunk and high and have sex as long as nobody was getting hurt. Of course, now you could nibble a square of chocolate and be high as a kite, so you didn't really need to sneak off to get wasted.

"Okay, then." Clay waved to the waitress and handed her his credit card when she came over. "I'll pay for these drinks, and put fifty bucks on Tommy's credit."

"Sure. What's your last name, love?" she asked looking at Tommy.

"Flanders."

"Tommy Flanders. I'll put it on the computer under your name. Treat it like a gift card." She walked off.

"You're not a regular here?" Clay asked Tommy.

"I, uh, well not at this time of day," he said. "I mostly come in after 5:00."

Clay nodded. "You a lobsterman, too?"

"No. I'm retired. But I try to not hit the bar until after 5:00. Got to keep some rules."

Murphy stirred to life. "Hey, I resemble that remark," he said.

The waitress came back over, frowning. "Declined your card, Mr. Wolfe," she said.

"What? Why? You try it twice?"

"Three times. No go. You got another one?" She handed him the worthless plastic.

Clay pulled out his phone, thinking that Citibank may have sent him an alert. Sometimes the fraud sensors thought that buying a pack of gum was out of the ordinary and raised red flags and shut it down until he texted back the okay. Nothing. He pulled a hundred out of his money clip and handed it over. He only had the one credit card.

"Keep whatever's left over for yourself," he told the waitress.

"Thanks, hon," she said, and winked at him with a sly smile.

"Gentleman, I've got to be going," Clay said rising to his feet.

"You taking this to the police?" Murphy asked. "Or going it alone?"

"No police," Tommy said. "You said you'd handle it yourself."

Clay paused. He hadn't planned on turning it over to the police, but he still asked, "Why no police?"

"One hint of the police, and that mean motherfucker puts a bullet in my boy's head and takes off."

"What if they go in quiet?"

"They don't know the meaning of the word. The fucking fuzz is all the same. Blue uniforms, sirens, and shouted commands. No, you promise no police, or my boy don't show up today."

"Okay, no police. Tell Jerry I'll come up on them with my gun, cuff Curtis Volkov, and turn him loose."

"Jerry?" Tommy Flanders said blankly, reinforcing the notion that he wasn't used to a few scotches this early in the day. "Oh, yeah, right. Thanks. I'll let him know."

"You need back-up?" Murphy asked.

Clay eyed the man who so resembled Dobby. Murphy didn't look like much, but Clay was betting he was tough as nails. At the same time, Clay knew that Curtis Volkov had been indirectly involved in the deaths of two, maybe three people. "Nah, I'm good."

"Don't forget to pay up once you nab the guy," Murphy said.

Clay nodded. "One week on me."

He walked out with a wave over his shoulder. What to do first, he wondered? He didn't really feel like spending hours of misery calling the credit card company and the fight to get to talk to an actual human being. Of course, if he stopped by the office, he could check in with Baylee and see how she was feeling, as well. That cemented the deal in his mind. What he'd forgotten was that she was down at the police station with a sketch artist, and thus there was no reward for the forty-five minutes it took to get an answer that so-and-so would look into why there was a freeze on his account. He tried calling Westy, but it went straight to voicemail.

Clay figured it was best to get some cash if he had no working credit card. Citibank was a bit far to walk so he took the Jeep and went to the drive-thru ATM. He hardly ever went to the ATM and wasn't surprised he got the PIN number wrong. Luckily, he had the number stored in his phone, but it still didn't work. He went on inside the bank. The line was eleven people long but there were four tellers hustling people through. Definitely better than calling the credit card company had been, but the result was no better. Both his checking and savings accounts had had some sort of a freeze placed on them the day before.

The manager was called. He was about four inches short of six feet but walked like he was four inches over. His mustache was carefully trimmed. Clay was brought to his office where he then proceeded to clack away officiously at the computer. The bluster leaked out of the man as he tried to resolve the situation with several calls, all to no avail. So-and-so had left early. Some lady named Jane Donahue was on vacation. The freeze had originated from the corporate headquarters in New York City, but the reason was unfathomable.

Clay's phone buzzed. It was a text from Baylee.

All done. Still want to run me by my house?

Sure. Pick you up in 2 min. He texted back.

"I've got to go," Clay said. He handed the man his business card. "Call my cell phone when you get this straightened out."

Baylee was standing on the curb in front of the station and got into the Jeep with only one jerk honking at him for stopping in the road.

"Hey, babe, give you a lift?" Clay asked with a smile.

"If you're going my way," Baylee replied.

"How'd it go?"

"That woman cop doesn't much like me. Don't know why. Or maybe that's just a cop thing. Everybody's a suspect, even the victim. Is that a cop thing?"

Clay licked his lips. "I guess victims don't always tell the whole story," he said carefully.

"Yeah, I guess you got a point."

"The house clear to go into?"

"Yeah. All good."

The bank had still not called after Baylee had filled up the food and water bowls for Ollie, packed a bag, dropped it off at Gene's house, made a bit of small talk, and they'd gotten back to the office. Clay checked the time. It was a few minutes past 2:00. He'd have to check in later. Now, he had to get out to the old and unused gravel pit.

"You okay here alone?" he asked Baylee.

She tugged at the sweater draped on top of the desk and showed him the barrel of her pistol. "I'm good. Wasn't sure I should bring that to the police station, but now we're reunited."

"I got some business to take care of," Clay said. He was careful not to give away where he was really going for fear she'd argue that it was suicidal to go out there alone, or worse, demand to come along.

"Hopefully it has something to do with tracking down that cocksucker who broke into my house and beat me up."

"My, my, such language from such a pretty mouth."

"Didn't I just show you my gun?" she asked.

"You did."

"Don't you think it best you shut up and get out of here?"

He did.

Clay had declined Murphy's offer to come along as back up, but he sure wished that he hadn't sent Westy off fishing this morning. He'd really like that particular SEAL covering his back right about now. He tried calling again as he sat in the parked Jeep, but, no service out on the water, straight to voicemail it went. Man, this just wasn't his day for getting through to anybody on the damn cell phone.

This Curtis Volkov was both dangerous and deadly. He was not afraid to kill from the sounds of it, and was very adept, even at a distance. If it was indeed he who had shot Lobbins, the man was good. Real good. Clay would need to get the drop on the man, and he best not let down his guard once he did. Else, Clay Wolfe was a dead man.

Chapter 24

STILL FRIDAY, JULY 10TH

After Clay left, Baylee resumed her research into Niles Harrington. She hadn't had a chance to look for an address for the mobile home transportation company, but that would have to wait. This Niles Harrington, she was learning, was quite the business phenomenon. He had grown his pharmaceutical company exponentially over the past ten years. The Harrington fortune had been spread out across a variety of interests until 2009, when Niles had bought a struggling generic pharmaceutical manufacturing company outright, renamed it Succor, and invested heavily in the marketing. Sales had bloomed. Of course, buying after the crash, his timing had been prescient, setting Succor up to profit enormously during the economic boom that had followed.

The company had been branded as a rural family business with good values whose mission was to bring assistance and relief to the suffering. As a matter of fact, their slogan was "Mother Knows Best." And the generic pain medication version of oxycodone, which soon became their biggest seller, certainly did bring comfort, even if at a steep price in both dollars and addictiveness, Baylee mused, thinking of her bout with Xanax.

Niles' wife of thirty-two years left him in 2015, taking half the family fortune with her, which was just about everything except for Succor, which Niles had kept as sole owner. Baylee wished that her marriage had ended with her as a rich woman, but then she would never have answered the advertisement to be Clay's receptionist. She had fended Tammy off by saying that Clay was too much of a pretty boy for her. The truth was that even if he dressed fancy and always smelled nice, he was one tough man from a fishing village in Maine. Everything about him excited her. Not that she was ready for any sort of relationship, much less one with her boss who had an entire closetful of issues, including the drinking.

Succor Pharma was now valued at five billion dollars and offered over 4,000 generic drugs, claiming to be a major contributor to the $254 billion in savings to the public by generic pharmaceutical companies. Sure, Baylee thought with a wry grin, they are part of the solution—even if a side effect was a lifelong addiction that people couldn't afford, driving them further and further into depression and poverty. But what about the tobacco companies? Liquor, beer, and wine distributors and makers, with their slick ads and lifestyle marketing, were as much pushers as pharmaceutical companies. Hell, what about people who made chocolate cake? All of these things were supposed to be bad for you, whether or not you chose to partake of them. Of course, bakers weren't prescribing cake to customers battling health issues as a solution to their pain.

Baylee wondered what Clay's appointment was, as it wasn't like him not to keep her in the loop. Was he meeting his mystery woman? Baylee could tell when Clay had been with her, more by intuition than anything else, but she also knew that the mystery woman was not *the one*. Or even very important. Clay did not walk around like a man in love. He didn't fall into the dreamy reverie of deep passion for another being.

She didn't think that Clay was seeing the mystery woman today, even though he'd been acting strange, hiding something from her. There was a fragility buried deep under the confident Clay Wolfe that Baylee hoped he might share with her at some point. She wondered if his mystery woman was prettier than she was. Did she have long blonde hair? Perfect white teeth? Large breasts? Were her legs long and slim? What was it about the woman that attracted Clay to her? This made Baylee think about her own bruised and battered face and body. She sure was a treat for the eyes right now.

Baylee focused on finding out anything unusual, lawsuits, legal settlements, something about Niles Harrington and his company that would be helpful to the investigation. Succor seemed to make most of their revenue from opioids, but it was all perfectly legal. As a matter of fact, by producing generic drugs, they truly were doing a service by supplying pharmacies with cheaper alternatives than the name brands. As it was a private company, it was hard to know much more than what they sold and their annual revenue.

She checked the time, wishing Clay was back. She missed his banter and wit, but most of all, the feeling of safety she felt when with him, even now, in the midst of this deadly investigation. Three o'clock on the dot. Hopefully, he'd be back soon. Maybe they'd have dinner together, now that they were practically living together. Maybe he'd take her into his bed. Maybe she'd take him into her bed. Baylee Baker knew that she and Clay Wolfe were destined to be together. She just wished it wasn't taking so long to take that next step. Maybe tonight...

·   ·   ·   ·

Clay got to the gravel pit half an hour early. The entrance was blocked by a chain. He envisioned that this was the spot that the exchange—drugs for money—would take place. He wondered if he should call Donna and have the police show up as well but mentally shook his head, knowing that he wouldn't. Clay wasn't even sure that Curtis Volkov would show up. If he did come sniffing around, any police presence might scare him off. Plus, he'd promised Tommy Flanders that he'd let his son drive away, avoiding any involvement.

That is what Clay told himself. In his heart, however, he knew that *he* wanted to be the one to confront and capture the man who'd beaten up Baylee. The man who'd most likely shot Lobbins just as the lobsterman had been about to come clean. The man who'd blown up Dylan Thompson in a firestorm of fireworks for having given Clay a name. And now, Crystal Landry, the hardworking grandmother grieving over the overdose of her granddaughter, had disappeared, most likely another Volkov victim. But more than anything, he wanted to avenge the wrong done to Baylee. Just the thought of the bruises surrounding her soft, brown eyes, her wounded shoulder and arm in a sling, the swelling along her jawline, and the fear in her eyes—all this, this trail of mayhem and death, it made his blood boil.

It was odd that Jerry Flanders was a lobsterman and his father had not been, as evidenced by his soft hands. Not only not a lobsterman, but a man who did little manual labor of any sort. Clay knew that the waiting list was long for anybody to get their foot in the door, and that, depending which region you fished, up to 4,000 traps had to be retired before a single new license was issued. This almost always went to a young person who'd completed the two-year apprentice program before turning eighteen, then worked as a sternman on his father's boat for some further years. This was a way to keep lobstering as a family tradition. A person over eighteen who wanted to get into lobstering without any family connections often had to wait up to twenty-five years to get to the top of the waiting list.

Of course, it was possible that Jerry Flanders had been taken out by an uncle or cousin or even grandfather. It just wasn't that normal for somebody to slip the blue-collar world and get a job that didn't leave heavily-calloused hands. And manicured nails. Clay should have been more persistent in finding out what Tommy Flanders had done for a career. The truth was that he had been in a hurry to leave, the brown liquor calling to him, as was the frothy beer. It wasn't like he was going to quit drinking entirely. But he certainly needed to get a handle on it, and now, in the middle of this deadly investigation, being buzzed or drunk was looking more and more like a very good way to get himself killed.

The sun had passed the midway point in the sky and begun its descent into the west. It would be best to approach from that direction to put the sun in their eyes. Clay got out of his Jeep and looked at the ravaged chasm torn from the earth that was the deserted gravel pit. There were four-wheeler tracks up the far side where it was not quite as steep, and he imagined there'd been a few tumbles taken here by the unlucky who stalled out before making it to the top. There was a small indentation to the left that was protected from view at the entrance, and that is where they used to have fires, coming out here to celebrate after football victories, or just for the hell of it.

The former owners had left several large boulders deposited on the left side of the entrance, flanked by a few scrub trees. Clay had no idea what kind they were, never having developed an interest in that sort of thing. That would be a good place to conceal himself so that, when the two men were in the middle of their exchange, he could step out with his Glock drawn, the sun at his back, and force Curtis Volkov to the ground to be handcuffed. He'd then deliver the man, along with the heroin, to the police station. Baylee would be avenged. But would that be the end of it? There was still the money and men behind the entire operation. Clay had a sneaking suspicion that man was Niles Harrington. Even if he were correct, how would he ever touch him? That kind of person always had somebody else do the dirty work, always hid behind a wall of lawyers and plausible denial.

The tracks of the four wheelers up the far side of the gravel pit reminded Clay that there was a path for all terrain vehicles up to the left, behind the boulders where he intended to hide, a path perhaps impassable, but probably not for his Jeep. He could faintly see tracks disappearing into the new growth since the pit had closed twenty-five years earlier. Clay eased his Jeep onto the rutted and rocky path that was just wide enough, bushes scratching at the sides. He thought about finding a spot to turn around, but a quick check of his watch convinced him it was time to get into place. He could back out of here later with Volkov handcuffed, not only at the wrists, but to the roll bar overhead.

He turned off the vehicle and got out. He walked the short distance to the entrance and looked from several angles to make sure that his Jeep couldn't be seen and then chose the best spot to hide. He slid into place, nestled between and behind the largest two rocks, a bit of shade from the trees providing him relief from the sun, and waited. They should arrive in fifteen minutes, he thought, wondering if drug dealers were punctual. If Volkov got here first, should he approach the man and handcuff him for the cops? No, he should wait until they were both here, out of their vehicles where he could see them, get the drop on them.

The warmth of the day made him sleepy, calming the adrenalin of the impending confrontation, and his mind turned to more idle thoughts. What was it that he wanted in life? He made his breathing slow and shallow, his eyes taking in the whole of the landscape in front of him, waiting, waiting, his mind wandering from thought to thought. This ability to be the calmest before the storm was a gift that had made him a football star and, later, an effective cop and homicide detective. So what did he want? He wanted his parents back, of course, but that wasn't a possibility. He wanted Grandpops to live forever, but that wasn't about to happen, either. When he was younger, he had wanted to change the world. He wanted to help people. Clay had dreamed of confronting the man who'd sold his father cocaine, his notion of justice a bullet in the head.

As a kid, he'd devoured Louis L'Amour books. The hero was always a loner hesitant to get involved, but with a sense of justice that dragged him into the melee. Once in, he was all in. This protagonist was often deeply wounded psychically, sometimes orphaned at an early age, and although admired by women, unable to connect with them. Except for the Sackett family, which became his favorite L'Amour reads, about an extensive family. They always had each other's back, no matter what, no matter how far they had to travel. Clay had spent many a day and night fantasizing about having a huge, caring family, brothers and cousins and uncles who would come to his aid when push came to shove.

That was not the case today. Clay Wolfe's present situation was more like a L'Amour plot where the hero is one against all and must prevail no matter the odds and the situation. He smiled to himself, because it was not an entire gang of villains he was facing today, but just one man. Of course, the L'Amour hero usually had to face down the hired gunslinger or beat the toughest man around with his bare fists. That often happened only after that poor hero had bashed his way through the lower echelon of scoundrels and just prior to sending the entire evil enterprise toppling to the ground.

Typically, the champion of these westerns would end up with the woman, and sometimes he would ride on, knowing his place did not lie in domesticity. Clay thought that perhaps he would like to fall in love, to settle down, to get married, and to have a family. He rather liked the notion of getting to know a woman better than he knew himself, another being who complemented his fractured self and who might make him whole again. But there lingered a sneaking suspicion that this was not to be so, that he was destined to be a loner, always breaking his own trail, traveling light, and pushing forward towards what, he knew not. Again, the image of the soft brown eyes of Baylee Baker sprang to mind, and his blood burned with a sensation that was not vengeance or anger.

Into this vision came a truck, turning down the road, and backing up to the chain fence. It was about twenty feet from Clay. A single man sat in it. It was not Curtis Volkov. The man looked to be about forty, had a thick beard and neck, and was smoking a cigarette. This must be Jerry Flanders, son of Tommy, lobsterman, and unwilling drug mule. He didn't look much like his father. Clay wondered if bringing Volkov to justice would indeed free this man from involuntary servitude trafficking heroin. Just as likely, the real person or persons behind the sordid operation would just replace Volkov with new muscle who would resume the relationship.

A black SUV with tinted windows pulled in next to the truck, nose facing the chain fence. It was a Cadillac Escalade, and Clay almost whistled. He committed the license plate to memory, just in case something went awry. The window of the luxury vehicle rolled down about six inches. Clay was not able to see the person or people inside, the truck blocking his view, and the window barely cracked. Jerry already had his window down, his large arm resting on the door. Jerry opened his door and stepped out, pulling a canvas bag behind him. He went around to the passenger side of the Escalade and got in.

Shit, Clay thought to himself. What to do? He'd thought that both of them would get out, and he'd walk up with his Glock and order them to the ground. This changed everything. He couldn't even be sure that it was Volkov, but who else would it be? It had to be that cold-blooded bastard. What if there were others in back? No, why would they be in back? Maybe Volkov was in back and had a driver? No, then Jerry would've gotten in back. So, it had to be Volkov and most likely was just the two of them. Clay knew that he should call it off. He could come back the next Friday and bring Westy for support. He could let the Port Essex police make the bust, now that he'd seen the exchange for himself. Every Friday at 3:00.

These were the thoughts shuttling through his head as he crawled over to the Ford truck and leaned his back against the door in a sitting position. What was he going to do? The door was most certainly locked, and he couldn't even see inside the tinted windows. Point his pistol at the driver side window and demand they open the door? No, Volkov would just shoot him as he tried to peer through the glass. He could walk up, smash the glass with his pistol, and cover them before they knew what had happened. No, because that thing looked like it had windows of bulletproof glass. If that was the case, they couldn't shoot through it any better than he could.

For some reason, he found himself worming his way around the back of the truck. He had no plan, but there was no way he was going to let that asswipe dickhead drive out of here. Not after what he had done to Baylee, and what he might do next time. No, this had to be settled. It came to him then that Jerry had most likely not locked his door. Here they were, in the middle of nowhere—why would he lock the door? The transaction was most likely almost over. He could creep around the back of the Escalade, and either yank the door open, or wait for the lobsterman to exit with his money and jump up and cover Volkov.

Hoping that Volkov wasn't looking at his side mirror, Clay squirmed over behind the Escalade and then up the side by the passenger door. He came up on one knee, his Glock in his left hand so that he could grab the door and jerk it open with his right. Dust and dirt covered his body, adhering to the sweat that had sprung from his pores. He needed a backup plan if the door was locked, but he didn't have one. That particular burden was erased as the door swung open.

Clay rose to a crouch, his Glock held in both hands, pointed into the interior of the Escalade. Jerry Flanders froze in shock. His broad face quivered in fear. Clay was not looking at him. His attention was focused on the driver. The man had a lean, ex-military type of carriage, a hatchet face, and mean eyes. He also had short-brown hair buzzed across the top. This meant he was most definitely not Curtis Volkov.

"Freeze," Clay said, feeling silly at the melodrama of his words.

Both men held their hands in plain view. Jerry had an envelope in his hand, most likely packed with money. The bag lay on the seat between them.

Clay stepped back. "Get out and lay on the ground. One at a time. You first." He motioned at Jerry with his pistol.

The large man looked unsure what to do with the envelope. He swung first one leg and then the other to the ground, partially blocking Clay's view of the other man. "On the ground, now," Clay said.

The lobsterman sprawled forward awkwardly on his face, still clutching the envelope, his hands over his head.

"What do you want?" the driver asked.

"Shut up. Toss that bag out, and then slide your ass this way and get on the ground."

"Money?" The driver motioned with his chin. "Plenty of money in that envelope."

"Roll over to your right." Clay nudged Jerry with his foot. "Two rolls."

"Drugs? You want drugs? Is this a holdup?" The driver went to grasp the bag.

"Put your fucking hands on the steering wheel," Clay said.

"Make up your mind." The driver said. There was no fear in his unflinching eyes. This was not his first rodeo. "Throw you the bag or put my hands on the wheel?"

Clay was guessing there was a decent chance there was a weapon either in the bag or under the bag. "Hands on the wheel," he said.

The driver shrugged, just a slight quiver of his shoulders, and put his hands on the steering wheel.

"Grab it tight." Clay stepped forward to grasp the bag, and the passenger window dissolved into tiny glittering pieces of glass.

There was no sound of a gunshot, but Clay had been here before. He took two steps and dove behind the Escalade before the thought had time to surge through his mind. Shooter. Up on the rim of the sand pit to the east.

He crawled behind Jerry's truck and came up running hard for the protection of the boulders and trees he'd previously lain in wait behind. There was no time to dwell and plan. If he let himself get pinned down, he was done for. Surely the driver of the Escalade had a gun, maybe even Jerry. By the time he reached the safety of the boulder a split second later, a few more thoughts had followed suit. He'd been set up. It was an ambush. He was the prey, not the predator.

Clay wormed his way along the ground back towards his Jeep. He had cover of rocks and trees and might just make it if he kept his head down. The driver was yelling for him to come out and give up. His shoulder was burning, and he realized he must've been grazed. Keep moving, he said silently to himself. To stop was to die. It must have been Volkov up on the rim. He was the sharpshooter. Only Clay's sudden move to grab the bag of drugs had saved his life. As he'd shown in the precise execution of Lobbins from a distance, the man was an excellent marksman.

The whine of an engine split the midafternoon air. Not the truck. Not the Escalade. It was of a higher pitch. A motorcycle, or more precisely, the spitting of a dirt bike engine. Clay stopped behind a tree, and from one knee, peered around the side. The driver was just coming around the truck, having decided it was safe to pursue on foot. Clay shot at him. Immediately several bullets clattered around him, presumably from Jerry, if that was even the man's real name as he was obviously not an innocent lobsterman but a hired thug playing a part. The driver fell back behind the truck. Clay didn't think he'd killed the man. The bullet had hit him high and on his right side.

There was no sign of the dirt bike, but the piercing noise was definitely approaching, the sound as formidable as a wailing cat. Clay knew that upon that particular feline rode Curtis Volkov, a deadly assassin and cold-blooded killer. But the man wouldn't be able to shoot from the back of a dirt bike, would he? Clay had been about to flee for his Jeep but stopped in his tracks. Maybe he could still take out Volkov, remove this scourge from the landscape of Port Essex. He again resorted to the army crawl to change location, grimacing at the mess he was making of his clothes.

Fifty feet to his right he rose and peered around a tree. The dirt bike was just about halfway to the parked vehicles when Clay stepped out into the open and brought the Glock to bear. The dirt bike was lime green, possibly a Kawasaki, Clay thought, as he lined up the pistol in the classic two-handed officer crouch. It was definitely Volkov, no doubt about that, his shaven head gleaming in the sun, goggles covering his eyes and his teeth bared as he came flying across the road leading to the sand pit.

Just as Clay squeezed the trigger, a bullet hit the tree next to him, sending splinters into the side of his face. He dropped to the ground, clawing at the wood chips driven deeply into his cheek, knowing he'd missed, the whine of the dirt bike abruptly silenced. He risked a peek around the other side of the tree and saw it lying on the ground, one wheel spinning in the air. Volkov was nowhere to be seen.

Clay was pondering his next move when it was made for him. The Ford truck bolted forward, Jerry at the wheel. He snapped a shot but didn't hold out any real hope of hitting the man. Was he fleeing, Clay wondered? But then the truck came to a stop just past Clay, and Jerry tumbled out the door before rising up aiming a rifle over the bed of the truck. Awful far for an accurate pistol shot, but well within range of the man's rifle as he sent a flurry of shots across at him. At the same time an automatic weapon began belting out from behind the Escalade.

It was now time to make his escape, Clay thought, and broke into a run, dodging trees, bushes, and rocks, as well as bullets. It was only seventy-five feet to the Jeep, but it seemed to take hours. The shooting ceased, suggesting that at least he was out of sight, and he heard the engine of the SUV kick into life. Clay jumped in the Jeep, turned the key, and floored it. The trail went up a rocky slope, rutted, and with small shrubs starting to grow up from lack of use. Clay looked in his rearview mirror just as the Escalade slammed into the back of the Jeep, snapping his neck and almost driving him off the path.

He steadied the wheel and again stomped down on the accelerator, pushing the Jeep to the limit on this rugged terrain. There was no way an Escalade could keep up with him, he speculated, not on this derelict trail. He thought about stopping, rolling from the Jeep, and coming up shooting, but it was too risky—and all those risks pointing towards his likely death. He took a quick glance in his mirror, and indeed the SUV was nowhere to be seen.

Clay considered setting an ambush of his own and pulled over, stopped the Jeep, and leapt out to seek cover behind some trees. But the SUV did not appear, and after ten minutes he gave up waiting.

His mind was racing, adrenaline coursing through his body as if he'd just crossed the finish at Daytona, and all he could think about was getting a drink and seeing Baylee. Brown liquor would be a balm to his battered soul and body, as would the brown eyes of his receptionist. With a grunt, he climbed back into the Jeep and threw it into drive.

Chapter 25

STILL FRIDAY, JULY 10TH

"You need to report this to the police," Baylee said for about the tenth time. She had a Tequila Sunrise in her hand as she sat looking out the large picture window of the function room of the Pelican Perch. Clay had called the owner to see if it was being used, and upon learning that it was vacant, had requested its use, privacy from prying eyes at a premium.

Clay was enjoying watching her try to drink the burning liquid around the stitches in her lip. He was also starting to come down from the rush of the shootout and was wondering if seeing her right then—and bringing the whole crowd in, even Grandpops—was actually a good idea. Murph, Westy, even Cloutier would turn up eventually.

"And say what?" Clay asked. He'd gone to the office, insisted that Baylee go with him, then to home for a much-needed shower—unfortunately alone—then fresh clothes. He'd bandaged the raw crease on his shoulder from the bullet, also by himself, not wanting to let on to Baylee that he'd even been grazed. "That I had a tip on a drug deal going down, didn't turn the information over to them, went out by myself and got ambushed? First, they'd laugh at me, and second, they'd say they'll look into it."

"Good. Isn't that what the police are for?" Baylee *had* picked the splinters out of his face.

"I turned Daigle over to them, and they did nothing, let him go on vacation."

"That was just bad timing. Don't you know somebody in the department?"

Clay took a sip of his Stowaway. "Gene knows the chief."

They both turned their eyes upon Gene Wolfe who had come along with them. All three of them were armed. Maine allowed concealed weapon carry without a permit; this was the first time Clay had thought it was a good idea.

"I can check in with Walter," Gene said. His eyes sparkled, excited to be part of this adventure.

"Better not." Clay sifted through his thoughts, forming his reply. "I think there's somebody from the police involved in this drug operation."

"Why do you say that?" Baylee asked.

"I heard that the chief wants me off the case," he said.

"Where'd you hear that?" Baylee asked.

"That doesn't matter."

"Tell me if I'm wrong, but the police never like private investigators interfering with their own investigations, now, do they?" Gene asked.

"Nope. They do not. And I have to admit, I got pretty ticked off a couple of times when I was BPD. So, yes, it stands to reason they don't want me sticking my nose in, but it's more than that." Clay paused, sighed, and shook his head. "It seems that Volkov is always one step ahead of us. And not only that. If this is as large an operation as we think it is, it's gotta have a lot of moving parts. Vehicles, bank accounts, drivers, ship owners, worker bees who actually dilute and package the drugs, what have you. Cops know shit about where they live and work. They know who's got money suddenly, and they check it out. I just can't believe not a single officer in Port Essex or Belfast, say, hasn't heard rumors at least, or caught a whiff of some of this activity."

"You think somebody in the police department is tipping him off?"

"I don't know."

"How about Niles Harrington?" Baylee asked.

"What about him?" Gene asked.

"That the funny fellow I saw you with at the bar the other day?" Murphy had suddenly appeared next to Clay.

"Murph. Glad you could tear yourself away from Lucky Linda's to come meet us," Clay replied. "When was that?" he asked with a furrowed brow. And then a few pieces of the puzzle tumbled together in his mind.

"Rough time shaving?" Murphy answered instead.

"How do you know Tommy Flanders?" Clay asked.

Murphy looked at his face again. Then he looked at Clay's shoulder where the bandage created a lump under his shirt. "Shit," he said. "I don't know the man at all. He was sitting next to me at the bar and started spilling his woes. You know the rest. I called you up. Never seen him before today. I take it the rendezvous with that Russian dude didn't go so well?"

"It was a set-up," Clay said. "Volkov tried to kill me. The waitress didn't know the guy either, did she? He was too soft to be part of a lobstering family."

"How'd he know to use me?"

"I got two options," Clay said. "The first is that you're working for the bad guys."

"I'll take door number two, Monty."

"You saw Niles Harrington last Friday at the Seal Bar," Clay said. "I came to meet with him, saw you, stopped to chat and then went over to join him."

"Yeah, you were asking about that Dante thing, or Rodin, the *Fourth Shade*. Looked that up by the way. Could be possible. Haven't heard anything about it, though."

"Well, he asked about you."

"Me?"

"I told Harrington that you were the nerve center of information and that I kept you on retainer for access to that information, of sorts anyway."

Murphy clambered onto a stool as if his legs had grown weary. "Are you telling me that that rich-looking dandy is a drug dealer?"

"I don't know," Clay said.

Gene smacked the tabletop. "He knows you use Murphy for information, so he sends in a guy to lure you into an ambush."

Clay had already come to the realization that he'd been played. Not just this afternoon, but every step of the way. The big question was, if Harrington was the big cheese pulling the puppet strings of people like Volkov, who was he getting his information from to know what strings to pull? Had to be a cop. He was saved an answer by Westy and Cloutier arriving together. He'd texted both of them an invitation to this particular conversation. At the same time, he let them know that he completely understood if they chose to not endanger themselves by being seen with drug cartel enemy number one.

"This is the entire war council?" Westy asked. "A beaten-up woman, a drunk, an old man, and a guy with a bad case of acne?"

"Looks like now we've added a fat guy and somebody from the fake news to the mix," Clay said.

"Wait," Murphy said. "Am I the old man or the drunk?"

"What's the deal?" Cloutier asked.

Clay brought them up to speed on the day's events and the latest evidence implicating Niles Harrington in the heroin scheme.

"Told you I should've taken the day off. Just like that game against Brunswick when the coach had me sitting on the bench when that monster d-end blindsided you and knocked you out," Westy said just as the bartender delivered a Bud to him and a Stowaway to Cloutier.

Clay refused another beer, wanting to keep his wits about him. This was definitely looking to be a one-beer day. No matter how much he wanted some brown liquor, he knew that it wasn't a good idea with so many people he cared about at risk from some very nasty people.

"So, all you got is an estranged daughter who said Harrington's money comes from Big Pharma and the fact that the guy hired you to find a statue?" Cloutier asked. "Pretty slim pickings."

"Also, he knew that I used Murphy for information," Clay said.

"Half the fucking town knows that, and the other half doesn't give two shits," Cloutier replied.

"Harrington is making a ton of money from drugs, but seemingly all legally," Baylee said.

"What'd you find out about him?" Clay asked.

"How much is a ton of money?" Westy asked.

"He is the sole owner of a company called Succor Pharma, which is currently valued at just about five billion."

"Fuck me," Westy said.

"What is a fellow worth that much doing in Port Essex?" Murphy asked. "We get our share of millionaires running through here, but no billionaires. They own private islands, frequent resorts, and cruise on mega yachts, but they don't make it to Port Essex."

"Family home," Clay said. "From back when he was just a millionaire."

"He bought Succor ten years ago when it was worth almost nothing," Baylee said.

"And now it's valued at five billion?" Cloutier asked. "That's pretty fast growth, even for a pharmaceutical company."

"Is Succor an acronym for something?" Gene asked.

"No, I had to look it up, but the basic definition of the word succor is 'assistance,'" Baylee said.

"Oh, I thought you were saying sucker, like you know, they sucker people into getting hooked on drugs," Westy said.

"They brand themselves as a family business," Baylee said. "Their slogan is 'Mother Knows Best.'" She made a retching noise.

"Fuck me," Westy said again.

"One more thing," Clay said. "It seems that my credit card and bank account have been frozen."

"You're just trying to get out of paying the bill," Westy said.

"Actually," Cloutier said, "that's quite a bit of clout if Harrington can freeze your credit card and bank accounts."

"So, what's the game plan?" Gene asked.

•   •   •   •

Baylee had not been very happy with Clay's plan to go right into the lion's den but had acquiesced when he said that Westy would come along as protection. He wasn't sure why he had to pander to Baylee's wishes, but he kind of liked her concern. And he certainly felt better about his ex-SEAL buddy having his back. Things would've gone quite differently earlier that afternoon if said SEAL hadn't been out on his boat fishing when Clay had tried to call him.

They first swung by Westy's house to load up on weapons. Clay called Niles Harrington while Westy drove. The man answered his cell immediately, almost like he was waiting for just such a call. He seemed angry that Clay had not been answering his phone. Yes, he very much wanted to get together to discuss the latest developments about the missing *Fourth Shade*. After Clay hung up, he looked at his call history. He'd indeed missed three calls from Harrington. After all, he had had a fairly busy afternoon.

Westy lived in what used to be his parents' cottage on Spruce Island, just about a mile further out the loop road from where Baylee lived. It was a post and beam home, nothing special, but well-built and tidy. His parents had retired to Edisto Beach in South Carolina and came back for just two weeks each August, when the summer heat was at its most oppressive in the South. Clay assumed that Westy had bought the house from his parents but was not actually sure that was true. Clay had been a regular visitor when they were growing up but had only been inside a few times since high school graduation.

Clay's earlier text inviting Westy to a war council had been the final straw. The man had packed his wife and son into the Subaru and suggested they go visit her sister in Rockland for a few days. They'd taken the Chihuahua with them. The interior of the house was an open floor plan, with twenty-foot-high ceilings that made it feel like a ski lodge. The living space blended into the dining space which blended into the kitchen. Westy had a gun locker in the corner of the main room. He went back into his bedroom and got the key and returned and opened it.

He took down a folded canvas bag from the top shelf, but Clay's eyes were drawn by the weapons that nestled into the racks of the lower interior. Westy took out an assault rifle and said, "M4. Much more versatile than the M16. Plenty of power and range." He put it in the canvas bag. He next selected a slightly longer rifle. "Mark 12 Mod 1. Sniper rifle. Also allows semi-automatic fire." Into the bag it went. "Benelli M4 Super 90. A.R.G.O. system makes it the most reliable shotgun out there." He selected a side-holster, just a regular one, not the entire tactical vest, and wrapped it around his waist and then slid a pistol into it. "Sig Sauer P226. Slightly better than your Glock. No offense." He grabbed a helmet with some sort of binoculars attached to the front. "Night vision. You need anything?"

"How about a missile launcher?" Clay asked.

Westy paused. "Don't you think that might be a bit much?"

"Yes. Yes, I do."

Westy laughed. "I'm just fucking with you. I don't have a missile launcher. Not in this weapons locker anyway."

"I'm fine with my Glock." Clay patted his shoulder holster.

"Let's do it, then."

They decided to pick up Clay's Jeep, and Westy followed him out. They did a drive by of Harrington's Estate, and then pulled down a small side street. "I'll leave my truck here," Westy said. He reached behind the seat and pulled out the sniper rifle and the night vision helmet and goggles. "Give me twenty minutes and then you can drive up to the front door."

Clay filled the time by calling Don who'd been tailing McKenny since yesterday. "Got anything for me?" he asked by way of greeting.

"Not much. The man seems to spend a lot of time at the Harrington Estate. Inside, I mean. Not much time doing any sort of landscaping work."

"Where is he now?"

"Home. He went home yesterday and today promptly at six, like he had a desk job or something. Like I said, I found him yesterday at a job site talking to his workers. He then went and spent the afternoon at Harrington's. Same thing today. Out the door at eight, check in with the guys, and then back to the estate. Leaves a little before 6:00 and goes home."

"Do you see him working outside on the grounds?"

"Nope. He's inside the whole time."

"Anybody else there?"

"Niles Harrington showed his face briefly both days. He's got a guy in a suit guarding the front door. He chats with him. Other than that, he hasn't left the house. Right before McKenny leaves, two new guys show up, one goes inside, one replaces the guy at the door."

"Around the clock security," Clay said. "And sounds like McKenny is part of it."

"That's what I'd say," Don said.

"Can you keep an eye on McKenny's house for another hour or so? Then you can kick off. I need to know if he goes on the move."

"Sure thing. I'll text you if he goes out."

It was time. Clay pulled back onto Point Road, and then left through the open gate of Niles Harrington's driveway. They had timed it for full dark. It was just nine o'clock, almost forty minutes past sundown. He couldn't see any bad guys, either off in the darkness, or at the door. Harrington must have told the guard to be discrete. It seemed odd to be able to just drive up to the front of the mansion, get out, walk up, and knock on the door. Especially knowing that the man was worth at least five billion. And that he ran a major drug ring.

There must be more security on the grounds than Don had seen,

Clay thought, or in the house. Niles had to have an entire crew, ex-military sorts exchanging duty to country for the love of money. And all Clay had was one man watching his back, somewhere out there in the darkness with who knew how many spooks.

Nothing to do about it now. He knocked and waited about twenty seconds before the door swung open. Niles Harrington stood there with the ease of a man without a concern in the world. He was dressed like he'd just come off his yacht, loose white canvas trousers and soft-looking blue and white striped shirt. The clothes were so simple, so well cut that Clay just knew they—together with the shoes and the heavy watch on his wrist—cost more than his Jeep. He had a glass of brown liquor in his left hand and shook Clay's hand energetically with his right.

"Come in, Clay. Let me get you a scotch. Bowmore okay?"

"Good to see you, Niles. Bowmore sounds fine." Now that he was here, Clay wasn't sure his plan was such a good one. Shake the tree and see what falls out, if you could call that a plan.

"I got your report, Clay. I thought maybe we could talk about the next step."

"From what your daughter says, it looks like Scott McKenny was fishing around for a buyer for an expensive piece of art." Clay didn't really believe this. It was too tidy.

"I wouldn't guess that possible. The man doesn't seem…refined or intelligent enough to understand the worth of the *Fourth Shade*."

"Maybe he was put up to it by somebody else?"

"What makes you say that?" Harrington looked at the door and then the window.

Clay was now sitting in the den, an immense room of wood-paneled walls and hardcover books filling shelves that reached from floor to ceiling. Various pictures also littered the shelves, in that organized way made to look haphazard. He had a glass of that smooth scotch, the occasional small sip sliding down his throat like bliss with a hint of danger.

"A professional thief who saw opportunity?" Clay shrugged. "Do you have any enemies?"

"I have no enemies."

"I don't think I've ever met a billionaire who doesn't have any enemies." Clay failed to mention that he didn't know any other billionaires, period.

Harrington coughed, and again looked at the window, the one right over Clay's shoulder, behind his back. "Sounds like you've been investigating me, and not the thief, Mr. Wolfe."

Clay had to trust that Westy would take care of whatever was outside. His concern was the two doors, presently closed. They'd come through the one, down a hallway from the foyer, but he wasn't sure where the other led. "I need to know who I work for, Mr. Harrington."

So now they were back to Mr. Wolfe and Mr. Harrington, brass tacks, indeed, Clay thought in passing.

"You need just ask," Harrington said coldly.

"Before we get into that, I have a confession to make." Clay spoke slowly, as if in no hurry, but his heart was racing. "My grandfather and the Chief of Police here in Port Essex, well, they're great friends from way back. The chief was at the house when I called you. I thought it wouldn't hurt to ask about Scott McKenny and tell him that I was investigating him for you."

"What?" Harrington tried to hide his incredulity, his mouth opening and as suddenly closing as he choked back a response.

"I didn't say anything about the *Fourth Shade*. I said that I was on my way over to speak to you about over-billing of hours, and maybe a few missing items, and I was wondering if the chief had heard any complaints from the other people McKenny works for."

"You told him you were coming over to my house? Tonight?"

"Yes. I know you wanted to keep our business secret, but the opportunity to ask in a casual manner was just too great. So I took it. He promised to ask around." He held up his glass. "Cheers, by the way."

As Harrington made to raise his, he put his hand to his pants pocket, drawing out a cell phone. He looked at it. "Sorry, I have to take this." He stood up and stepped out of the room.

Clay let out a generous breath. By his estimation, he'd just been minutes, maybe seconds, from being exterminated. He stood up and browsed the shelves, staying out of the angle of the windows, at least until Harrington was able to call off his assassins. He'd thought it unlikely that the man would try to have him killed here in his house, for the truly rich never got their hands dirty—weren't in the same room much less in any close proximity to the crime they'd ordered.

But the tension in the room had been palpable, and so he'd layered in the fake story to prevent himself being picked off in plain sight like one of those floating ducks at the fair that people shot at. He was fairly certain that Harrington's goons were better shots than most of the people at the fair. Of course, Harrington's fake phone call might just have been a ruse to get himself out of the field of fire, but Clay didn't think so. As a matter of fact, he was willing to bet his life on it—hell, he *was* betting his life on it. There was no way he'd take out Clay now, or so Clay hoped.

There was a picture of a woman who Clay recognized as the ex-wife, and then another one of her and Niles at their wedding. He thought it odd that Harrington would still have it on display some five years after the divorce. There were pictures of a teenage Charly with a boy who must have been her brother. Then Charly graduating from college. It appeared that Niles was not yet ready to say goodbye to his family. Clay walked over to the door he had not come through, and with a deep breath, opened it. There could be a gunman behind it, but he doubted it. He was interested to know if perhaps the *Fourth Shade* was there, getting dusty in a corner, out of sight, its supposed theft just a ruse.

The room was a magnificent office, and Clay flipped on the lights, again noting the dark wood and antique furniture. There was a painting of a young woman with a blurred face in a rugged coastal setting that Clay thought might be an Andrew Wyeth, but what did he know of art? Certainly nothing about the strange art created by Charly Harrington, that was for sure. At least he could grasp the works of Wyeth, if not the worth. The desktop was clear, and the drawers were all locked. Who locked their desk drawers at home?

There was another door and Clay was just opening that one when he felt, rather than heard, somebody come into the office behind him.

"What are you doing?" It was Harrington, a shorter, athletically-built fellow behind him.

Clay turned around with an apologetic look plastered to his face. "Sorry. I was just looking for the bathroom?"

"I'll have my butler show it to you. It's down the hallway." Harrington turned. "Please show Mr. Wolfe to the lavatory, Jacob."

Like the man who had been behind the wheel of the SUV at the gravel pit, this one man had the ramrod posture and hard look to his eyes of an ex-military officer. Clay doubted that he was a butler, but the name Jacob did seem to fit the position. As a profession, Clay would guess the man was ex-special forces and hurt people for a living. He worried that Harrington had decided to go ahead and kill him and then plead ignorance with the police. Fortunately, they made it to the lavatory, and a grand bathroom it was, and then back to the den without incident.

Chapter 26

STILL FRIDAY, JULY 10TH

"Sorry to bother you at this time of night, Walter." Gene sat on his friend's porch watching the sky darken as the sun plummeted to the west. Clay had agreed to Gene visiting the chief as long as he didn't share any details of the afternoon shooting.

"Not a problem." Walter Knight was a few years shy of seventy. His short-cut hair was a grizzled gray. He had that stoop that taller men often had, especially as they aged, but he still played a pretty good game of squash and could out-swim more than half the men in his department.

"How's the wife?"

"Mary is doing fine. She'd say hello but is already getting ready for bed."

Gene nodded. Mary was struggling with some early signs of dementia. And it was late. Too late to be bothering them. "Tell her hello for me. I won't be long," he said.

"This about that drug investigation your boy is in the middle of?" Walter asked.

"He might be in over his head."

"What can I do for you?"

"I heard you told him to drop the case."

"I did no such thing."

Gene didn't blink. "Hmm. He must have gotten a wrong

impression. Have your people been able to make any progress in the investigation?"

"Lieutenant Smith has assembled a task force. I get a daily briefing. It seems the local dealer may have fled to the islands. If he comes back, we'll scoop him up. If he doesn't, we'll put out a warrant for his arrest."

"Are you aware how deep this goes? How complex this organization is?"

"What are you telling me?"

"Clay tells me that it's more than a local problem. He says that a group of lobstermen are smuggling heroin and fentanyl through their traps, and somebody is then transshipping those drugs all throughout New England. From here. Little ol' Port Essex."

Walter cleared his throat. "Who's his source?"

"Crystal Landry."

"The grandmother of the little girl who died?"

"Yes," Gene said.

"Who else?"

"That's it."

"You tell me my town is the conduit for much of New England's drug supply 'cuz a former heroin addict who works in a laundromat told your son that?"

"There's other circumstantial evidence," Gene said. "One, Jake Lobbins is shot and killed by a highly trained marksman. Two, Dylan Thompson is killed in a fiery murder—"

"First of all," Walter interrupted. "Lieutenant Smith has found no evidence that Lobbins was even smuggling drugs. Secondly, Thompson was probably smoking heroin and set off his own fireworks."

"I know," Gene said. "I couldn't make it to trial with what we have, much less win a case. That's why I'm here."

Walter sighed and stood up. "What do you want from me, Gene?"

"I don't know. Just be aware that something's not quite right."

•   •   •   •

Joe Murphy walked up to the Side Bar. One of the things about drinking all day was it was generally a bad idea to drive. He lived on the edge of town. Drank in town. Had no real need to leave Port Essex. He had a truck but rarely used it, not since he'd stopped clamming, anyway. He knew the bartender at the Side Bar, as he knew most of the bartenders in town.

Murphy figured he might as well reward himself with a whiskey for the walk up the hill. Especially as it seemed to be all for naught. Unfortunately, the bartender knew nothing, only that he hadn't seen Crystal Landry since she had been in the day before having drinks with Clay Wolfe. She'd finished her drink after he left, tried to cadge a free one, and then left in a huff. He promised to keep his ears open and let Murphy know if he heard anything. Murphy threw back a quick shot and went back out the door.

The trailer park was just down the road, heading away from his home, but nonetheless, Murphy walked the few hundred yards necessary. There was still an empty spot where Crystal's trailer had been. He knocked on fourteen doors. Nobody knew anything. One guy claimed she owed him ten bucks. Seven people didn't even know her. Five people weren't home on this Friday evening, quite possibly amongst the small crowd back at the Side Bar.

The last lady said she'd seen Crystal walk in the day before in the afternoon and stand stock-still for five minutes staring at the empty spot where her trailer used to be. The lady figured that she'd come to check out that everything was in order but wondered how it was she'd walked. She thought maybe Crystal had parked at the trailer-park office and walked over as a sort of goodbye to her old home. Then, Crystal had shaken her entire body as if rousing from a bad dream, looked all around, and walked hurriedly off.

At least Murphy was able to get the name of Crystal's boyfriend from the lady. Dale McCormick. A helluva lot of walking for a name.

He stopped at the Side Bar for another whiskey to get him home. It was late for Joe Murphy.

•   •   •   •   •

"Okay, where do we start?" Baylee asked Cloutier.

The two were in the empty newsroom of the *Port Essex Register*. The *Register* was an afternoon paper that went to press Monday to Friday. If anything happened Friday night or Saturday, it was old news and thus, often irrelevant by Monday afternoon's edition.

"As I understand it, Niles Harrington is a legal *and* illegal drug seller," Cloutier said.

"We know for a fact that Succor sells drugs," Baylee agreed. "But we are only theorizing that he has an illegal component to his empire."

"From nothing to five billion dollars in ten years is hard to believe."

"The thought being that the illegal drug trade must have been used to boost company growth."

"It's a private company. It wouldn't be that hard to do—or hide," Cloutier said.

The two women sat at a long table with computers. They were side-by-side, logged in and scrolling for information as they talked.

"Or vice versa," Baylee suggested.

Cloutier paused and looked over at her. "What?"

"A legitimate pharmaceutical company privately owned could certainly hide the source of the money used for its growth—"

"But the legitimate company also could boost the illicit opioid trafficking with drugs." Cloutier burst in and interrupted with an excited look on her rosy face.

Baylee nodded. "That was my thought. A private company can keep a great deal of their finances secret, making it a perfect place to launder dirty money and grow a business."

"Meanwhile, the legal business is funneling drugs, say fentanyl, into the illegal operation, bolstering immensely the illegal drug trade."

"A perfect complement for each other."

"So, how do we tie the legal together with the illegal?"

"It says here that China has maybe as many as 400,000 chemical companies operating across the spectrum from legal to illegal. Most of them are somewhere in between, a sort of purgatory or murky ground, legally and regulatory-wise," Baylee said.

"It was just recently that China even outlawed fentanyl for private use," Cloutier said.

Baylee was listening, typing, reading, and all the while thinking that she liked this woman, multitasking like a bird flitting from branch to branch. She knew that the woman was the newspaper's editor, a friend of Clay's, and lived with a woman named Denise. This was the first time she'd exchange more than the most basic of pleasantries with Marie Cloutier and was discovering that she had a razor-sharp intellect softened by a genuine friendliness.

"It seems that anybody in the U.S. can find a source and have fentanyl mailed to them pretty cheaply if they go on the dark web. It is basically undetectable, and besides, nobody is really looking for it. It seems the DEA is just now catching on to its proliferation in the market," Cloutier said.

"Yep. They've got offices all over Mexico working in conjunction with their government, but just two minor offices in China."

"And that includes the embassy."

"Not that Harrington would even need back-door channels," Baylee said. "He can get all the fentanyl he needs legally. Couldn't be too hard to fudge a number here or there and out the back door goes a case, or box, or however its packaged."

"There must be a pretty strict oversight."

"Like you said, the DEA is just now catching on to the problem, but it is probably easy to do on the other end. Put on the paperwork that you are shipping a thousand kilograms and add another hundred and who knows the difference. It says here that China has only two-thousand inspectors to oversee the $100 billion industry."

"That 100 kilograms mixed with heroin could turn a profit of 200 million," Cloutier said.

"Doctor the paperwork, mix it up, sell the drugs for a bundle, and feed a big chunk of the profit back into expanding and growing the legitimate business. Voilà, the perfect business marriage." Unless one mate shoots the other, Baylee thought.

"Why does China have a corner on the market, anyway?"

"Little to no laws restricting production and sale. And, unlike heroin, cocaine, or marijuana, you don't need sunshine, rain, and hardly any workers. Just a small factory."

"Yeah, it says here it's a low-cost investment that just about any entrepreneur can capitalize on," Cloutier said. "One sale and I could put my daughter through college."

"It's been around for sixty years. Why is it just becoming a problem now?"

"Big Pharma pushing their product leading to over-prescription, which in turn leads to addiction. Simple economics. If there is a demand, the supply will follow."

Got that right, Baylee thought to herself. It was crazy how easy it was to get hooked. The real pushers were the doctors, not the dealers. "So, we have absolutely no concrete evidence of any sort of wrongdoing. But," she paused dramatically, "but we *have* established that if Harrington wanted, he could easily get his hands on fentanyl. By mixing that with heroin and selling it on the street, he could have an incredibly lucrative business."

"Where does the uncut heroin come from?" Cloutier asked. "I mean, the fentanyl is practically legal, with just a bit of fudging. But he still has to get the heroin to lace with the fentanyl."

"His main home is in Houston, which is also where Succor is based," Baylee said.

"Which is not far from the Mexican border."

"So, he's buying heroin in bulk from the cartels and fentanyl from the Chinese, combining them, and then shipping them somehow up the Atlantic to be dropped off in lobster traps off the coast of Port Essex and then distributed throughout New England," Baylee said. "Seems improbable."

"But plausible."

"So crazy that it might just be genius."

"I doubt the DEA is keeping close tabs on Port Essex, Maine."

"How do we unearth any actual proof?" Baylee asked.

"Well, we either catch him red-handed with the drugs, which I find highly unlikely, or we build a case compelling enough to cause the DEA to investigate further."

"We could call it Operation Denial," Baylee said.

"Like, Duh-Niles?" Cloutier asked.

Chapter 27

SATURDAY, JULY 11TH

Clay Wolfe woke up Saturday morning feeling extremely frustrated. It might have been due to the fact that he'd gotten absolutely nothing out of Niles Harrington the evening before. At least he'd stayed alive. Westy confirmed that there were three armed men outside the windows, lurking with evil intent. He claimed that he could've taken them out easily enough. He'd called them amateurs. And then they'd suddenly stood down, two of them returning to guard duty on the perimeter, and the third keeping watch outside the window, never knowing how close they'd come to death.

The fact of the matter was that they had nothing on Harrington. If Westy had killed those three men, he would have gone to jail for murder. It'd be the word of a billionaire against two men trespassing on his property who killed his security detail. Plus, they'd have tipped their hand. Or maybe not. Harrington had certainly been suspicious finding Clay nosing through his office under the false pretense of looking for a bathroom.

Afterwards, they'd met up with Baylee and Cloutier to compare notes. The two women had come up with potential scenarios for how Harrington ran his drug operation, but there was nothing close to real proof and certainly not a whit of hard evidence. Murphy had called with the name of Crystal Landry's boyfriend and that she'd been spotted by a neighbor after her house had been stolen, but that was all. Clay made a note to try to find the man today. He was also supposedly a lobster mule for Volkov—and Harrington, if the man really was involved.

Clay had a sneaking suspicion that his frustration had nothing to do with the concrete wall that his investigation had run into but was rather something different altogether. He was avoiding the notion to the best of his ability, but the unbidden thoughts kept penetrating his consciousness, drowning out the drug trafficking case with its complex cast of characters and scenarios.

No, the cause of his vexation was lying right upstairs in his childhood bed in the form of one Baylee Baker. Her lithe figure, dressed in very little, he imagined, was safely ensconced in the bed he'd spent ten years in before going off to college. Try as hard as he might, he couldn't stop, slow, or distract himself from the image of her asleep. Her hair would be tossed lightly across her face, a face overspread by the shy smile he imagined she slept with. Then she'd roll over onto her back, tossing the sheet back, to reveal that she slept in just a T-shirt, white, no bra, and light-purple panties. Her breasts rose and fell with each breath.

With a silent curse, Clay rose from the couch and went out the door and across the driveway to the stairs to his apartment above the garage. He doubted there'd be any murderous attempts at 6:00 in the morning. He had time for one very long, and very cold, shower. It took ten-plus minutes of icy water to banish the image of Baylee sleeping, her skin so perfect, her legs sliding away under the sheets, her hair sexily across her face, leaving uncovered that shy half-smile.

He shaved, wanting for some reason to look his best. It felt good not to have the dusty aftermath of a hangover lurking in his head. Clay felt good. He felt alive. He breathed deeply and patted his hard stomach. It was going to be a good day. He pulled on tan slacks and a turquoise button-down shirt. A pair of white Chuck Taylors. It was Saturday. No need for more. With an energetic step he bounced down the steps and back across the driveway.

Gene—Grandpops—was in the kitchen, pouring a cup of coffee. He handed it to Clay and got another one. They went out to the porch and sat without yet having said a word. The sky across the harbor was gray, covering the sun, yet the morning was already sticky, with no wind to clear things out. It being the weekend and most tourists and visitors sleeping off Friday night's booze, there was almost no movement in town at this hour.

"What time did you get in?" Gene asked.

"Close to midnight."

"How'd it go out to Harrington's?"

Clay shrugged. "About as I figured. He was smooth and friendly, and I got nothing out of him." He neglected to mention that by his estimation he had been seconds from a violent confrontation when he'd headed off the action by mentioning the chief of police.

"You still like him for the kingpin?"

"Yep. His butler looks like he just walked off the Afghanistan desert yesterday after several tours."

"You slept on the couch. Does that mean Baylee is upstairs in your room?"

Clay ruminated on that statement. Images of Baylee sleeping in his bed edged into his mind again. "Yep."

"She's a fine young lady."

"Yes, she is."

"You think you might take her out to dinner sometime? Just the two of you?"

"She works for me."

"Maybe you should fire her."

Clay smiled. "How'd things go with the chief?"

"About how you'd expect. He was skeptical, to say the least."

"At least we got it on his horizon."

"For the record, he says he did not give orders for you stay away from the case."

"Hmmm. Interesting," Clay said.

"What's the plan for the day?"

"We need some witnesses."

"Live ones would be best," Gene said.

"Yeah. Murphy got the name of Crystal Landry's boyfriend. The one being forced into smuggling. Trying to figure out if I should hunt him up."

"The last few people you hunted up, somebody else hunted down."

"Yeah, that's what I don't understand. How can the chief be skeptical when so much shit is going down in Port Essex?"

"He's got Lieutenant Smith running a task force looking into the Lobbins murder. He believes that Thompson was just a stupid accident by a heroin addict. It's all pretty thin."

"I gave them Daigle on a silver platter, and they let him slide away."

"Maybe you should ask them." Gene nodded to the street.

A black and white police car pulled in the driveway behind Clay's Jeep. Two officers got out as a Ford Police Interceptor Utility vehicle pulled in behind them. The driver of this vehicle was a patrol officer, the passenger Donna—looking none too happy. She got out and walked up to the porch.

"Good morning," she said.

"What's going on?" Clay asked.

The officer who had arrived with Donna stood about ten feet behind her, his hands on his belt, while the other two policemen stood behind Clay's Jeep, one looking at the house, the other watching the street.

"We picked up Dale McCormick about an hour ago. We'd been monitoring him for smuggling drugs through his traps."

"Who's Dale McCormick?" Gene asked.

"Crystal Landry's boyfriend," Clay said.

"We're pretty sure he brought in heroin yesterday."

"Yesterday?" Clay asked. "Why'd you wait to arrest him until today?"

"We had him under surveillance. We were hoping he'd lead us to your guy. The mysterious Russian."

"And did he?"

"He gave us the slip this morning. We scooped Dale up when he showed up on his wharf to go out on the boat. But there was a window of thirty minutes where we didn't know where he was."

"So, you decided to go ahead and arrest him anyway?"

"We were concerned that he'd made the drop. We figured we'd missed our opportunity but maybe we could get him to talk. Either he still had the drugs in his possession, or he would have a wad of cash." There was a hardness to Donna's eyes that was even colder than Clay was used to.

"And did he?" Clay asked.

"Drugs were gone but he had $5,000 in a manila envelope in the glove compartment of the car he was driving."

"Suspicious but not incriminating," Gene said.

"So, he made the drop during the half hour he was missing?" Clay asked.

"Why are you here telling us this?" Gene asked.

"He confessed. Told us he made the drop this morning," Donna said.

"Now do you believe me about the smuggling going on in town?" Clay asked.

"He admitted that he'd been told he was being watched. Said the dealer called him and cancelled the exchange yesterday. Left a rental car around the corner from his house with the keys under the bumper. Told him to sneak out his back door at 5:00 this morning and meet the dealer at the old Messier sand pit."

"So did McCormick give you anything you can use?" Clay asked.

"Just one thing. Then, they made the exchange and went their separate ways."

"He gave you something on Volkov?" Clay asked.

"He didn't mention anybody by the name of Volkov," Donna said. "He said that the dealer was you. Clay Wolfe."

"Me?" Clay asked. He took the two steps down to ground level.

"Were you out to the Messier sand pit?" Donna asked, or was she Lieutenant Smith?

"No, well, um, not today," Clay said. "This is ridiculous."

"What do you mean not today?"

Clay hesitated. "I was out there yesterday."

"What were you doing out there yesterday?" Donna asked.

"I had a tip that Volkov was doing an exchange out there with a mule."

"You sure you weren't meeting with Dale McCormick like he said?" Donna asked.

"C'mon, you know better than that." How was it possible that he'd been sleeping with a woman for months who could even consider that he was a heroin dealer?

"Okay." Donna nodded. "What was the name of the mule?"

"Jerry Flanders."

"Where'd you hear about this exchange?"

"His father, Tommy Flanders, contacted me. Said his boy was being forced into the smuggling thing by Volkov. Said he wanted out. Told me they were meeting out to the sand pit for their regular Friday afternoon exchange."

Donna wrote the names down in a notebook. "I'll check into them."

"Thanks."

"And?"

Clay sighed. "It was an ambush."

"An ambush?"

"They had a sniper. When I went to approach the vehicles, he took his shot. He missed. I ran." Clay wondered if he should mention shooting the one man, but it certainly didn't seem to be a time to be offering up information.

"It appears you got away."

"You sound skeptical."

Donna scuffed her foot on the ground, took a deep breath, and looked Clay square in the eye. "We got a man in custody who just named you as the man trafficking drugs in Port Essex and that he met you out at the Messier sand pit first thing this morning. When I confront you with this, you tell me about some wild shootout there yesterday. Sounds a bit suspicious to me."

"Whoa," Clay said. "I didn't say wild shootout. I said a sniper took a shot at me and missed."

"That's a wild shootout in Port Essex," Donna said. "And you didn't report it?"

"No."

"Why not?"

"I doubted anybody would believe me." Clay wasn't sure how he was so quickly put back on the defensive. "I know it seems a bit far-fetched."

"I agree," Lieutenant Smith said.

"Volkov knows I'm closing in on him, and that's why he's throwing red herrings out there to slow me down."

"I have to ask you something," Donna said.

"What?"

"Do you mind if we search your Jeep? And maybe your apartment?"

"You'd need a warrant for that," Gene said.

"I don't have a warrant," Donna said. "That's why I'm asking. Just to clear this up."

"That's fine," Clay said. "Go ahead."

Donna nodded at the two officers who moved to the Jeep and began the search. The glove box was rifled through, as well as the center console with a variety of junk that Clay didn't even know was in there. A collection of tools he didn't remember owning, a smattering of gift cards, and some sunflower seeds amongst other things. Floor mats were pulled out, and they ran their hands under the seats. Clay stood next to Donna on the walkway, and Gene remained sitting on the porch.

It was while they were rummaging in the back of the Jeep, in the space for miscellaneous tools, that the two officers suddenly paused.

Clay could feel the tension in the air, a heavy pressure like the moment before a summer thunderstorm broke.

"Lieu, we got something here," one of them said, raising his hand.

Lieutenant Donna Smith walked away from the porch, while the driver kept his eyes pinned on Clay. She went to the back of the Jeep and peered into the opening. She did not reach her hand in.

Clay tried to remember what was in there. A ratchet and screwdriver set he used to switch from the hardtop in the winter to the soft top in the summer. That was about it, he thought. He went to follow Donna over to the Jeep. The driver put up a hand for him to remain where he was.

Donna came back over and stood in front of him. "Are you carrying?"

Clay shook his head. His Glock was in his shoulder holster, draped over the chair he'd been sitting in on the porch.

"What's going on here?" Gene asked.

"There is a sealed plastic bag of what looks to be a great deal of heroin in the back of your Jeep." Donna took out a set of handcuffs. "I have no choice but to arrest you."

"I know nothing of this," Clay said, then angrily, "Come the fuck on, Donna, don't you see what this is?"

Donna held up her hand, cuffed him, and read him his Miranda rights. "Is there anything you want to tell me?"

"He has nothing to say," Gene said.

"I haven't been out this morning," Clay said.

"Is there anybody who can verify where you were a bit more than an hour ago?"

"He would like to exercise his right to remain silent," Gene said.

"Did you exchange money for the heroin in the back of your Jeep with Dale McCormick this morning?" Donna asked.

"What's going on?" Baylee stepped out onto the porch.

Donna looked at her with surprise, suspicion, and anger. "Can you confirm the whereabouts of Clay Wolfe about an hour ago, Miss Baker?"

Baylee was not in the bra-less white T-shirt and light-purple panties that Clay had been envisioning earlier, but was nonetheless possibly even more sexy than he'd been imagining, her sleep-tousled hair, vast brown eyes filled with worry, and instead of the shy smile there was a curl of confused concern to her pouty lips.

"An hour ago, we were all asleep," Gene said, cutting off any reply.

"So, you cannot verify Clay Wolfe's whereabouts?" Donna kept her eyes pinned on Baylee.

Baylee did not reply, taking in the scene, Clay handcuffed, the officer on the walkway on his radio, the two in the driveway setting up a perimeter of police tape. The Jeep, with all the doors open as well as the tailgate.

"Were you asleep an hour ago?" Donna redirected her attention to Clay.

"No."

Another patrol car pulled up. "Okay, let's go," Donna said. She grabbed his arm and led him across to the car. One officer got out and opened the back door, and Donna ducked his head and slid Clay into the backseat.

Chapter 28

SUNDAY, JULY 12TH

Clay sat across a small table from his grandfather. They were in the expansive office of the Chief of Police. It certainly beat the cell that Clay had slept in the previous evening. The room was tastefully decorated with dark wood furniture, soft lighting, and pictures of Chief Knight's family. Nice-looking wife and kids. There were no windows in the room, perhaps why they were allowed to meet there. It would seem that Gene still had a great deal of pull with the man. But, maybe not enough sway to clear Clay completely.

"The Bail Commissioner has refused you bail until you appear before a judge at the arraignment," Gene said.

"When will that be?" Clay askd.

"Tomorrow morning at 10:00."

"Meanwhile Harrington is tidying up his heroin trafficking operation. He's probably sending Volkov out to put the fear of god into the smugglers. Heck, you and Baylee are in the gravest danger."

"Why me and Baylee?" Gene asked.

Because you're the only two I really care about in the whole world, Clay wanted to say. You two and Westy, but that dude can take care of himself. "Because I got you involved," he said instead.

"There were four bags with about a hundred grams of heroin. Plenty enough to charge you with drug trafficking instead of just using or dealing," Gene said after a pause.

"What am I facing?"

Gene shrugged. "Judges have a lot of latitude in Maine. As long as the Feds don't step in and take over."

"Can they do that?"

"If they prove you crossed state lines in the operation, or if they want to link this to a larger case, they will, and they can."

"Will they?"

"I don't know. I doubt it."

"So, if I face a Maine judge, what are we talking?"

"Up to forty years. Big fine."

"Let's try to look at the positive side."

"You have no prior convictions. You served as a police officer. You are a regular part of the community." Gene drummed his fingers on the desk. "I'd say five years, maybe as little as a couple of years in jail."

"Harrington," Clay said. "When he missed his opportunity to kill me last night—two nights ago, rather—he went to his plan B, which was to set me up."

"They lifted several very clear prints from one of the bags. The other three were clean as a whistle."

"How long until they get an answer?"

"They put a rush on it. Either tonight or first thing tomorrow morning."

"They have anything else?"

"Other than a material witness and a hundred grams of heroin in your Jeep? Not so much," Gene said.

"They're going to find shell casings from my pistol out at the sand pit if they look around," Clay said.

"You already told them you were out there the other day," Gene said.

"I didn't say I fired a weapon. I said I ran."

Gene nodded. "Anything else I should know?"

Clay licked his lips. Started to talk and then stopped.

"What is it?" Gene asked.

"I find it odd that the morning after you pay a visit to Chief Walter Knight at his house raising suspicion that there is a huge drug trafficking problem here in Port Essex, that the very next day, first thing in the morning, the police show up at my house and bust me with a large quantity of heroin."

"You're back to thinking the chief is in on it?"

"Somebody obviously planted it," Clay said.

"Yes."

"When Lobbins was shot, he said something to me as I helped lay him on the gurney. He said, 'watch police.'"

"Watch police?"

"It's been in the back of my mind ever since. The guy had just surrendered, and I saw the resignation in his eyes. He was going to tell me everything he knew."

"Your point is?" Gene appeared nettled.

"I think he was warning me that the police are involved."

"In smuggling drugs?"

"Hey, I worked with my fair share of corrupt cops in Boston. Most of us were there to uphold the law, but you get some bad apples in every barrel."

"You're telling me that Walter Knight, who I've been friends with for over twenty years, is part of this drug trafficking?"

"I don't know." Clay massaged his temple with his thumbs. "I just think it's pretty weird that you pay the chief a visit sharing what we suspect, and the next morning I'm in jail."

"And this McCormick fellow? He's taking one for the team?"

"What if he names me and in return the charges against him are dropped?"

Gene Wolfe had not made a name as a fierce lawyer by closing his mind to options. He'd been surprised to learn that his only son was addicted to cocaine. He had not been taken unaware since. "Okay, let's play that out."

"A huge drug smuggling ring that circles all of New England is centered right here in Port Essex, and yet the police haven't made a single arrest. It wasn't until a baby girl overdosed on heroin that it was brought to anyone's attention, and that was because of an ex-junkie hiring a private investigator."

"Not very impressive," Gene agreed.

"I turn up Allen Daigle as a local dealer and turn him over to the police. The next thing we know the man is 'off in the islands,' supposedly on vacation, but more likely, tipped off."

"Who'd you report him to?"

"Lieutenant Smith," Clay said.

"Donna Smith? The one who arrested you this morning? The one you've been sleeping with?"

Clay blanched. How did the old man know that, he wondered? "Yes."

Gene nodded. "The bag with the fingerprints—what do you want to bet they're yours?"

"No bet. I can't bet against myself, now, can I? But I sure hope not."

"Yeah, I hope a lot of things, but every time I turn around, this case of yours gets a little more complicated."

"That it does. Will they free me tomorrow?"

"You might be stuck in here for the next forty years," Gene said.

"I need to get out on bail and clear my name."

Gene sighed. "Judge Wilson has been assigned your case. She's an old friend. I'll see what I can do. First offense. Pillar of the community. Extenuating circumstances. Blah-blah-blah. I'll see what I can do."

●   ●   ●   ●

Baylee had been stunned. Freshly awoken, she'd watched as Clay was taken away in the police car. Gene told her about the man, McCormick, who'd said that he had delivered a shipment of heroin to his dealer just this morning, and how that man was Clay. How the police showed up and searched his Jeep and found four packets of a substance they believed to be heroin.

She'd watched from the kitchen window as a swarm of officers had come and searched his apartment, and once the warrant arrived, had sat on the porch while they searched the house. A tow truck had come and taken the Jeep away. She had been interrogated. Gene had been interrogated. And then they had all gone away and left a mess in their wake.

Baylee helped Gene pick up the house and then went and straightened Clay's apartment above the garage. She hadn't wanted it to be a mess when he came home. She had carefully folded and put clothes back in drawers, thinking all the while of the man who belonged here, next to her, and not in jail.

Westy had stopped by. Cloutier stopped by, too. They had made plans to get together the next day. Somehow, in a daze, Baylee found herself again laying down in Clay's childhood bed and trying to sleep, the day having flashed by like a fast-moving storm, thick, quick, heavy, and over before you even knew it was there.

A little before noon the following day, Gene Wolfe donned his lawyer's cap and had been on his way to the station when Baylee remembered Ollie, her cat, who had been left at home with no company, and who had probably almost finished his bowl of food. She convinced Gene that she would be fine, that there was no threat to her now that Clay was in jail, and he had dropped her and Flash at home.

Baylee, Flash, and Ollie now sat on the living room couch, as the late afternoon turned to early evening, reflecting on all that was, and trying to devise a strategy for all that was to come. Surely the charges against Clay could not stick. Or, could they? There were no witnesses, no alibi. Clay, according to Gene, had been in his apartment alone, showering, at the particular time that McCormick claimed he'd exchanged the heroin with him for the cash.

McCormick was lying. Baylee imagined that a good defense lawyer would be able to rip his testimony to shreds, if her knowledge of television courtroom dramas equated to real life. And Gene Wolfe was the best. She was convinced that if it came to trial, McCormick's credibility would be demolished.

But the fact remained that a vast quantity of what was most certainly heroin had been found in Clay's Jeep. 'In his possession,' so to speak. "What do we do about that, Flash?" she asked the basset hound.

There was no answer. Baylee wondered if no answer *was* actually an answer. No, she said to herself, there is always a way out.

Then she heard a car in the driveway. She went still, Ollie the one-eyed cat, sensing her tension, yawned and stretched, his claws expanding from his paws like that Marvel character, Wolverine. Could it be Curtis back to finish the job? Baylee disengaged herself from her tangled pets and went and retrieved her purse from her desk.

George had been a total prick, but at least he taught her one important trick. To think that she'd ever been Mrs. George McManus. Baylee McManus. She wrinkled her nose. Baylee Wolfe. She liked the sound of that better. Anyway, she thought, thank you George for the trick. Of course, it hadn't worked out so well for him in the long run. He'd bought her the gun when he was going off on a fishing trip with some buddies for ten days. It sounded like an awfully long time to stay drunk, and she'd wondered if there had been women involved, but didn't really care.

George had bought her the gun and told her to keep it in her purse. Were anybody to attack her, he advised, just tilt the purse and shoot the bastard. And she had. There was no need to waste time and motion pulling it out of the purse. Tilt and pull the trigger. That was the best and worst advice George ever gave out in his entire life.

There was a knock at the door. Light. Two taps.

Baylee looked through the living room window. There was a non-descript silver car in the driveway. On her doorstep stood that police officer. Lieutenant Smith. Donna. The one she suspected that Clay was sleeping with. The one who had arrested him this morning.

She was not in uniform, but rather wore knee-length shorts and a white V-neck with a floral pattern of summer flowers curling lazily upon it. She looked fantastic. Her blonde hair cascaded loosely, out of the bun she wore when on duty, spilling down and onto her shoulders. Baylee found herself staring at the woman's full and rounded breasts and put a hand up to her own, as if measuring, judging, and coming up short. The woman's body was sculpted, her butt filling the backside of the shorts, her calves rounded in a gentle curve, and even her fucking ankles looked fantastic.

The dilemma, for Baylee, was how could she open the door, hold her purse, and keep her hand on the pistol? Perhaps she was being overly cautious? The woman was, after all, the police. Yet, she was also the enemy. The mystery lady who was sleeping with Clay. How Baylee was certain of this fact, she had no idea, but she was absolutely convinced that Clay had been intimate with this woman. Nay, not intimate, she thought, merely friendly fucking, beautiful and impersonal like the woman's ankles.

She put the purse over her shoulder, as if about to go out, and opened the door just as Donna went to knock again. "Hello."

"Hello, Baylee."

"Lieutenant Smith, isn't it?"

"Donna." She smiled a wide and conspiratorial grin. "I'm off duty."

"Donna, then. What are you doing here?"

"Can I come in?"

Baylee thought of telling her that she was on her way out, that she had business in town, but truth be told, she wanted to talk to this woman. She wanted to know what made her tick, whether she was witty, sarcastic, intelligent, and most of all, why Clay was fucking her.

"Sure, come on in," she said stepping aside. "Can I get you something to drink?"

"Sure. What do you have?"

"I could open a bottle of red. I believe I have a Malbec aging in my wine rack." By aging, she meant it had been there since early in the week.

"That'd be great."

Baylee nodded at the couch. "Make yourself at home. I'll be right back."

When she returned with two glasses of wine, Donna was on the couch with Ollie nestled in her lap. Traitor, Baylee thought, handing the woman a glass of wine. She sat in the armchair kitty-corner to the couch. Flash, who'd followed her to the kitchen and back, curled up on her feet.

"How are you doing?" Donna asked.

"I'm fine."

"Clay asked me to check on you and make sure you were…safe."

That was before you arrested him, Baylee wanted to shout. "You know that Clay isn't a drug dealer."

"I know."

"Why'd you arrest him?"

"He was accused of being a dealer by a man suspected of being a smuggler and was then found with a hundred grams of heroin in his possession." Donna shrugged. "I had no choice."

"He's being set up."

"I have no doubt of it."

"What are you doing about it?"

"Well, for one, I'm talking to you."

Baylee thought that perhaps her face was a bit too square but could find little else to fault in her appearance. She had the fit look that came from exercise and not starvation.

"Do you have any idea who might be framing Clay?" Donna asked.

"Curtis Volkov," Baylee said.

"Ah, yes, the mysterious Russian who doesn't show up in any databases."

"He's real."

Donna flinched, looked around the living room, the very place that the mysterious Russian had beaten and could have easily killed Baylee. "Yes, of course. I'm sorry. Maybe that's not his real name, though."

"How about Allen Daigle, can't you arrest him, ask him?"

"Daigle has, uh, disappeared."

"To the islands?"

"He and his wife flew to St. Croix and checked into a resort. They were supposed to fly back yesterday. He never got on the plane. He's checked out of his resort. We don't know where he's gone."

"How about McCormick? Can you squeeze him? Make him tell the truth?"

"He's sticking to his story, so far, anyway. The DA has suggested we cut a deal with him, offer him a reduced sentence for his testimony."

Baylee stared at her, empty, at a loss, for there seemed to be no way out. Was it possible that Clay would actually go to prison for a crime that she knew he did not commit?

"That's why I'm here," Donna continued. "Is there anything else that Clay shared with you? Anything at all?"

"Niles Harrington."

"What's that? Who? What about him?" Donna leaned forward, setting her glass down on the coffee table.

"Niles Harrington owns a summer home here in Port Essex."

"What about him?"

Baylee looked out the window. She leaned over and scratched Flash behind one droopy ear, the Basset Hound groaning in appreciation. "We think he is the one behind the whole thing. He is the bank. He is Volkov's boss. It's him behind the entire drug trafficking operation."

Donna pulled a notebook out of her purse. "H-A-R-R-I-N-G-T-O-N?" she asked.

"Yes."

"So, why? Why do you think so?"

Baylee shrugged. "He made billions on Big Pharma in a relatively short period of time."

"That's it?"

"Pretty much," Baylee admitted. "That's why we haven't brought this to the police—to you—before this. We were hoping to build more of a case, but then Clay got arrested."

"Who else knows about your suspicions?"

It was all so far-fetched when spoken aloud to a stranger, to a policewoman, to Clay's lover, Baylee thought. "Nobody. Just Clay and me."

"How about his grandfather? Gene Wolfe? Has Clay confided in him?"

"No."

"You're sure?"

"Why?"

Donna licked a speck of red wine from her lip, which might have been a bit on the thin side, Baylee thought. Thin lips and a face too square.

"Why does it matter who knows?" she repeated.

"Anything that Clay claims now will be suspect, but if there are witnesses who can testify to his suspicions before his arrest, it would be much more credible," Donna said.

"It was just me. We talked about it the night before you arrested him."

"Where did…" Donna began, stopped, and composed her face, a visible shift back to a professional. "You're sure he didn't share his suspicions with anybody else?"

"I'm sure."

"I'll look into it immediately." Donna stood up. "I'll run a background check and see what I can turn up."

"Thank you," Baylee said. "I wasn't sure you'd believe me."

"Do you mind if I use your bathroom before I go?" Donna picked up her purse from beside her.

"Down the hall to your left."

Baylee went to the front door and opened it to look out at the lengthening shadows created by the sun dripping down behind the trees to the west. She hoped that she hadn't been betraying Clay's trust by sharing their suspicions about Niles Harrington. She hadn't intended to bring him up but had realized that not doing so out of spite over Donna and Clay's relationship was petty and childish. If Clay trusted her, shouldn't Baylee as well? But there was certainly no reason to involve any of the others in this mess, not yet anyway.

The woman was the police. If anybody could help clear Clay's name, it was her, and now, that seemed to be the most pressing issue. Sure, it would be great to reveal the true bad guys and see them go to jail and end the drug epidemic gripping their small town. But, first and foremost, she did not want to see Clay go to prison. She could bear the thought of him being with Donna Smith, even if it made her insides twist, but she couldn't even imagine him in jail, a convicted drug trafficker. No, his innocence must be proven, and to do this, her own petty jealousies had to be set aside.

At the same time, she'd been careful to involve nobody else. "Why?" she whispered into the shadows. Donna had said that the more that she knew, the better for Clay, yet Baylee hadn't told her that others were in the know. Westy. Gene. Cloutier. Murphy. A whole passel of people. Why had she not told Donna this? And then, suddenly, she knew. Because she didn't trust her. There was something more than petty jealousy. Why was she really here, prying? Was it really to help Clay, or was there another, more nefarious purpose?

Baylee heard footsteps coming down the hallway, into the living room, across the floor towards her. She turned and there was Donna, just three feet from her, stopped, her purse in one hand, her other hand in the purse. Would she pull the gun out and shoot her or just tilt and pull the trigger, Baylee wondered? The purse was a Salvatore Ferragamo, she knew, had instantly noticed when Donna had been at her door knocking. She'd been down in Boston a few years earlier, shopping at Neiman Marcus when she'd seen a whole display. The least expensive was sixteen hundred bucks, probably more than what a cop earned take-home in a week, she thought. What she hadn't put together was that it was far too expensive a handbag for a policewoman's salary. She'd been focused on her relationship with Clay, and of course this stunning beauty sleeping with Baylee's love had the most gorgeous purse ever.

No, she wouldn't tilt and shoot. It would be too much of a shame to ruin such an elegant accessory. Baylee's eyes fluttered to her own purse, on the floor next to Flash. A better-trained dog would sense her need and trot the handbag, gun and all, over to her. Not Flash. She looked back at Donna and saw her eyes tightening and then the sound of car pulling into the driveway broke the silent tension of the evening.

Chapter 29

MONDAY, JULY 13TH

Clay wondered how good of a friend Grandpops was with Judge Wilson after being released on his own recognizance Monday morning just before noon. She claimed that he was an established member of the Port Essex community and was not a flight risk, set a court date for August 19th and cut him loose. The drive back from Wiscasset was quiet, both men lost in their own thoughts.

When they got back to the house, the crew was already assembled and waiting. Baylee gave him a lingering hug that made his blood race. Murphy had a glass of what was most likely Gene's best scotch. Westy was twirling and tossing his Ka-Bar, the deadly steel glinting. Cloutier had her laptop open, and Clay got a glimpse of her Facebook page. Even Don, his investigator, was there.

"How's the big house?" Westy asked.

"Piece of cake," Clay said. "Time flew by."

"Forty-eight hours is a bit shorter than forty years," Cloutier said.

"I assumed that's why you're all here?" Clay asked. "To make sure I don't go back. Because, to be honest, forty-eight hours was just about two days too long."

"I found Tommy Flanagan," Murphy said. "Except his name was really Jamie Long."

"Who is Tommy or Jamie or whatever his name is?" Cloutier asked.

"Guy who set me up and sent me into that ambush at the sand pit,"

Clay said. "Go on." He looked at Murphy.

"I was back over to Lucky Linda's and noticed Justine waiting on tables, you know, the waitress that brought us drinks when we had that chat with Flanders?"

Clay nodded. He had not known her name. "Go on."

"Well, I had the thought to ask the lass if she had seen Flanders since, you know, because you put the fifty on his credit in the computer, not that you put anything on my credit." Murphy eyed Clay, but when he didn't bite, he resumed his story. "Anyway, if you remember, she'd never seen him before. He claimed that he usually came in later, but she told me she often worked the night shift and had still never seen him before. But, when she came in for her Saturday shift, there he was, large as life, sitting at a high top, probably 'cause the bar was full. Guess he wanted to collect on his credit. Only, he spilled a little bit over before he was done and owed another twelve bucks. He hands her a card, only the name isn't Tommy Flanders, now is it?"

"Jamie Long." Baylee said.

"Bingo. Jamie Long. I'd been asking the fellows around if anybody knew a Tommy Flanders and kept drawing a blank, but when I started asking about Jamie Long, well then, just about everybody had a story about him. Seems like he owes half the town money and stole from the other half. Regular dirt bag is what the general consensus was. What's more, he's a junkie."

"I got a court date of August 19th if you could move the story along," Clay said dryly.

"Okay, okay," Murphy said with his hands raised.

"Bad Dobby, bad Dobby," Clay murmured.

"What?"

"Nothing. Get on with the story."

"Okay, so I get the address for this fellow Long and pay him a visit. He's willing to talk because Volkov had promised to hook him up with a month of junk but hadn't been around since he put him up to it."

"What? Two days?"

"Yeah, he was a pretty impatient fellow. Said he had to pay a buddy double for a high earlier in the day, and he was pretty pissed off."

"Does he know where Volkov is?" Westy asked.

"Yes. He's scared to death of him. Talked tough, but he wasn't going to pay him a visit. But he did say if we put the fucker behind bars, he'd testify against him. No dice if the man is walking around on the free side, but if he was locked up? He'd sing like a bird. I think Volkov has fun knocking ol' Jamie Long around once in a while."

"Murph, where is Volkov?" Clay asked. His voice was patient, but his eyes were not.

"One Point Road."

"That's Niles Harrington's address," Clay said.

"Thought it might be. Didn't get a chance to check it out. Long said that Volkov is staying in the guest house of some big estate."

Clay wracked his mind and a blurry image of a house down back of Harrington's mansion flitted vaguely into his mind.

"Let's go brace him," Westy said.

"Slow your roll," Clay said. "We don't have any proof against the man."

"Murph just said that this Long dude was in for the ride if we put him behind bars," Westy said.

"*If* we put him behind bars. We need proof before we start pointing fingers. Plus, it sounds like Jamie Long is less than a reliable witness," Clay said.

"I might be able to help with that," Cloutier said.

All heads swiveled to her. "What?" Clay asked.

"I found Daigle, or rather, I found his wife, though truth be told, she found me."

"Allison? Allison Daigle?" Clay asked. It was less than two weeks ago that she had hired him to investigate whether or not her husband, Allen, was having an affair. He wondered, idly, if it was better in her eyes that he was a heroin dealer than a cheater.

"That's the one. Called me up yesterday out of the blue and said she had a story for me. How her husband surprised her with a vacation to St. Croix, and while there, confessed everything to her. Crying and all that stuff. Said they were going to lose the house, he'd made some bad gambling decisions, owed the wrong people too much money, blah, blah, blah. They told him they were going to kill her first, and then him, if he didn't agree to sell heroin for them. They said nobody would suspect a local lawyer of also being a junk dealer."

"And nobody did until Clay had me follow him," Don said. "Just a respectable professional chatting it up here and there. But if you looked closely, there was always some sort of exchange."

"He told Allison that he had fake passports for both of them. That they could disappear and start a new life," Cloutier said. "They went round and round all week. He was more afraid of Volkov than of having to face the music with the police. She finally convinced him to come back, though."

"He's back in Port Essex?" Clay asked.

"Yep."

"Where?"

"She wouldn't tell me. She said that she was willing to cut a deal. Wants me to be the go-between them and the police, and when it's done, the story is mine to print."

"No way he's walking free," Westy said.

"She said he'd be willing to take a couple of years but no more. In return, he'd testify against Volkov. She said that he could also put Volkov's boss behind bars. Said he had video and audio of the man that would slam the cell door shut on him for quite some time."

"Harrington?" Clay asked.

"She wouldn't say."

"You believe her?"

"I don't know what else the play would be," Cloutier said.

"So, we take it to the police," Don said. "We know where Volkov is. We got two people willing to testify against him. They go out to the end of Point Road and arrest the guy. Case closed." His voice was high, and it was obvious that this was getting a little more intense than he cared for.

"I had a strange visit yesterday," Baylee said. "From the police."

"Who?"

"Lieutenant Smith paid me a visit. Donna Smith. She was off duty, checking up on me, wanting to help clear Clay's name," Baylee said. "Supposedly."

"Supposedly?" Clay asked.

"She was asking a lot of questions," Baylee said. "About what we know and/or suspect."

"Isn't that what the police do?" Murphy asked.

Clay looked from face to face. The room was spinning with memories, thoughts, insinuations, and plots. Was Donna part of the drug trafficking? That was the central question nagging at him, but there were so many others… Why? Was she using him? And, how could it be true? All these nasty thoughts competed with the image of Donna naked in bed.

"Yeah, that's what I thought at first. She wanted to know what I knew. What Clay suspected," Baylee was saying. To Clay, the words sounded as if they were coming from a million miles away.

"If she is truly trying to clear Clay and bring the perpetrators to justice, isn't that exactly what she would be doing?" Don asked.

"Yes, I suppose," Baylee replied. "But she got real odd when I told her that we suspected Niles Harrington."

"You cast suspicion on a local billionaire pillar of the community who has donated to every charity in town and paid for the high school's new gymnasium, and you expect her to take that in stride?" Gene asked.

"I guess."

"But what?" Westy asked.

"Tell them," Cloutier said.

"Tell us what?" Murphy asked.

"She seemed more interested in who we'd told about suspecting Harrington than any of the details as to *why* we suspected him," Baylee said.

"What'd you tell her?" Clay asked, banishing the images, memories, and misgivings from his mind.

"I told her that you'd only shared that information with me," Baylee said.

"And then what happened?" Cloutier prompted.

"She asked to use the bathroom and when she came out, she walked up behind me with her hand in her handbag."

"And?" Murphy asked.

"She had a gun in there," Westy said.

"That was my thought," Baylee said. "But maybe it was just because I had a gun in my handbag?"

"You felt like she was going to shoot you?" Clay asked.

"I don't know. It was strange. And then Marie pulled into the driveway, and the moment passed."

"You should probably tell everybody," Gene said, looking at Clay.

Clay looked around the circle of friends who had pulled together around him and who he was imperiling, and knew that he didn't have the luxury of secrets, even if he didn't want Baylee to hear him speak the words, to know, to be hurt by his words and what they signified.

"I've been sleeping with Donna Smith for the last six months," he said.

Murphy barked a sharp laugh and shook his head. "Don't that beat all."

"You're in a relationship with that woman?" Cloutier asked.

Clay looked at the floor. "No. It was just sex. And it's over."

"So, she's the afternoon delight," Westy said.

The phone buzzed in Clay's pocket. He pulled it out with the intention of silencing it, but then realized this was not the time to be ignoring calls. He hit the button and put it to his ear without saying anything.

"I need to speak with you," the voice on the other end said.

"Hello, Crystal," he replied.

Chapter 30

STILL MONDAY, JULY 13TH

"That was Crystal Landry," Clay said, hanging up the phone. "I'm going to meet her in an hour." He looked at the time. "At two o'clock."

"Where?" Gene asked.

"Koasek Park."

"I'm going with you," Westy said.

"She said to come alone."

"Fuck that," Westy said. "Last time we let you go off alone you almost got killed."

"Last time I was with you I almost got killed."

"I had the situation well in hand."

"Neither one of you should go anywhere near Koasek Park," Gene said. "Perhaps you're forgetting that it was Crystal Landry's boyfriend who just got Clay arrested? This is a set-up if I ever saw one."

"I don't think so," Clay said. "I think she's on the up-and-up."

"Let's get the police involved," Cloutier said. "Maybe not Lieutenant Donna Smith, though."

"I've got my questions about the chief, to be honest," Clay said. "This is all going down on his turf."

"You don't think Donna is involved?" Baylee asked, eyes flashing.

"That's not what I'm saying," Clay said hurriedly. "I'm just thinking there might be others on the take, you know, even if just to look the other way, and possibly to pass on information."

"Okay, so, no police," Gene said. "But that doesn't mean you should go out in the middle of the woods and meet with some former junkie whose boyfriend just framed you."

"She has something important to tell me. And I trust her. Strange as it sounds, she's the only one who hasn't lied to me or tried to manipulate me or buy me."

Gene snorted. "Not that you could say the same for her boyfriend."

"Believe me," Clay said emphatically, "I'm going to ask her about that."

"And I'm going with you," Westy said. "Seeing as your Jeep was impounded you probably need a ride."

"Take Westy," Baylee said.

"Okay." Clay caved in. "In the meantime, what's the plan?"

"I need to get together with Allison Daigle and work out the details of her husband surrendering to the—" Cloutier seemed on the verge of saying *to the police* but stopped herself. "Of his surrender."

"I'll go with you," Baylee said. "Let Operation Denial commence."

Cloutier snickered. "Duh-Niles."

"Inside joke," Baylee said.

Clay wanted to say no, that he didn't want her in danger, but he knew better. "Okay, then. Murph, how about you go pick up Jamie Long and bring him back to your place for safekeeping."

"How do you suppose I manage that?" Murphy asked.

"Tell him you got a handle of whiskey," Westy suggested.

"I don't keep liquor in my house," Murphy said.

The entire group looked at the man who spent most of his waking hours in bars. Clay realized that it made a certain amount of sense, for if he was never home, why would he need liquor there? "I'll give you the money to pick up a bottle," he said. He reached into his pocket and pulled out his money clip. There was a five and two ones. He really needed to figure out his banking situation.

Gene pulled out his wallet and peeled off three twenties and handed them to the man. "What do you want me to do?"

"Maybe have a conversation with the chief? Tell him we have several potential witnesses who want guarantees. See what he has to say," Clay said.

"That's a sure way to get them all killed if the chief is in on things," Westy growled.

"Yeah, I had a thought on that. You know the other night when we went out to Harrington's?" Clay waited for Westy's nod before he continued. "I told Harrington that the chief knew where I was. That's when he backed off having me killed."

"Which wouldn't have mattered if Walter was in on the whole thing," Gene said excitedly.

"And you'd be dead," Baylee said.

"Westy had my back," Clay said. "All the same, let's hold off on involving the police for now."

"Why don't you come with me instead?" Don said to Gene. "I was going to go back and keep an eye on the Harrington Estate, see if there's anybody coming or going. I could use somebody riding shotgun. Especially if you bring a shotgun."

"I can help with that," Westy said. He was not smiling.

Crystal had told Clay to park in the back-parking area for Koasek Park and then to take the path on the left and just begin walking. She would find him. Westy pulled over well short of the lot and slid out of the car. He reached into his bag of tricks behind the seat and came out with the M4. He'd indeed given the Super 90 shotgun to Gene as he rode off in Don's Toyota Corolla. Clay slid over into the driver's seat; Westy thumped the door to let him know he was all set, and the two went their separate ways.

Clay couldn't help but smile as he thought of Grandpops riding off with a shotgun across his lap and a blanket over it. Westy had tried to convince him to put it in the trunk, or at least in the back seat, but the old guy had asked what good it would do him in either of those places. Clay's grin dried up as he realized that Gene and Don were going to stake out a drug kingpin and his sick and twisted henchmen. He should have tried harder to steer them clear of the center of the inferno. This brought him back to the *Fourth Shade*. He wondered if any part of the story that Harrington had woven for him was true; more and more he was coming to the conclusion that it had been nothing more than a concoction to distract him while at the same time keeping tabs on him.

Once Clay was parked at the trailhead, he picked up his phone and sent a quick text to Don and Gene in a group message. **Stick with McKenny if he goes anywhere.** That would certainly be the safest alternative.

Clay had put on a light summer jacket, more to hide his shoulder holster than for appearances, and he now patted the Sig Sauer P226. He wished it were his Glock, but the police currently had that pistol in their possession. Truth be told, there wasn't much difference between the two weapons. Time to go find Crystal Landry and try not to get killed at the same time, he thought, as he climbed out of the truck and started down the path.

Not so long ago he'd wandered down this same path with Donna as he told her about unmasking Allen Daigle as Port Essex's local drug dealer. Then, they'd fucked in a small clearing. Now, in his mind, she was a prime suspect in one of the largest drug-trafficking operations—what Baylee had called Denial, or Duh-Niles—in all of New England. He'd sure screwed the pooch on this one, literally and figuratively. Now he was meeting an ex-junkie whose boyfriend had just framed him, and he was in danger of getting fucked again.

"Over here."

Clay looked to his left, and there, behind a tree, was Crystal Landry. He veered off the path towards her.

"Follow me," she said. She led him to the same small clearing that he'd rolled around with Donna in. It was, indeed, a small world.

"What's the deal?" Clay asked when she stopped, turned, and faced him. He could feel the hair on the back of his neck prickle. Was there a gunman lining him up in his sights even now, he wondered?

"Heard you got arrested for dealing heroin," Crystal said.

"Because your boyfriend framed me," Clay replied.

"It wasn't him that framed you. He was just the one that pointed the police in your direction."

"Why?"

Crystal looked at him like he was a moron. "So they wouldn't torture and kill him, of course."

Put that way, Clay thought, he couldn't really blame the guy. "Who?"

"Curtis Fucking Volkov," she said.

"What does this have to do with me?"

"Dale doesn't want any part of this. He wants out. But he doesn't want to go to jail, and he certainly doesn't want to end up upside down, gutted like a deer."

"Understandable. Again, so what do you want from me?"

"I want you to do the job I hired you for," she said.

"Didn't you also fire me?"

"C'mon, I was just testing you. I didn't really fire you."

"And this doesn't have anything to do with the fact that Volkov is now trying to find and kill you?" he asked.

"Fuck that peanut-head," she said.

Clay grinned. He couldn't but help like this feisty lady. "Okay. You want me to find the people that supplied the heroin that killed your granddaughter and put them in jail."

"Kill the fuckers if you have to."

"Things have gotten a little bit bigger and more complicated than I thought," Clay said. "I believe that a very wealthy man by the name of Niles Harrington is the money behind the trafficking."

"You get a gold star, Mr. Wolfe. And that is where Curtis Fucking Volkov is staying right now."

"I knew that. In the guest house."

"Did you know that they've been holding off on making shipments because the heat has been too hot? You sure stirred up a hornet's nest for them. They think now that the spotlight has been thrown on you, it's the time to move the product. Then they're going to take a breather. No more heroin in, no more heroin out, not until this blows over."

"How do you know all of this?" he asked.

"Dale," she said with a shrug of her shoulders. "They got him by the balls. I been hiding out at his place."

"They haven't been making any shipments out?"

"When they had him set you up for the fall, Dale heard Volkov asking when they were going to move the junk, said that two weeks of product had the bunker filled to the gills, and that rich snob was telling him to relax, everything was going to be okay."

"The bunker? The bunkhouse? Is that what they call the guest house?"

"No fucking clue."

"So they're going to have to move it, and soon. When?"

"Tonight. As soon as it gets dark."

"How do I trust you?"

"You got any kids, Mr. Wolfe?"

"No."

"You ever held a baby girl in your arms?"

"Sure." A few times, never for long, he thought.

"They killed my grandbaby, Mr. Wolfe. And I want them to pay for it. And you're my only hope."

"Okay, Crystal. If you find out anything more, you got my number. Anything at all."

Clay walked out the path hoping that he had not just been fucked for the second time in a week in those woods. He didn't think so. Crystal Landry might be rough around the edges, but he liked her.

Chapter 31

STILL MONDAY, JULY 13TH

Clay returned and picked Westy up where he'd dropped him earlier. Clay slid over, letting the man drive his own truck. He started to tell Westy about the conversation, but his friend said he'd heard. Clay started to reply, opened his mouth, closed his mouth, and wondered how the heck this former SEAL had gotten close enough to hear their conversation when he'd actually been wondering if Westy had eyes on him at all.

Clay's phone buzzed.

Text from Gene. McKenny and some goon on move. Should we stick with them?

Clay replied. Yes. Find out where he goes and then come back to the house.

"What do you think?" Westy asked. "Is she telling the truth?"

"She sounded sincere to me."

"Crystal was hell on wheels as a young woman, but she's had her nose to the grindstone for a few years now."

"So, you think we should trust her?" Clay asked.

"I don't trust anybody, brother. Not even you."

"What?"

"You'd sell me out in a second if that hot receptionist of yours asked. She's got you twisted in knots."

Clay nodded. "You got a point there. I'd sell your ass out if the paper boy asked, though."

"Good to establish lines in the sand," Westy said. "So, we go take them down with the drugs tonight, but we go expecting to be ambushed."

Clay texted Baylee. Tell Allison Daigle that Volkov should be out of commission by TMRW.

"Do we bring the police in?" Clay asked Westy.

"Hell, no. It sounds like they're rotten to the core. Especially that tamale you been dipping your wick in."

"Yeah, I think you got that right," Clay said. "What do you think about the chief?"

"He seems like a good guy, but either he's in the know or he's seriously bad at his job," Westy said. "Small town like this, smuggling in a shitload of heroin regularly, then shipping it out all over New England—and he doesn't have a clue?"

"Grandpops said something about his wife having health issues. Like maybe he's been distracted."

Clay's phone buzzed with a text from Baylee. Will do. Should be back within an hour.

As they pulled back into the driveway of his grandpops' house, Clay asked one final question. "If we do capture Volkov, Harrington, and a few other thugs tonight, what do we do with them? Turn them over to the police? If the chief is involved, that wouldn't do a damn bit of good."

"You figure that out. I got an errand to run," Westy said.

"Errand? Like what? Pick up a gallon of milk?"

"I'm going to swing by and sneak-and-peek the Harrington estate. It was dark the other night. Never even realized there was another house."

"Sneak-and-peek?"

"Recon."

"Want me to go with you?"

"You know how you slow me down when we go scuba diving together?" Westy asked.

Clay got out of the truck and went inside, pondering.

He'd made no headway in his quandary of what to do with a passel of bad guys if, indeed, the Port Essex Police Department was corrupt, when a car pulled into the driveway. It was Baylee, alone.

"Where's Cloutier at?" he asked.

"Had to do something with her girlfriend. She said she'd be back here by 5:00."

"What did Allison Daigle say?"

"We told her that we were going to blow this thing wide open tonight, and Cloutier was running the story tomorrow afternoon in the *Register*. She said that Allen would turn himself over to the DEA first thing in the morning if Volkov was out of commission. He'll cooperate fully if they're willing to deal, which I imagine they will be."

"The DEA is a great idea. Isn't there somebody working out of the Lincoln County Sheriff's Department connected to the DEA?"

"Detective Sergeant Barry Howard."

"You're on top of this," he said.

"Not sure how it should be handled." Baylee sat down on the couch and he joined her. "I mean, we should probably just turn the whole thing over to him now. He can call in the troops, and they can arrest the whole kit and caboodle of them."

Clay shook his head. "First of all, even if they were inclined to believe us, they're not going to barge into a billionaire's house without dotting their i's and crossing their t's. Just that single warrant would take way too long, and how many other houses and cars does the man own? Plus, unless they have very good reasons to compartmentalize, people in law enforcement talk to each other, especially when something big is afoot. They would definitely contact the Port Essex Police Department. But I tend to think neither of those things matter, because they're not going to believe us, not until we produce Daigle, Long, and McCormick. And none of those fine citizens are going to dare come forward until Volkov is behind bars."

"Yeah, how'd that go? McCormick is willing to testify as well?

What else did Crystal have to say? How exactly are we blowing this drug operation up tonight?"

Clay told her about the meeting with Crystal. Once he was done, they sat silently, chewing over the details.

"The plan is to take them down just after dark?" Baylee asked.

"Yep."

"Is that even legal?"

"I've been hired to expose the drug operation in Port Essex. That gives me the legal right to go where the case takes me." Clay said the words with much more assurance than he felt, not actually sure how well that would stand up in a court of law. Still and all, he had a feeling that if this went well, the authorities weren't going to be looking too closely at legal niceties given their own obliviousness. "If I have reasonable suspicion that a crime is taking place, I have every right to go onto Harrington's estate without a warrant."

Clay's phone buzzed with a text from Gene.

McKenny rented a U-Haul and is now back at Harrington's with it.

Clay texted back. Are they loading it?

No.

Come back to the house. We have plans to make for tonight.

K.

"Sorry to put this on your plate," Clay said to Baylee. "You can walk away. Take a trip. I bet your boss would give you a couple of days off."

"Don't you try to coddle this little woman," Baylee said. "Volkov didn't knock you around and kiss your mouth with his stanky breath."

"Sorry." Clay raised his hands in surrender.

"Besides, I doubt my boss would give me time off. He's kind of a dick."

"Probably has to be to keep you in line."

"He sexually harasses me," she said.

"How so?"

"Words, mostly."

"Has he ever touched you inappropriately?"

They both sat as if frozen to the edge of the couch, about a foot apart, staring at each other, even their breathing having fallen into rhythm, the rest of the world falling away.

"No."

"What would you do if he did?"

"Hard to say."

"What if he kissed you?" Clay leaned in a fraction of an inch.

"I guess I'd know if he did." Baylee tilted her chin and ran her tongue over her lips.

The sound of a truck pulling into the driveway pushed them away from each other. Clay stood and went to the window. "Westy," he said.

Westy was finishing up drawing out a map. Don and Gene were also back, and Clay was filling them in on all the updates. Gene, particularly, was adamant that they should involve the DEA—and as soon as possible. Clay relented for a couple of reasons. He rationalized that he didn't want his grandpops around for the potential violence brewing at the Harrington Estate. He also had to admit that it made sense, but he didn't want them interfering in what had become a very personal matter.

Gene called the sheriff's office in Wiscasset and managed to get put through to the cell phone of Detective Sergeant Barry Howard who was under contract to the Maine Drug Enforcement Agency, working out of the Lincoln County Sheriff's Department. It seemed that the name Gene Wolfe still carried some weight, and Howard agreed to meet with him at seven o'clock. Gene would lay their cards on the table and wait for a text from Clay to pull the trigger that would bring in the cavalry. If he didn't hear anything by nine, he was to share the final piece of information that a huge drug shipment was currently on the road out of Port Essex in a U-Haul. This would mean that Clay and the others had failed.

They had been unable to reach Marie Cloutier, not that Clay

wanted her at the showdown. She'd probably come to the realization that she was in over her head. Perhaps she'd shared what was going on with her girlfriend, Denise, who had promptly told her she was crazy and convinced her to step away and merely write the follow-up story, not *be* the story. At least, that's what Clay was hoping.

It was just about six o'clock when Joe Murphy walked in the door carrying a rifle. The weapon was short, squat, and deadly looking. The stock was folded down, allowing Murphy to easily conceal it under the light jacket he wore.

"What are you doing here?" Clay asked. "You're supposed to be keeping an eye on Jamie Long."

"He's taken care of," Murphy replied. "And I'm not going to miss this shindig."

"What do you mean 'taken care of'?"

"He's more than halfway into a handle of Allen's. He's pretty content right now."

"You don't have to be part of this," Clay said.

"It's been some time since I shot anybody," Murphy replied.

Clay's phone buzzed with an incoming call. He looked at the screen. It was Cloutier. It appeared everybody was going to show.

"Hello," he said.

"Clay? I'm sorry," Cloutier said. "I think I saw the *Fourth Shade*."

"What?"

"She's sorry that you have to die," Curtis Volkov said. Clay recognized his nasty tone immediately; the voice was like fingernails on a chalkboard. "Do you know who this is?"

Clay put his cell phone on speaker. "A woman-beating, drug-dealing, baby-killing scumbag," he said. The others drew closer to listen. This had gotten their attention.

"Ha. That could be any of a number of people," the discordant voice said. "But in this case, I am Curtis Volkov."

"What do you want?" Clay mouthed the words 'he's got Cloutier' to the crew.

"Do you know what Volkov means in Russian?"

"Dickhead?"

"It means 'wolf,' Mr. Wolfe. You see, you and I are not so very different."

"Other than the fact that you are a psychopathic pig-fucker?"

There was the whack of a blow followed by the sound of Cloutier screaming in pain. "Let's try to be a little bit more civil, Mr. Wolfe. It would behoove us all," Volkov said, the manic edge of a sociopath limning his words.

"Okay. I'm sorry," Clay said. True, he'd been venting his anger and frustration, but he was also trying to buy time to think. "Please tell me. How is it that we are the same?"

"Well, for one, we both like that pretty kitten of a receptionist of yours, Baylee Baker."

Gene put a hand on Baylee's back to reassure as well as to caution silence. It would not do for the man to know they were in the middle of a war council to plot his downfall in just a few hours. Clay was forced to bite his lip. He drew a deep breath and blew it out.

"And we get a rush out of hurting people, don't we, Mr. Wolfe?" Volkov said. "Tell me it didn't feel good when you shot my man at the sand pit the other day."

"There was a certain satisfaction," Clay said.

"It is not so wrong to hurt some people, don't you think? Your enemies, for instance?"

"It depends who your enemies are."

"Why is that? You, I am sure, have heard the old adage that there are two sides to every story. The world is not black and white, Mr. Wolfe. Why should you decide who is good and who is bad?"

"I am going to suggest that the man who is a heroin dealer and is currently holding a woman hostage is bad," Clay said.

"But you want to hurt me and my employer. Should I not take steps to protect myself? Would you not hurt somebody to protect yourself? How about to save that Miss Baker? More importantly, don't you want to kill me because I have your friend and will likely torture her?" Volkov's voice dripped from the phone with false comradeship.

Clay did not know how to respond. He worried that anything he said would only inflict pain upon Cloutier, so he said nothing.

"I will take your silence for agreement," Volkov said. "It is okay to hurt your enemies, to protect yourself and those you care about. How about if it is your duty? As a police officer, did you ever shoot somebody? Put them in a choke hold? Taze them?"

"Yeah, I guess so. What is it you want?"

"Who determines your rules, Mr. Wolfe? Who is it that decides the police should increase their enforcement against crack in the ghetto while at the same time turning a blind eye to cocaine littering your college campuses? Who decides why the rich get tax breaks and the middle class do not? Why does O.J. Simpson walk free and Donald Trump get elected your president, Mr. Wolfe?"

"The Constitution," Clay said. "Rule of law, Declaration of Independence. Judicial precedents…." His voice trailed off weakly.

"Don't be an idiot. Those are pieces of paper to be interpreted any way you like, much like the Bible."

"Congress, then."

"They are just mouthpieces, Mr. Wolfe."

"Yes, for the people," Clay said.

A harsh, barking laugh that sounded like a seal erupted through the speaker. "True, Mr. Wolfe, they speak for the people, but not for all of the people. Not even for most of the people. They are the conduit by which the wealthy control this nation of yours. It is the rich who make the rules. It is the moneyed aristocracy that imprisons the poor and glorifies those of means."

"I suppose you could look at it that way," Clay said carefully.

"Much like your wars, Mr. Wolfe. Korea? Vietnam? The Persian Gulf? Afghanistan? Hundreds of thousands of people being killed because your government directed it. Your soldiers kill those that your Congress says need killing. Is it for democracy? Revenge? Oil? Or maybe just to make the wealthy wealthier."

"What is it that you want from me?"

"I want you to admit that you would kill somebody if you thought it was your duty and that that duty might itself be misplaced," Volkov said.

"Okay, sure. I guess that can happen."

"Could you be mistaken, Mr. Wolfe, is the question?"

"I could be."

"So, you would kill for self-preservation, to protect those you care about, to defeat your enemies, and for a possibly misplaced sense of duty," Volkov's voice dripped over the phone. "It sounds like we are not that different. And from there, it is a short jump to the next level."

"Next level?" Clay asked.

"Killing those of impure blood, the weak, the mentally deficient."

"And who has impure blood?"

"Do you know that Hitler was also a wolf? His family name means 'father wolf'. The three of us are all, each in his own way, like the mythical werewolf, stalking this earth, stamping out the evil vampires who are trying to take our way of life. Isn't that the saying, here in Maine? The Way Life Should Be."

"I thought you Russians hated Hitler and the Germans for what they did to you in WWII," Clay said.

"Not at all. Hitler attempted to free us from our oppression by the Jews. After the war, my grandfather walked away from the army while in Germany and disappeared. A few years later he surfaced in the United States. It was Hitler who freed us from the gypsies and Jews overrunning our lives."

"Who do you work for, Volkov?"

"I work for myself."

"Your kind always does the dirty work for somebody else. Who is it?"

"My grandfather worked for the KGB. My father worked for the CIA. Me? I am a freelancer."

"I find no record of a Curtis Volkov in any database."

"Ah, of course, Mr. Wolfe, that is not my real family name. My father had a different name than my grandfather as I have a different name than my father. It is a matter of convenience. I took it on a few years back to honor my hero and idol, Adolf Hitler. Unfortunately, 'father wolf' had to die, as now, do you."

"Where are you?" Clay asked. "Are you even in Port Essex?"

Again, the seal barking laughter. "Wouldn't you like to know?"

"What do you propose?"

"Her life for yours, Mr. Wolfe. A simple trade."

"Okay. Where?"

"Not so fast, Mr. Wolfe. I will call you at 9:00 this evening to tell you where to go. Any funny business, and the woman dies."

The phone went dead.

"What are we going to do?" Baylee asked. "I mean, you can't give yourself up to that sadistic fuck."

"He's not going to let her go," Westy said. "Not a chance. She knows too much, is a pillar of the community, and a journalist. He plans on killing you both."

"He's buying time until the U-Haul is loaded and on the road. Then he'll set up a meeting to kill me and make it look like I killed Cloutier," Clay said.

"Most likely he'll plant evidence making it look like you did it to shut her up," Westy said. "We have to move forward with our plan. We strike at 8:00."

"That's a death knell for Cloutier," Gene said, shaking his head. "We have no idea where they might be holding her."

"She's with them," Clay said. "At the guest house on the Harrington estate."

"You can't be sure of that," Gene said.

"Yes. She's there. Her first words on the phone: she told me she'd seen the *Fourth Shade*. I had no idea what she was talking about, but it gradually dawned on me she was giving me a clue as to her location.

Of course, that is where Harrington put it while pretending it had been stolen. In his guest house. She was letting me know where she was."

"I don't know how that helps us," Gene said. "As soon as we show up to confront them, they'll put a bullet in her head."

"We could intercept the truck after it leaves the house. Once on the road," Westy said. "Then go back and save Cloutier."

"Can we manage that without the men in the truck putting out a distress call?" Clay asked. "I think not. Plus, I want Harrington to go down for this as well. If we can't tie him directly to the drugs at his house, all of his money is going to buy a plausible deniability case that will wreck any sort of prosecution."

"We have three witnesses that will name him," Baylee said.

"A drug mule, a junkie, and a dealer?" Clay asked. "Harrington's legal team will tear them apart. It will be their word against a respected billionaire with a long history of generous donations to local charities, including policemen's widows and orphans' funds and volunteer fire fighters, the whole shebang. No, the drugs have to be found at the Harrington estate, and that, along with the testimony of the witnesses, might be enough to at least concern the man."

"I think that was the point of that conversation," Murphy said.

"What?"

"That money makes the rules."

"Not always," Clay said. "Sometimes the little guy wins."

"Not in real life," Murphy said.

"You want out?"

"Nah. I've always believed in lost causes."

Clay stood up and walked to the window looking out over Port Essex and the harbor beyond. Just on the other side, out that long tip of land, was the Harrington estate. That was where the bad guys were. That is where the drugs were. That is where Marie Cloutier was. And thus, that is where they must go.

"Here is what we're going to do," he said, turning back around.

Chapter 32

STILL MONDAY, JULY 13TH

Weston Beck thought about taking his boat but opted to launch instead from a private cove he knew about a mile from Harrington's estate. It had been ten years since his last combat mission, but he dove regularly. He pulled his scuba gear out of the back of the truck. The LAR V Draeger rebreather ran on 100% oxygen. Unlike typical scuba equipment, it recycled the exhaled breath into a closed circuit where it filtered for carbon dioxide. The reason was simple. This prevented expelled bubbles which might rise to the surface and give away the diver's location. It was only good up to depths of seventy feet, but that wouldn't be a problem today. The system was small, compact, and front-loaded, making it an excellent choice for shallow water operation.

Into a waterproof bag he packed his sniper rifle and his assault rifle along with his field glasses and a roll of duct tape, essential equipment for any campaign. It took only minutes for him to gear up, and he wasted no time easing into the water. It wouldn't do to have some teenagers drive up looking for a bit of privacy come upon a frogman disappearing into the ocean. The team certainly didn't need the Coast Guard to come patrolling the shore looking for him and messing up the operation.

On a good day, the ocean just off the shore in Maine was murky, and he used a muted flashlight. He had his Rocket Fins on but was unable to go full speed due to the rugged coastline. It was not exactly open-ocean swimming. He had to pick his way through rocks, while hugging the coastline. Still, he made the distance in under an hour. He eased from the water into the rocks east of the Harrington guest home. They provided plenty of cover for him to discard his scuba gear, stowing it neatly away in the bag once his weapons had been removed. He stowed the bag under a rock, up high, and secured it just in case the tide rose that far.

Westy checked his watch. Clay arrived in half an hour. One hour until sundown. He slung the Mark 12 Mod 1 sniper rifle over his back and cradled the M4 as he went up over the lip on his belly and wormed his way forward to a small copse of spruce and scrub brush. He took his field glasses from his belt and did a careful surveillance of the target and the area around it. The house and grounds were quiet. Too quiet.

•   •   •   •   •

Baylee rode shotgun as Don drove the back way to the Harrington manse, Murphy in the back with the short squat assault rifle he called the 'widowmaker' across his lap. She held her Smith & Wesson Shield in her right hand, the short pistol molded into her palm. Westy had offered her a rifle, but what did she know about shooting a rifle? No, she would stick with what she was familiar with.

Don pulled to the side of the road. Westy had carefully gone over the details of the rough map he'd made of the estate with them. Just around the bend, about 200 yards ahead, was the entrance to the guest house, which had a separate driveway than the main house. Right next to them, behind the bushes, was a hole in the fence Westy had cut on his earlier visit. Baylee and Murphy got out of the car with a caution from Don to be careful. He would be keeping watch on the entrance to the driveway.

Sure enough, a hole big enough for Westy lay behind the bushes, making it spacious for both Baylee and Murphy. With a wave of his hand, Murphy moved off to the right. His destination was the cover of several large rocks. Baylee had to go further, to get within range for her small pistol. There was a circular stone well about fifty yards from the front door of the house with a wooden roof over it. Baylee idly wondered if this was to stop rainwater from getting into the well, or was it just for aesthetic purposes?

If there was anybody patrolling the grounds, there would be little cover. Still, she couldn't be seen from the house until the last twenty yards, the view blocked by a line of fir trees. Baylee worked her way slowly forward staying as flat as she could, all the while feeling the small hairs on the back of her neck rise up, waiting for the bullet that would leave her twitching on the ground. She wondered what had been on George's mind as he lay dying after she shot him. She wished she had a Xanax, just one, to take the edge off, to settle her anxiety, and to calm her mind.

Baylee reached the fir trees. This was the test. There was no cover at all for these last twenty yards. There was nobody visible in the driveway. No movement from the house. She turned to look back over her shoulder but could not see Murphy. She took a deep breath, one last look, and then sprinted forward in a crouched position, driving her legs and diving behind the stone well, her breathing ragged with adrenalin, exertion, and fear.

Once she'd settled her breathing, Baylee risked a glance over the top of the well. There was no movement. No sign of life. It was all very quiet.

* * *

Clay pulled up next to Don and asked if everything had gone smoothly. The man told him everything was to plan so far and that nobody had come or gone from the guest house of the Harrington estate in the last twenty minutes.

This next part was the test. There was a small gate across the end of the driveway, and more than likely there would be guards. After all, they were moving what Clay guessed would be at least 500 kilos of heroin with a value of upwards of 150 million dollars. Much less than that and they wouldn't have needed a U-Haul to move it, Clay had reasoned.

The plan was to drive through the gate, which wasn't built to withstand a two-ton automobile traveling thirty miles an hour. From this direction the entrance of the drive would be easier to hit at that speed, also giving him the element of surprise and getting past the guards before they could shoot him. Once past, Murphy would provide covering fire to prevent them from following him.

With a deep breath, Clay pressed the accelerator to the floor and went hurtling forward, cutting the wheel for the forty-five-degree entrance and slamming through the wooden gate. He saw no guards. That was strange. He passed by Murphy who had come to a crouch next to a boulder, his widowmaker at his shoulder. The dirt driveway ended in a cul-de-sac in front of the house and he came to a skidding halt in a cloud of dust.

Clay opened the door and rolled from the car, pulling the Sig Sauer from the shoulder holster as he came to one knee over the trunk with the pistol aimed at the front door. Nothing. Where was the U-Haul?

His phone buzzed in his pocket. With one eye still on the house, the pistol in his left hand, he wrestled the cell out with his right hand. He recognized the number as the one that Crystal Landry had last called him on.

"Crystal?" he said as he answered it.

"I know where they're hiding the heroin," she replied. Clay listened, shaking his head grimly, then pocketed the phone.

"We gotta go," Clay yelled waving his arm over his head. Westy was already coming at a jog, and Baylee came around the well at a run. "I'll tell you in the car," he said. They piled into the Subaru, Westy riding shotgun and Baylee in back. They stopped for Murphy farther down the drive. At its entrance, Clay honked and waved for Don to follow them, and then squealed onto the road as he called Gene.

"Are you with the DEA right now?" he asked.

"Yes. What's up?" Gene asked.

"We had the wrong location for where the heroin is being stored. The correct place is Country Lane, number 54. Still in Port Essex. Tell them to come now. We're going to be tight for time, don't have a plan, but we'll try to slow them down and save Cloutier. It's a ranch, but there is an underground bunker out back. Tell them to come now."

"We're a half hour away," Gene said. "You want me to call the chief?"

"No. If he's in on it, Cloutier is dead. We'd be walking into an ambush." Clay hung up the phone. "You get all of that?" he asked the car occupants.

"How do you know all that?" Westy asked.

"Crystal called. They just had Dale McCormack make his last drop out there. They were too busy to meet him. Kinda shows how desperate they are, using a guy who just got out on probation to run more stuff in."

"We just driving in shooting?" Westy asked. He lounged comfortably in the spaciousness of the front seat, even with an assault and a sniper rifle.

"We'll make a plan when we see the lay of the land, but they're set to transport in twenty minutes." It was four miles to the address. They did it in under ten minutes.

Somehow Don managed to keep up with them, and they were standing in the trees at a corner of the road looking across at the ranch house before the nine o'clock deadline. The last remnants of twilight allowed them to see the U-Haul in the driveway. A man was shutting the back door and latching it. It looked like it might be Volkov. Two others were climbing into the truck. There was nobody else in sight.

"Okay, here's the plan," Westy said. "Clay, you and Baylee hustle around the back and find the entrance to the bunker. That is where they'll have Cloutier. Don, you and Murph get down there across the road in cover. Don, you take my sniper rifle. I won't be needing it. I'm going to block the U-Haul in with the car. Let's go." He clapped his hands lightly as if he'd just given out the fishing assignments for the day.

Clay and Baylee scuttled across the road, she with her Smith & Wesson and he with the Sig Sauer. They disappeared into the dusk and trees. Don and Murphy were working their way down the road to get into a better spot for cover fire, careful to not expose themselves as they did. Westy went back to the Subaru, hoping that Clay had left the keys. He had. He laid the M4 on the passenger seat, and then moved it so the barrel was on the floor and the stock came up at an angle that would make it easier to grab.

Without a second thought he pulled the car onto the road and drove under the posted speed limit of forty-five to the front of the ranch. The U-Haul had been started and Volkov was at the driver's window when Westy pulled across the driveway blocking the truck from leaving. He grasped the M4 and stepped out bringing the weapon to bear across the top of the car.

"Freeze," he yelled.

At the same time a gunshot from the house exploded the windshield. He dropped to his knees, rolled, and came to a prone position with the M4 peeking around the back of the car. There was no movement in the house. The truck was empty. Volkov was nowhere to be seen. He knew that they would have to come to him, if they wanted the heroin out of the front driveway. He could be patient.

A man came in a crouching run alongside the truck where Westy had no clear sightline. From across the street a shot rang out, and the man dropped to the ground. This was followed instantly by a muzzle flash from the house, and Murphy stumbled forward and fell in the road.

Westy sent a burst into the house, and the tire next to his head blew out. He rolled back the other way, to the front of the car.

A man came running across the yard firing an automatic weapon, and the Subaru shook with the impact, the top peeling back like a tuna can being ventilated by a can opener. Several bullets erupted out from where Don was in position, and the man turned the barrage across the road into the trees.

Westy came to his feet and put four rounds in him just as the U-Haul lurched forward and smashed into the car, shoving it into the middle of the road. Westy was knocked to the ground and lost his grip on the M4. The truck reversed, cut the wheel, and started to accelerate down the street.

There was no rifle fire from Don. There wasn't time to retrieve the M4. Westy came to his feet, took three running steps, and jumped up onto the passenger-side running board of the U-Haul. He yanked the door open, and Volkov, one hand on the wheel and the other holding a pistol, put three shots past his face. He swung out wide on the door to avoid being hit, grasping the mirror, and then rolled up over the hood.

For a split second Westy and Volkov were staring wide-eyed at each other with only the windshield separating them, and then Westy's hand found the driver's side mirror and he twisted around, his feet finding the running board on that side. With his right hand, he delivered a blow through the open window. The vehicle lurched into the ditch but then back onto the road as Volkov again turned the pistol back towards Westy.

He slammed his open palm into the Russian's neck, but it had little effect. In desperation, Westy let go of the mirror, preventing himself from falling backward off the running board by clasping Volkov's neck, and reached his left hand into the truck, grabbing the man's wrist just as he pulled the trigger. The bullets whistled past his ear, way too close for comfort, deafening him. He grunted and then twisted the wrist savagely, the pistol clattering to the floor.

That's when they hit the tree. Westy was flung forward, his hands wrenched from Volkov's neck by the impact, and his arms bruised as they were wrested free of the window. He was brought up short by another tree, the young birch exploding into fragments, faring slightly worse than Westy's ribs. With a groan he came to his feet and stumbled back to the truck. The whistling noise of the bullet from earlier was the only sound he could hear, whining in his ear like a giant mosquito.

The airbag had deployed, filling most of the interior. Volkov was lying flat across the seat, and Westy thought at first he'd been knocked unconscious. Then he realized the man was searching for his pistol on the floor of the passenger seat. Westy grabbed both of his feet and snatched him out of the truck. It was easier than he thought, and he fell backwards.

The two men came to their feet, and Volkov pulled a blade. Westy pulled his own Ka-Bar free from the sheath at his back. They circled warily, the steel glimmering in the faltering light. Volkov stepped to his left and slashed out with his right. Westy bobbed his head and punched the man hard in the jaw. He felt the bones crunch under his knuckles. Most people forgot that you could also throw punches in a knife fight.

In pain and desperation, Volkov brought the knife back across in a slashing movement throat-high, but Westy parried it with his arm, deflecting the steel upwards, and again punched the man hard in the gut, the air leaving his body with a whoosh.

He clung to the knife weakly, still deadly, and Westy had no intention of dying. He gashed the bicep of the knife arm and threw another punch, this time into Volkov's throat, and the blade went clattering free, the man collapsing to the ground like a suddenly deflated balloon.

Chapter 33

Clay and Baylee were behind the ranch house when the first gunshot split the air. They froze momentarily.

"C'mon. Westy knows what he's doing," Clay said. "Aren't the doors to these places usually in the side of a hill or something?"

They both looked around. The backyard was flat as could be.

"How about that shed back there?" Baylee asked pointing.

"That sounds about right," he said.

They skirted the edge of the yard, staying in the shadows, listening to the gunfire out front. When they reached the shed, Clay pulled on the door. It was locked from the inside.

"What kind of shed locks from the inside?" he asked.

"I don't imagine we have much of an element of surprise now," Baylee said.

"Fuck it."

He stepped back and then forward, kicking the wooden door. It wobbled but remained intact. He put his shoulder into it, and it cracked, and another kick splintered it. He was about to put his shoulder through the remaining door when Baylee held up her hand for him to stop, reached in, and unlocked it. They looked at each other, nodded, and she pulled the broken remnants open on the hinges.

Out front there was the sound of a revving engine and then grinding metal on metal. They both paused to listen. The sound of a truck flooring it down the road could clearly be heard. Clay looked at Baylee and shrugged, and they went into the shed.

There was a workbench along one side with tools, a wheelbarrow leaning against the wall, and a lawnmower in the center of the small space. It all looked very normal. Except for the knothole in one of the boards underneath the mower. Clay hooked his finger in the hole and pulled up the three-foot board. And then two more. There was a trapdoor. It was locked.

"The DEA should be on the way. They won't kill her if they're trapped down there. Not if they know that we know where they are," Baylee said. "We can just sit right here and make sure nobody leaves."

"If the truck gets away, Harrington will probably slide on the drug trafficking charges," Clay replied. "So, why would he go down on a murder charge if he didn't have to?"

"Right now, he's thinking it's kidnapping at the worst, and his legal team will tie that up in court until nobody cares anymore. Then he pays a fine and walks away."

"That is, unless he thinks he won't be found down there." Clay banged on the door. "What if they have another exit?"

"That would be a problem." Baylee stepped to the door just as the sound of a lock turning could clearly be heard from the trapdoor.

Baylee stepped back and centered her Smith & Wesson on the trapdoor. Clay grasped the handle, looked up, and mouthed the words *one*, *two*, *three*, then pulled the door open. Light spilled out from the opening, illuminating a ladder that led fifteen feet down into the earth. The sides appeared to be concrete, not much bigger in diameter than a trash barrel.

"Clay Wolfe. Come on down," a voice boomed up hollowly from below.

Clay looked around the shed. There must be a camera somewhere.

"And bring your pretty receptionist with you."

"That sounds like a pretty stupid idea," Clay yelled down. "Why would we do that when the DEA is on their way?"

"Because if you don't, I'll kill the journalist."

It was definitely the slightly arrogant and condescending voice of Niles Harrington. "You wouldn't do that. Do you really want to go to jail for murder?"

"Do you really believe, Mr. Wolfe, that I would build a safe haven with only one way in and one way out?"

"How do I even know Cloutier is down there?"

There was the sound of rustling about and then a scream that lingered in their ears long after it was over.

"It will be so much harder for her to type now that she only has nine fingers. She will only be able to write stories now that don't require q, a, or z."

"I'm going down there," Clay whispered to Baylee. "You stay up here."

She nodded, as if agreeing, and he started down the ladder towards the light below. He held his pistol in his hand as he clambered downward, his eyes watching for any sign of movement.

"In here, Mr. Wolfe."

Clay dropped the last few feet into a crouch, pistol extended in front of him. The cylinder opened into a room that could have been the living space of any middle-class house in America. Except there were no windows. Niles Harrington sat in a leather recliner, his feet up on a footstool. His elbows were on the armrests and his fingers were interlaced underneath his chin. He might have been welcoming a guest for tea. In the doorway behind him stood one of his goons, the short-wiry man who had acted the part of butler the other night. He held a pistol in his hand and looked to know how to use it.

Standing in the opposite corner was Scott McKenny with his arm crooked around Marie Cloutier's neck and a pistol pressed to her head. She was holding a red-stained rag to her hand. Tears were flowing down her cheeks, and her eyes were angry. There was an open doorway out both sides of the room. Clay pointed the Sig Sauer at Harrington.

"That isn't very pleasant of you," Harrington said. "Where is Miss Baker?"

"She had an appointment and had to go," Clay said.

And then he heard feet drop behind him, and he risked a glance over his shoulder. Baylee stood there with her pistol leveled at McKenny. She sidled past him and into the room, her Smith & Wesson never wavering in her hand, aimed directly at McKenny.

"Ah, there you are, Miss Baker. I am so glad you could join us," Harrington said.

"Looks like a Mexican standoff," Clay said. "Speaking of Mexico, is that where you get your heroin from?"

Harrington laughed. "Right to the point, Mr. Wolfe. That is where it initially came from. Not across the border, but like most of the immigrants, through the port of entry, in this case, via ship."

"Do you mind telling me why?" Clay asked. "I mean, you were already rich. What was the point?"

"Things were a little dicey there at the beginning, Mr. Wolfe. I had everything I owned tied up in Succor trying to get the company in the black. I'd gambled my entire family fortune, and the heyday of opioids and other pharmaceuticals had not yet bloomed. It was then that Jacob here," Harrington tilted his head back to indicate the man behind him. "Jacob, as you may have guessed, is not really my butler, but is the head of my security detail. He came to me with the suspicion that one of our employees was stealing small amounts of fentanyl. When we looked into it, we discovered he was mixing it with low-grade heroin and making a killing."

Clay nodded. "Where some saw theft, you saw opportunity."

"Exactly, Mr. Wolfe. That is why I like you. You have that rare ability to think outside of the box. We took the concept, multiplied it by thousands, applied modern business methods, harnessed the power of our legal businesses, and voilà, we had a winner."

"And you were able to cook the books, mix the heroin with fentanyl you were importing for your legal drug trade, just dropping a zero here and there so that nobody would notice," Clay said, trying to buy time. If the DEA showed up, a shootout would certainly attract attention.

"Don't worry, Mr. Wolfe. The trapdoor has been shut behind you and this bunker is completely soundproof. Nobody is going anywhere." Harrington leaned forward in his chair. "But I do admire that you have done your homework. What else is it that you think you know?"

"You load the heroin laced with fentanyl into commercial ships that drop a speedboat over the side off the coast of Port Essex and load up the pots with more than just lobsters. You pay, coerce, and force lobstermen to smuggle the drugs to you. I assume you bring the heroin to this bunker before dispersing it throughout New England." Clay took another step closer to Harrington.

"Bravo, Mr. Wolfe, bravo."

"You have Allen Daigle deal locally, and Donna Smith keeps you out of trouble with the police, sweeping any dirty laundry under the rug."

"I understand you and Donna had a bit of a fling," Harrington said.

"You sent me out to Los Angeles to get me out of town for a few days while you cleaned up a few items. Does it bother you that your daughter, Charly, detests the ground you walk on?"

Harrington laughed. "Charly and I have a perfectly good relationship. As a matter of fact, she told me that the two of you had a bit of a roll in the sack. You do get around, Mr. Wolfe."

"She told you that we...?"

"I asked her to...delay you, Mr. Wolfe. I didn't ask her to fuck you. I guess she must have found you interesting."

Clay felt his cheeks burn. "You said...." He trailed off in embarrassment. "It was her that turned me onto you being behind the drug trafficking, you know."

"How's that?"

"She mentioned that she wanted no part of you because your money came from Big Pharma."

Harrington clucked his tongue. "Silly girl. She always did talk too much. But, did you really think that anybody would turn their back on five billion dollars? You are the foolish one, Mr. Wolfe. Did you think she could live in L.A. on an artist's income?"

"Is there even a *Fourth Shade*?"

"Yes, Mr. Wolfe. When weaving lies, it is always best to wrap them around a truth, don't you think? It is currently right upstairs in the house, sitting in plain sight in the living room."

"What now?" Clay asked.

"Now? Well, now you drop your guns. And then we kill you, Mr. Wolfe. Why would you drop your guns, you ask, if we're just going to kill you? I give you my word that I will let the two women walk out of here, as soon as things quiet down and I am safely on a plane to…let's just say a place where there is no extradition, if that becomes necessary."

"And if I refuse?"

"Then I have McKenny shoot the journalist in the head. I will save Miss Baker to give you a second chance to change your mind."

"Not before I kill you." Clay saw Harrington's eyes flinch.

"Are you willing to exchange the lives of these two women for the satisfaction of killing me, Mr. Wolfe? I think not."

Could he really trust Harrington to not kill Baylee and Cloutier, Clay wondered? Perhaps. Perhaps not. Was there any chance of winning a shootout? Maybe, but Cloutier would certainly be dead. "Have you ever killed anybody, Scott?" he asked.

"Sure," McKenny replied. "I did a tour in Afghanistan."

"Up close and personal? Brains all over you. A woman's brains, Scott." Clay risked a look over and saw McKenny's eyes shifting nervously in his broad face. He also saw Lieutenant Donna Smith now standing in that doorway with a pistol pointed at Baylee.

"Your gun, on the floor, now, Clay," she said.

She still looked beautiful. Evil, yes, but damn good looking. "Okay. I'm going to lay my gun on the floor," he said.

"No," Baylee said. "If you put your gun down, I'm going to start shooting."

"We have no chance," Clay said.

"I am not going to lose you," Baylee said. "I need the job."

Cloutier dug her elbow halfway to McKenny's spine and dropped to the floor as his grip on her neck let go. Baylee shot him, the bullet shattering the elbow holding the pistol.

Donna pulled the trigger and missed a lunging Baylee completely.

Clay shifted his gun and snapped a shot at Donna. He missed as she dove back out through the doorway.

The butler goon behind Harrington shot Clay, the bullet glancing off his hip. He was knocked back against the wall by the force of the blow. Another bullet hit the concrete by his face, sending chips like angry bees into his cheek, for the second time in the past week. Wood splinters on one side and concrete chips on the other. He steadied his hand and shot the goon in the face.

Cloutier stood up and punched McKenny in the neck, which turned his screaming in pain into a wet gurgle.

Baylee went through the doorway after Donna like a lioness closing in for the kill.

The doorway led to a bedroom. A king-sized bed dominated the room. There was a bureau on the left and a door on the right. Baylee approached the door with the pistol in her right hand. The cop had to be behind the door. The woman who had been sleeping with Clay. There was nowhere else to hide.

There was no sound from the main room. Everything had grown chillingly quiet in this buried bunker in the woods of Port Essex. Her own breathing loud in her ears, Baylee crept slowly forward. She called for Donna to come out. There was no answer. She reached out her left hand, counted to three, grasped the knob of the door and yanked it open. As the door swung open with a bang, she felt a hand grab her ankle and jerk, sending her crashing to the floor. The fall knocked Baylee's gun from her hand, and it went clattering into the corner.

Donna rolled from under the bed and came to a knee with a pistol extended in front of her. Her finger was tightening when Baylee lashed out with her foot and kicked the woman in her perfect fucking calf, sending the shot into the ceiling, and Donna tumbling forward onto her face. Baylee scrambled for her gun in the corner, but felt her foot grasped and twisted, spinning her from her knees onto her back. She again kicked out with her free leg and heard a splat as her foot connected what must have been Donna's face.

The hell with her gun, Baylee thought, she was going to kick this bitch's ass without it. She lunged towards the woman and wrapped her hands around her neck and slammed her head back into the floor several times. Donna's eyes rolled back in their sockets, and Baylee rose to a crouch, one hand entwined in the luscious blonde hair, pulling the bitch to her feet, and then smashed her fist into that pert nose sending Donna sprawling onto the bed. Baylee grabbed her by the belt and pulled her up to meet another crashing blow to the mouth.

Donna whimpered, covering her face with her hands and begging Baylee to stop. Her rage not yet muted, Baylee pulled her to her feet and slammed the palm of her hand up under her chin, and then threw her to the floor. She dropped with her knee into Donna's solar plexus and heard the rush of air explode from the woman's lungs.

"I think she's had enough."

Baylee looked over her shoulder to where Marie Cloutier stood in the doorway.

●   ●   ●   ●

Harrington was gone. Clay had to trust that Baylee would be fine. He couldn't let the kingpin escape. Cloutier seemed to have McKenny well in hand. He had to go after Harrington.

Clay limped through the doorway the billionaire had disappeared through. It was a small kitchen, what you might find in a tiny New York City apartment. There was a door on the far side that could be a pantry. Clay took two steps across and jerked the door open, the Sig Sauer steady in his other hand. There were stairs leading up. Of course there *was* a second exit, Clay thought, as he dragged himself up the stairs.

At the top, there was a steel door creaking back and forth on hinges that had not recently been in use, or not until that minute. Through the opening he could see the three-quarter moon shining brightly. A light breeze rustled the leaves of the trees. Clay stepped out through the side of a small knoll behind the backyard and into the woods.

He sensed, rather than heard, movement on his right. Clay jerked backward as there was a flash, and he heard the angry whizzing of a bullet passing in front of his face. He stepped out and around the door looping a roundhouse left at the shadowy figure, his blow connecting with cheekbone and causing another shot to go astray. Clay brought the pistol barrel sweeping overhead and down across the skull of his attacker, and the body crumpled to the ground.

Clay grasped the man's arm and turned him over. Illuminated in the moonlight was Niles Harrington. He was unconscious from the gash to the forehead. Clay felt for a pulse. The man was alive. He doubted that he would be going anywhere soon, so he turned and hobbled back down the stairs, across the kitchen, and into the underground living room. McKenny lay on the floor in apparent shock from his shattered elbow, and perhaps a few additional blows from Cloutier, a low whine keening from his lips as he lay wide-eyed and twitching. There was no gun on him or nearby.

"Cloutier? Baylee?" Clay called as he approached the doorway on the far side.

"In here."

Clay stepped through the doorway. Baylee was straddling Donna's lower legs as she cuffed her hands behind her back with what must have been the policewomen's handcuffs. She slid off her and rolled her over. Donna's face was battered and bloody.

"Everybody okay?" he asked.

"Not everybody," Baylee said smugly.

"Let's bring her with," Clay said. "We need to go check on Westy and the boys."

They went back across, leaving McKenny where he lay, up the stairs, and out. Harrington was beginning to stir.

"I best tie him up," Clay said. "Anybody see any rope downstairs?"

Baylee shrugged, and then after a moment, unhooked her bra and pulled it out through her sleeve. Clay had just a moment to marvel at that but then got busy tying the man's hands, and when he was done, Cloutier handed him another bra for the feet.

"I would've taken this bitch's bra, but I was worried one of her fake tits would explode," Baylee said.

"Is everybody okay?" Westy stepped out of the shadows with his M4 at the ready.

"Yeah, more or less," Clay replied. "How about you? Where's Murph and Don?"

"What?" Westy stepped closer. "Here, say it in this ear. The other one is acting like the cable went out with the volume turned all the way up."

"All good here. Where's Murph and Don?" Clay mustered his loudest voice.

"Murph took a good one to the shoulder, and Don is tending to him while they wait for LifeFlight. They're in the house," Westy said. "You're sure you're okay?" He was looking at Clay's bloody hip.

"Yeah, I think it was just a glancing blow. Let's get in the house. McKenny's down there with a mangled arm."

They all turned at the sound of sirens in the distance. They limped into the house where Murphy was sitting in an armchair with a whiskey in hand while Don busily wrapped a ripped sheet around his shoulder in a crude sling. Don's face was white, and his hands were shaking as he bandaged Murphy. Baylee said something about moving her car back out of the middle of the road where the U-Haul had pushed it. She slipped outside and came back a moment later.

That is where the DEA, the EMTs, and the police found them, sitting in the living room of a ranch in rural Port Essex.

Lieutenant Donna Smith was handcuffed and face down on the floor. There was a Russian assassin whose real name nobody knew secured with zip ties, bloodied and bleeding, next to her. There was a dead man by the front door and another in the yard. There was a third dead man in an underground bunker, lying alongside a local contractor crying in pain. At the back entrance to the bunker there was a billionaire trussed up with lingerie.

Clay was being tended to by an EMT when the Chief of Police arrived with Gene Wolfe at his side. "You want to tell me what's going on here?" he asked.

"I sure hope I didn't violate my bail," Clay replied.

TWO WEEKS LATER

Clay knocked on the door. After a few moments, Baylee opened it, Flash at her feet. Ollie, the one-eyed cat was on the couch glaring at him.

"I brought a bottle of wine." He wished it was a bottle of brown liquor, but he was trying to give that stuff up.

"Come on in," Baylee said. "You must've finally gotten your bank account and credit card sorted out?"

"Yep. Another thing the investigation is looking into about Niles. Seems that banking violations are taken almost as seriously as heroin dealing." Clay stepped into her living room, his eyes immediately going to a statue on the corner of her desk. It was a nude male, head bowed, left arm reaching or pointing downward. "Is that new?" he asked.

"Yep," she said.

"Where'd you get it?"

"I picked it up at a bunker sale a couple of weeks ago. The owner was indisposed, and I got it for a steal."

"What do you call it?"

"I was thinking 'Shady' was about right," Baylee said. "Do you want to open up that bottle of wine and pour a couple of glasses?"

Clay smiled. He thought back to that night two weeks earlier and remembered Baylee moving her car from the road. That was when she must have walked out with the *Fourth Shade*.

"I tracked down Crystal's trailer today," Clay said, "and made arrangements for it to be returned and hooked back up first thing tomorrow."

"She'll be happy about that."

"Yeah, well, I think Gene was starting to like having her around." Crystal had been staying at the house for the past two weeks. "He always did like his women younger and a little on the trashy side, so to speak."

"How about Kelly Anne?"

"Looks like they're not going to prosecute. She moved up the coast some where everybody doesn't know her. Load off of Crystal, I imagine."

"You going to uncork and pour that wine or just stand there talking all day?" Baylee asked.

Clay limped past her to the kitchen, Ollie eyeballing him all the way. He was supposed to be using a cane but refused, even though Grandpops had offered up his. The bullet had torn some flesh off his hip but somehow had otherwise done no real damage. He was due for exploratory surgery in a couple of weeks but was thinking of skipping it.

"How does oysters and steak sound?" Baylee asked.

"Sounds like I should have brought a white as well as a red."

"Except neither one of us drinks white."

"That's true. I guess we just don't tell anybody we drank red wine with oysters. Where'd you get them?"

"Place down the road. Said they came from a company in Brunswick. Mere Point Oyster."

Clay popped the cork and poured two glasses. "Sounds fabulous."

"Let's go down to the water and sip, and then I can open the oysters and you can barbecue."

Flash followed them down to the outdoor hanging bench swing on the ocean. "How's Murph?" Clay asked once they were settled in, just inches apart.

"Itching to get home. Said they won't let him drink whiskey in the hospital."

"That's too bad."

"I did bring him a water bottle filled with Jameson," she said.

"It's important to stay hydrated."

"Cloutier's story keeps running."

Once she had finished giving her statement and had her amputated finger bandaged, the journalist and editor of the *Register* had gone to the office and banged out the first of several breaking stories. *The New York Times* had hired her as a stringer to see it through its course, even as newspapers all over the country picked it up as well.

"She deserves it," Clay said.

"Don gave his notice?" she asked.

"Yeah. Said he didn't think he was cut out for this line of work. I tried to promise him we'd be back on workman comp fraud cases, but he couldn't be swayed."

"Any word on Volkov?"

"Not a peep. Not since that hint of a whisper about the Patriot Act."

"Not sure I'm a big fan of the Patriot Act, but it couldn't happen to a nicer guy," Baylee said.

"Hope they're waterboarding the shit out of him right now," Clay agreed.

"Speaking of acts, I heard they were going to hang the Kingpin Act on Harrington."

"Yep. Going to freeze all of his assets. Seems he graduated from Mexican mud to the white powder from the Golden Triangle of Southeast Asia."

"Will he go to prison?"

"The case against him is pretty airtight, but I'm sure he'll string it out in the courts for years to come. Nice to know he won't have any of his five billion to play with until they can put him behind bars."

"Where does that leave us?"

"I need a new lead investigator now that Don is gone." Clay avoided the question hanging in the air. He knew that he had too many issues to resolve to become romantically involved with Baylee. "Thought maybe you'd like to fill that position?"

She leaned her head against his shoulder, and they sat silently, looking at their town of Port Essex over the harbor. It looked no different today than a month earlier. But it was.

About the Author:

Matt Cost aka Matthew Langdon Cost

Over the years, Cost has owned a video store, a mystery bookstore, and a gym. He has also taught history and coached just about every sport imaginable. During those years—since age eight, actually—his true passion has been writing.

I Am Cuba: Fidel Castro and the Cuban Revolution (Encircle Publications, March, 2020) was his first traditionally published novel. *Mainely Power*, the first of the Mainely Mysteries featuring private detective Goff Langdon, was published by Encircle in September, 2020, followed by book two, *Mainely Fear*, in December, 2020, and book three, *Mainely Money*, in March of 2021. Also forthcoming from Encircle Publications are his Clay Wolfe / Port Essex Mystery series: *Wolfe Trap*, *Mind Trap*, and *Mouse Trap*; as well as his new historical fiction novel, *Love in a Time of Hate*.

Cost now lives in Brunswick, Maine, with his wife, Harper. There are four grown children: Brittany, Pearson, Miranda, and Ryan. A chocolate Lab and a basset hound round out the mix. He now spends his days at the computer, writing.

If you enjoyed reading this book,
please consider writing your honest review
and sharing it with other readers.

Many of our Authors are happy to participate in
Book Club and Reader Group discussions.
For more information, contact us at info@encirclepub.com.

Thank you,
Encircle Publications

For news about more exciting new fiction, join us at:

Facebook: www.facebook.com/encirclepub

Twitter: twitter.com/encirclepub

Instagram: www.instagram.com/encirclepublications

Sign up for Encircle Publications newsletter and specials:
eepurl.com/cs8taP